which?
essential guides

SA
IN

Please return/renew this item by the
last date shown to avoid a charge.
Books may also be renewed by phone
and Internet. May not be renewed if
required by another reader.
www.libraries.barnet.gov.uk

BARNET
LONDON BOROUGH

“ Increasingly we are all expected to look after ourselves financially – investing for emergencies, for our children, for our future. The best way to make good saving and investment decisions is to understand the products on offer and match them closely to our needs and views about risk. ”

Jonquil Lowe

About the author

Jonquil Lowe is an economist who worked for several years in the City as an investment analyst, and is a former head of the Money Group at the Consumers' Association. She now works as a freelance financial researcher and journalist and holds the Diploma in Financial Planning. Jonquil writes extensively on all areas of personal finance and is the author of several other books, including the *Which? Essential Guide to Giving and Inheriting,* the *Which? Essential Guide Pension Handbook, Be your own Financial Adviser, Money in Retirement* and, as co-author, *The FT Guide to Personal Tax.*

SAVE AND INVEST

JONQUIL LOWE

Which? Books are commissioned and published by Which? Ltd,
2 Marylebone Road, London NW1 4DF
Email: books@which.co.uk

Distributed by Littlehampton Book Services Ltd, Faraday Close, Durrington, Worthing,
West Sussex BN13 3RB

British Library Cataloguing in Publication Data
A catalogue record for this book is available from the British Library

The Which? *Essential Guide Save and Invest* went to press in spring 2008 and includes
measures announced in Budget 2008. Although the author and publisher endeavour to
make sure the information in this book is accurate and up-to-date, it is only a general
guide. Before taking action on financial or legal matters you should consult a qualified
professional adviser, who can consider your individual circumstances. The author and
publishers cannot accordingly accept liability for any loss or damage suffered as a
consequence of relying on the information contained in this guide.

Author's acknowledgements
The author would like to thank the Money Research Group at Which? for patiently
reading the draft of this book and their helpful suggestions.

Project manager: Claudia Dyer
Edited by: Emma Callery
Designed by: Bob Vickers
Index by: Lynda Swindells
Cover photographs by: Alamy
Printed and bound by VivaPress, Barcelona, Spain

d at Arctic Paper
ably managed forests.
C certified Chain of

ccess our website at

Contents

Introduction   6

1 Getting started   9
Financial planning • Know the risks • Managing risk • Other considerations

2 Tax, wrappers and wraps   27
How you are taxed • How investments are taxed • Tax-efficient wrappers •
Wrap accounts

3 Savings   49
Your financial plan • Easy access savings • Savings for growth • Savings for income •
Other savings products

4 Pensions   69
Pensions as an investment • Pensions and risk • Work-based pensions •
New national pension scheme • Personal pensions

5 Stock market direct   91
Shares: the basics • Shares: a mixed bag • Buying and selling shares •
Tax and shares • Gilts and bonds

6 Investment funds   115
Fund versus direct investment • Types of investment fund • Choice of funds •
Comparing funds • Timing your investment

7 Property   139
Buy to let • Buy to let abroad • Property funds

8 Income investments   155
Income and risk • Annuities • Insurance bonds • Equity release schemes

9 Unusual investments   175
Collectables • Derivatives • Hedge funds • Business angels

10 Building your portfolio   189
First principles • Manage your own portfolio • Getting help • Protection for the investor

Glossary   207
Useful addresses   212
Index   217

Introduction

The Dotcom Crash confirmed what most investors already knew – shares are risky. But the run on Northern Rock Bank and cooling of house prices from autumn 2007 onwards may have left you wondering whether there are any safe havens for your money. The answer is: no.

All savings and investments have some element of risk, but not necessarily the **capital risk** that newspaper headlines often focus on. The Government's actions over Northern Rock show that you are, as a depositor, very unlikely to lose cash outright through a bank crash, but that does not make bank and building society accounts the safe choice for all occasions.

The interest from a bank or building society account is barely enough to keep pace with inflation and sometimes lags behind. Moreover, choosing the 'safe' option of a bank or building society for long-term savings generally means losing out on better returns elsewhere. A study by Barclays Capital found that £100 invested in a building society in 1990 would, with gross interest reinvested,

have grown to £137 today in **real terms**. Over the same period, £100 invested in shares would have grown to £337. Missing out on better returns on this scale is not simply annoying – it can mean the difference between: paying off your mortgage in full, or not; having a comfortable retirement, or not; giving your kids a good start to adult life, or not. Playing it too safe can be downright reckless. To be financially secure, you need to take some risks.

❝ Playing it too safe can be downright reckless. To be financially secure, you need to take some risks. ❞

At the other extreme – and equally reckless – are investors who pile all their money into a single sure-fire asset that, because it has performed well in the past, is bound to carry on doing so in the future. Of course, everyone learnt the lesson of the Dotcom Crash so no one does that any more – or do they? How about the 1 in 14 people who, in a survey by Baring Asset Management, said their home will be their pension? In order to be financially secure, you need to diversify.

WHY DO PEOPLE SAVE AND INVEST?

Too often 'risk' is used to mean just capital risk. In reality, there are different kinds of risk and the trick is to play off each against the others, according to your own goals, circumstances and personal risk comfort zone.

Three-quarters of people who save do not have any particular goal, according to a survey by National Savings & Investments (NS&I). Of the rest, the most popular goals are saving for an emergency, a deposit on a home, to pay off a mortgage or for home improvements, a holiday or other special occasion, retirement or for your children's future.

Some of these are short-term goals, some medium-term, others long-term. This makes a difference to the risks that are appropriate and the types of investment that are suitable. Given a wide range of goals, you would expect the UK public to hold a broad spread of different savings and investment products.

HOW DO PEOPLE SAVE AND INVEST?

Over half of the financial wealth of UK households is invested in pension funds and life insurance. Much of this form of saving is made automatically through pension schemes at work.

When it comes to the investment decisions that households more actively make for themselves, by far and away the most popular choice is cash and accounts with banks and building societies. Direct investment in shares and indirect shareholdings through **mutual funds** (such as unit trusts) make up a relatively small part of the total. **Gilts** and **bonds** hardly register at all.

Jargon buster

Bonds Loans you make to a company, government or other organisation. But instead of keeping the loan until it is repaid, you can sell it on the stock market (see Chapter 5)

Gilts The common name for bonds issued by the British Government (see Chapter 5)

Mutual funds Unit trusts and similar investment funds where you pool your money with that of lots of other people to buy a wide spread of different shares and/or other stock market investments

Unit trust An investment fund where you pool your money with that of other people to buy a wide spread of different shares and/or other stock market investments

Wrap An administrative arrangement that lets you manage different investments through a single account. Some wraps have tax advantages

Moreover, government surveys show that half of UK households have less than £1,500 in total in any savings and investments. The picture suggests that, overall, UK households are not planning their savings and investments sufficiently to meet their financial goals.

IMPROVE YOUR INVESTMENT DECISIONS

Save and Invest will help you review your own savings and investments and make them work harder for you.

A key theme throughout the guide is risk: your attitude towards risk, the risks inherent in different types of investment, how to spot risks, when to avoid them, how to manage risk and how to make it work to your advantage.

Risk is not the only factor you need to consider, but it is fundamental to getting your investment decisions right. Underestimating the risks inherent in strategies and products, failing to match risks to your comfort level and a lack of transparency that hides risks are at the heart of many investment scandals and disasters.

Therefore Chapter 1 starts off by looking at the type of investor you are and the types of risk you will meet in the investment world. Try the quiz on page 12 to find out if you are, at heart, a cautious, balanced or adventurous investor. Knowing this will help you to work out when to follow your instincts and when to compensate for them. Chapter 1 also includes a quick-start guide to the most popular investments for achieving different financial goals.

> **❝** Try the quiz on page 12 to find out if you are, at heart, a cautious, balanced or adventurous investor. **❞**

Chapter 2 considers the important role that tax should play in your investment decisions and looks at putting '**wraps**' around your savings and investments.

Chapters 3 to 9 look in depth at different sorts of savings and investments and how they fit into your financial planning. Along the way, *Save and Invest* dispels common investment myths and signposts you to sources of further information.

Chapter 10 completes the journey by showing you how to put together an effective portfolio suitable for your goals and circumstances. It also guides you on when and where to get specialist advice and how to get the best from a financial adviser.

With *Save and Invest* as your guide, you will be well set to achieve your financial goals.

Getting started

Before financial advisers can give advice, they must 'know their customer'. The same is true for you. The first steps in deciding where to save and invest are to take stock of where you are now and to understand yourself and your goals.

Financial planning

Saving and investment decisions are likely to be most successful if made within a framework of sound financial planning. When making any financial decision, it pays to work through the basic steps below. This is as true when considering savings and investments as it is for any other financial decision.

- **Step 1** Define your goal. Often, you will be saving or investing for a specific purpose: to build up an emergency fund, save for a deposit on a house, for your children, for retirement. This may be an open-ended goal or you might have a particular objective in mind, for example, building up enough to pay off a mortgage in 25 years' time. Sometimes, you will have no specific purpose, but you still need to think whether this is money for the short, medium or long term.
- **Step 2** Consider all the factors that are relevant to your saving or investment decision. This may include other demands on your money (see Are you ready to invest?, opposite), other financial arrangements you already have, the amount you can afford to save or invest, your tax position, your attitude towards risk, your age and health and whether you have dependants. Your religious or ethical views may also shape your choices. For example, if you are a Muslim, you may be interested in sharia-compliant products.
- **Step 3** Develop suitable strategies and identify the generic products that would be appropriate.
- **Step 4** Choose specific products and companies.
- **Step 5** Keep your strategy under review and adjust or adapt it as necessary. For example, if you want to save a target amount over so many years, check each year whether you are on target. If not, consider, say, boosting the amount you save or switching to other products. Apart from regular reviews, revisit your decisions whenever your circumstances change – for example, you inherit money, get a new job, get divorced – or there is a major change to the wider world around you – for example, tax rates change or some new products are launched.

 To help you check your budget and work out how much you can afford to save, try the budget calculator at www.moneymadeclear.fsa.gov.uk/tools.aspx?Tool=budget _calculator. To find out more about sharia-compliant products, go to pages 57 and 130.

ARE YOU READY TO INVEST?

Investing is fun but needs to be done from a firm financial base and with expert help when you need it.

Have you sorted out the basics?

Any saving and investment should be made within the context of your overall financial health. If you have any debts that are growing uncontrollably or whose repayments are so large they stop you achieving other goals, paying off these should be your top priority. Next, your first savings goal should be to build up an emergency fund. Experts suggest a fund equal to three months' take-home pay, but smaller sums will still help with unexpected bills. Don't take risks with this money (see Chapter 3).

Could you manage financially if you were ill?

Make sure your finances would be protected if you were off work sick for an extended period. Check the sick pay scheme at work and consider your own income protection insurance if it's low or you are self-employed.

Is your family protected?

Life insurance is a must to protect anyone financially dependent on you if you were to die. Check what's available through work. Take out your own policy to top up.

Are you planning to buy a home?

If you are planning to step onto the housing ladder, building up savings to cover a deposit and buying costs may be a top priority. Usually this is a short-term savings goal (see Chapter 3).

Are you on track for retirement?

Retirement is expensive. The earlier you start to save, the more manageable the cost. Because of favourable tax treatment, pension schemes are usually the best option (see Chapter 4). If you are approaching retirement or already retired, see Chapter 8 for ideas on maximising your income.

Do you have spare cash to save or invest?

You may be looking to rearrange your existing savings and investments. Perhaps you have come into a lump sum, for example, through inheritance, retirement or redundancy. But for many people saving means finding some surplus cash each month.

Do you know what you want and where to get it?

If, at any of the steps in the financial planning process (see opposite), you do not feel confident doing the research or making the decisions yourself, consider getting financial advice. See Chapter 10 for details on using an adviser.

 For guidance on sorting out debts, see the *Which? Essential Guide* to *Managing Your Debt*. For help with problem debts, contact your local Citizens Advice Bureau or one or the other organisations listed on pages 212-16.

The Risk Quiz

An important part of taking stock of your personal circumstances is being aware of your attitude towards risk and how this may colour your decisions. Answer the following questions to test your instinctive approach to saving and investing. It will help you decide what sort of investor you are.

Imagine yourself in each of the situations described and choose the answer that best fits what you would do or how you would feel. Then see overleaf to check your score and what it means.

1 You usually have a bit left in your bank account each month. What would you be most likely to do with the money?

a) Put the money in a savings account.
b) Spend the money.
c) Use the money to buy Lotto tickets.

2 You are in your forties, haven't thought about your pension yet and inherit £20,000. What do you do?

a) Invest the money in a pension scheme.
b) Put the money in a savings account.
c) Invest the money in the shares of small, high growth companies.

3 You have a portfolio of shares. The stock market is falling and your portfolio has lost a quarter of its value. What do you do?

a) Sell your shares.
b) Do nothing.
c) Buy more shares.

4 Some shares you bought as a long-term investment have fallen in price, losing a quarter of their value. How would you feel?

a) Very worried.
b) Bit concerned.
c) No particular feeling.

5 Some shares you bought as a long-term investment rise in value. How would you feel?

a) Delighted.
b) Relieved.
c) No particular feeling.

12

" Some shares you bought as a long-term investment have fallen in price, losing a quarter of their value. How would you feel? "

6 You lose your job and receive a large redundancy payment. The stock market is buoyant. What would you do with the money?

a) Invest all the money on the stock market.
b) Put all the money in a savings account.
c) Put half the money in a savings account and invest half on the stock market.

7 The government introduces a new yearly tax allowance to encourage investment in new and growing companies. What would you do?

a) Invest straightaway so as not to lose any allowance.
b) Wait a few years to see what the scheme is like before investing.
c) Do nothing.

8 You have a new grandchild and want to save regularly so the child has a lump sum when she reaches 18 years. How would you invest the money?

a) All in a savings account.
b) All on the stock market.
c) Half in a savings account and half on the stock market.

9 The government introduces a new yearly tax allowance to encourage people generally to save more. What would you do?

a) Invest straightaway so as not to lose any allowance.
b) Wait a few years to see what the scheme is like before investing.
c) Do nothing.

10 You have a portfolio of shares as a long-term investment. How often would you check the share prices?

a) Daily.
b) Weekly.
c) Monthly or less.

How did you score?

Mark the answer to each question as follows then add up your total score. Check below for what your score means.

Question number	Score if you answered a	b	c	Your score
1	5	10	10	
2	5	0	10	
3	0	5	10	
4	0	0	5	
5	10	0	5	
6	10	5	10	
7	10	10	5	
8	0	5	5	
9	5	0	0	
10	0	0	5	
			TOTAL	60

Score 15 to 35

You seem to be a cautious investor. You don't like taking risks with your money. That's fine for short-term goals, like an emergency fund. But when it comes to longer-term goals, like investing to pay off a mortgage, building up a nest egg for your children or saving for a pension, you run a serious risk of missing your targets. The safe investments you prefer are very unlikely to deliver high enough returns, making your goals impossibly expensive. You're also likely to run into problems if you are investing to provide an income. As you draw off the income, inflation will eat into the value of your capital and will reduce the buying power of your income year after year. So be a bit wary of your natural caution and try to focus on the full range of risks rather than just capital risk when working out your long-term investment strategies.

Score 36 to 65

You seem to be a balanced investor. This is the ideal type of investor. You appear to have a good appreciation of the different risks involved in saving and investing. Your short-term strategies are sensibly cautious. You are willing to accept a bit of capital risk in order to improve your chances of a return that will beat inflation and make your long-term goals affordable. Focus on identifying the particular savings and investments that will help you put this strategy into practice.

Score 66 to 80

You seem to be an adventurous investor. You like to spot good chances for profit and then put your money where your hunch is. That's fine if you are playing with money that you can afford to lose, but you may need to tone down this approach when you are investing for the short term or pursuing an important goal like an adequate pension. Think more about tailoring the risks you take to the type of goal and be prepared to spread your money across a range of different investments so that you don't always have all your eggs in one basket.

Know the risks

Understanding risk is fundamental to building a sound savings or investment strategy and to choosing suitable types of financial products.

THE FIVE RISKS

When you save or invest your money, you expose yourself to some or all of these five risks:

- **Capital risk.** The risk that you will lose some of the money that you originally invested. Also the risk of losing some or all of the gains that you have built up so far. The most obvious investments that carry capital risk are stocks and shares whose prices can fall as well as rise.
- **Inflation risk.** The risk that the buying power of your money will fall even though you don't lose any actual pounds. See pages 16–18 for more about the impact of inflation. Bank and building society accounts and most NS&I products are particularly exposed to inflation risk.
- **Shortfall risk.** The risk that your savings or investments will not grow by enough for you to reach a particular target. See page 18 for details.
- **Fixed/variable risk.** The risk, if you lock into an investment offering a fixed return, is that you will miss out on better deals later on. Equally, the risk, if you opt for a variable return, that it will fall below the level you need. This can be a problem especially for income investors (see Chapter 8).
- **Longevity risk.** The risk that you will live longer than your investments last – a risk with pensions and other strategies for providing retirement income (see Chapters 4 and 8).

The main trade-off is between capital risk versus inflation plus shortfall risk. To reduce inflation and shortfall risk, you need higher returns. To achieve higher returns, you have to accept extra capital risk (which may come in the form of exposure to stock market movements and/or extra charges).

> **❝ Bank and building society accounts and most NS&I products are particularly exposed to inflation risk. ❞**

To check out current investment scams that are doing the rounds, visit the Financial Services Authority's (FSA) consumer website at www.moneymadeclear.fsa.gov.uk/news/scams/scams_and_swindles.html.

Every investor would ideally like to achieve high returns with no capital risk. Investments like that do not exist. If someone offers you a deal that looks too good to be true, it will be a con. Look for the hidden risks, the hidden charges or downright fraud. Don't touch deals like this and report them to Consumer Direct on 08454 04 05 06.

The trade-off can be roughly illustrated by the risk ladder opposite. The investments at the bottom of the ladder have the lowest capital risk but are also likely to offer the lowest returns, making them more vulnerable to inflation risk and/or shortfall risk.

At the base of the ladder are index-linked investments, which, as you might expect, offer returns that are linked to inflation and so protect you from this risk. But usually the return from such investments is relatively low, increasing the shortfall risk.

Absent from the ladder is cash. In 2007, when there was a run on Northern Rock Bank, stock markets were volatile and the housing market looked to have peaked, you might have wondered if keeping cash under the mattress was not the safest bet. Keeping your money in cash, on the face of it, seems to have low capital risk. However, inflation risk is very high – any increase in prices reduces the buying power of cash with no return to offset the damage. Shortfall risk is guaranteed, since cash under the mattress cannot grow. And what about capital risk – is it really nil? If cash is stolen or lost in a fire, it is completely gone with virtually no chance of compensation. So cash does not fit into the trade-off of risks – it is simultaneously exposed to all the risks and not a good 'investment' on any count.

THE IMPACT OF INFLATION

Inflation means a sustained rise in price levels. It is the enemy of savings because it erodes the value of your money over time. One pound today buys significantly less than it did ten years ago and one pound in ten years' time will buy less than it does today. For example, if inflation averages just 2.5 per cent a year (broadly, the Government's inflation target) for the next ten years, one pound will then buy only the same as 78p today. In other words, your money will have lost over one-fifth of its value. If inflation is higher, the loss will be greater, see the How inflation eats into your money, overleaf.

Therefore, a basic requirement of any savings and investments is that they protect the buying power of your money over time.

Jargon buster

Corporate bond Investment where you lend to a company and can sell the loan on the stock market
Index-linked investment Investment where the return you get is designed to grow in line with inflation
Investment fund A ready-made portfolio of investments that you and lots of other investors collectively invest in

The risk ladder

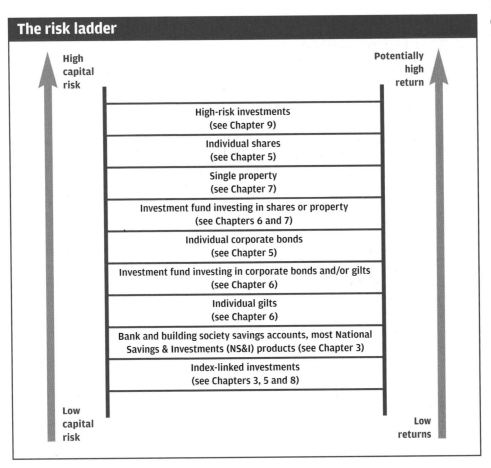

High
capital
risk

Potentially
high
return

High-risk investments
(see Chapter 9)

Individual shares
(see Chapter 5)

Single property
(see Chapter 7)

Investment fund investing in shares or property
(see Chapters 6 and 7)

Individual corporate bonds
(see Chapter 5)

Investment fund investing in corporate bonds and/or gilts
(see Chapter 6)

Individual gilts
(see Chapter 6)

Bank and building society savings accounts, most National
Savings & Investments (NS&I) products (see Chapter 3)

Index-linked investments
(see Chapters 3, 5 and 8)

Low
capital
risk

Low
returns

How inflation is measured

The UK Government uses several measures of inflation. The most commonly referred to in the investment world is the Retail Prices Index (RPI). This is a weighted average of prices for

"A basic requirement of any savings and investments is that they protect the buying power of your money. "

For an estimate of your own personal inflation rate, try the Government's Personal Inflation Calculator at www.statistics.gov.uk/pic/index.html.

How inflation eats into your money

The table shows in today's money how much you could buy with £1,000 in the future given different rates of inflation in the meantime.

Looking ahead this number of years:	This is what the buying power of £1,000 nominal would be if inflation averaged:				
	2% pa	4% pa	6% pa	8% pa	10% pa
5	£906	£822	£747	£681	£621
10	£820	£676	£558	£463	£386
20	£673	£456	£312	£215	£149
30	£552	£308	£174	£99	£57
40	£453	£208	£97	£46	£22

around 650 goods and services collected every month. The RPI is based on average spending patterns, so the inflation that you personally experience is likely to be different from the measure for the UK as a whole.

SHORTFALL RISK

Shortfall risk is a problem where you have a particular savings or investment target in mind and is mainly associated with large, long-term investment goals.

For example, if you take out an interest-only mortgage, usually you simultaneously pay regular savings into an investment product with which you plan to pay off the mortgage at the end of its term. Shortfall risk is the risk that the proceeds will fall short of the amount needed to pay off the outstanding loan.

Shortfall risk can occur because the long-term investment chosen is linked to the stock market. This means the return from the investment is hard to predict and can fall as well as rise.

In theory, you could avoid shortfall risk by choosing an investment that offers a safer, more predictable return. But risk and reward go hand in hand. Choosing a safer investment inevitably means accepting a lower return. This increases shortfall risk and can make the investment goal impossibly expensive (see the table, left).

Saving to meet a target

How much you might need to save to provide £100,000 in 25 years' time

If investment grows at an annual rate of:	Monthly saving required	Total amount invested over 25 years
4%	£195.88	£58,764
5%	£170.03	£51,010
6%	£147.15	£44,145
7%	£126.99	£38,097
8%	£109.31	£32,793
9%	£93.87	£28,161

Managing risk

The appropriate amount and balance of inflation risk, shortfall risk and capital risk depend on the nature of your saving and investment goals, in particular, the timescale involved.

INFLATION RISK

Sometimes, protecting your money from the ravages of inflation is a high priority. For example, when you rely on your savings to provide an income year after year and cannot afford to see the buying power of that income fall.

Only a few investments guarantee to protect your money against inflation. The main ones are NS&I index-linked savings certificates (see Chapter 3), index-linked gilts (see Chapter 5) and **RPI-linked annuities** (see Chapter 8). They do not necessarily offer much extra return over and above inflation and other features of these investments, such as investing for a fixed term, can be restrictive. Therefore investors looking for some real growth in their money typically turn to other savings and investments that offer the chance of higher returns, albeit without an inflation-matching guarantee.

The chart overleaf is based on data from surveys by Barclays Capital. It shows that, dividing the last 100 years into decades, shares have only twice failed to beat inflation. The failure rate is higher for the lower-capital-risk investments: gilts and cash. Index-linked gilts have been available for just the last 20 years, so are shown only for the last two decades in the chart.

Jargon buster

Annuity An investment where you exchange a lump sum for income, either for a specified term or, more usually, for the rest of your life. See Chapter 8

Cash Commonly used in the investment world to refer collectively to savings-type products that earn interest

Equities Another name for shares or share-based investments

RPI-linked annuity An annuity where the income you get increases each year in line with inflation. The drawback is that the starting income is lower than you would get from an annuity that is not linked to the retail price index

❝A few investments guarantee to protect your money against inflation.❞

Real investment returns 1906–2006

The table compares the real returns from equities, gilts, index-linked gilts and cash. A negative figure means that over the decade concerned, the return failed to beat inflation.

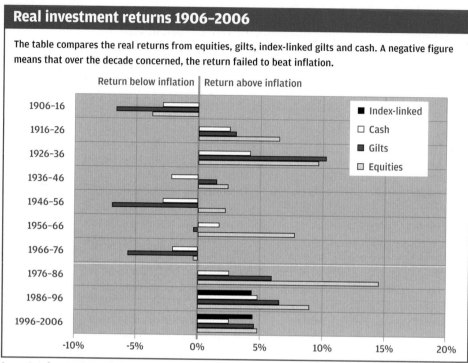

Source: Data from Barclays Capital, *Equity Gilt Study 2007*

SHORTFALL RISK

If you are investing to reach a specific target, there are two facets to managing shortfall risk:

- **The amount you invest.** Your budget might be a constraint, dictating the maximum you can afford to invest. Possibly you have had a forecast showing an amount you might accumulate years ahead if you invest a specified amount now. Crucially, the amount you need to invest is likely to be lower if you choose investments that offer a higher return but with some capital risk (see page 18).

- **Keeping your investments under review.** Especially if your investments expose you to capital risk, it is essential that you regularly review your progress towards your goal. If you are falling short of your target, you may need to increase the amount you invest or consider other changes. If you are ahead of target, you might choose to leave your strategy unchanged or even reduce the amount you invest.

YOUR TIMESCALE

Accepting some capital risk is the main way of offsetting both inflation risk and shortfall risk. It generally means

Jargon buster

Dividends Income from shares

putting at least some of your money into stock market investments. But this is not an appropriate strategy for short-term goals.

Long-term goals

Over the long-term, an investment in a broad portfolio of shares tends to increase in value. There are sound economic reasons for this. Companies are a main generator of economic growth. The fruits of growth may be shared with employees through wages and salaries and with company owners through **dividends**. Investors are the owners of the companies whose shares they hold. Share prices tend to reflect investors' views about the future prospects of companies, so in a growing economy, share prices tend to rise.

The chart opposite shows that equities have in nearly every decade over the last 100 years produced better returns than gilts or cash. Other analysis from the same Barclays Capital survey shows that, looking at every period of ten consecutive years over the last century, equities have outperformed gilts 83 per cent of the time and outperformed cash 93 per cent of the time.

Short-term goals

Over short time periods, shares are volatile. If you need to sell shares within the next few years or on a particular date, there is a risk that your particular shares or the stock market as a whole may be in a downturn at that time. A slump in the stock market is not a problem if you can ride it out and wait for share prices to bounce back. It is a problem if you have to sell.

For short-term goals, such as an emergency fund or building up a lump sum over five years or less, you generally need to stick to savings in the second step of the risk ladder (see page 17). These are bank and building society accounts and most NS&I products. These are all savings with very low capital risk. Within this broad category, there is a wide choice of individual products.

❝ A slump in the stock market is not a problem if you can ride it out. ❞

Jargon buster

Short-term goal Usually defined as five years or less
Medium-term goal Approximately five to ten years, but not precisely defined
Long-term goal Usually defined as ten years or more

 To find out more about individual savings products, see Chapter 3, which sets out the most popular of these.

CAPITAL RISK

A sound strategy for saving or investing over the medium to long term involves some capital risk. But how much risk and how do you adjust the amount of risk you are taking? This is not a precise art and there are no hard and fast rules. But there are general guidelines that can help. They are very much an application of common sense.

Diversification

The main guideline is: diversify. As we have seen above, investing in shares – although they are subject to capital risk – opens up the opportunity of superior returns compared with simply putting your money in the bank or building society. So too, for example, does including property in your portfolio. Basically, diversification means:

- **Do not invest in the shares of a single company.** It might hit bad times or even go bust. Spread your money across a range of different companies. Similarly, do not invest in a single property.
- **Do not choose companies all in one sector of the economy.** It may be hit by world events or government policies. Spread your money across different sectors. Similarly, consider properties in different geographical locations and/or mix residential and commercial holdings.
- **Be wary of investing in just one country.** It may hit a downturn. Consider investing across several different countries.

- **Do not invest in just shares or just property.** Spread your money across different 'asset classes'.

Asset classes

Traditionally, diversification and striking a balance between risk and return are achieved by spreading your money across four distinct asset classes:

- **Cash,** such as bank and building society accounts, NS&I products, sharia-compliant accounts (see Chapter 3).
- **Bonds,** such as gilts and corporate bonds (see Chapters 5 and 6).
- **Property,** such as real estate investment trusts (REITS) and similar funds (see Chapter 7).
- **Equities** – shares in companies and share-based investments such as many unit trusts and investment trusts (see Chapters 5 and 6).

See Chapter 10 for more about asset classes and how to build a diverse portfolio of investments.

❝Asset allocation accounts for over 90 per cent of the variation in return you get. ❞

Other considerations

Suitable strategies and investments will also depend on factors, such as existing financial arrangements, your personal and family circumstances and your ethical and religious beliefs.

OTHER FINANCIAL ARRANGEMENTS

When setting your goals and strategies, take into account any arrangements that you already have. For example, if you belong to a pension scheme at work, this may reduce any extra you need to save for retirement and may also increase your choice of ways to save. An old endowment policy could perhaps help towards achieving a lump sum investment goal.

The financial arrangements of other family members might have an impact on you. For example, if your husband, wife or partner has their own savings, you might be able to save less.

Bearing in mind that a high proportion of relationships end in divorce or separation, you should consider carefully whether to pursue savings and investment goals on an individual or a household basis.

DEPENDANTS

Whether or not you have dependants can affect your investment decisions, particularly the amount you need to save or invest and, in some cases, the products you choose. For example, if you are saving for a deposit on a home, you are likely to need a larger amount if you need a family home rather than a single-person flat. If you are investing to provide an income, you will need a larger income if you are supporting others as well as yourself. You might want investments that give your dependants a lump sum or continuing income if you die.

❝Consider carefully whether to pursue savings and investment goals on an individual or a household basis.❞

Chapters 2 to 9 consider alternative investments that may be important if you have dependants.

HOW MUCH YOU CAN SAVE OR INVEST

Some products have a minimum investment that may put them out of reach, depending on how much you can afford to set aside for the savings or investment goal.

With some other products, there are dealing charges. Although you could invest small amounts, the charges make this uneconomic.

TAX

Your tax position and how different products are taxed is an important factor affecting your choice of suitable savings and investments. Chapter 2 looks at tax in detail.

YOUR AGE AND HEALTH

Health can come into your investment decisions in two ways. First, it may affect your overall strategy. For example, if you are investing to provide an income in your later years, your life expectancy may dictate whether you are planning for the short- to medium-term or the long-term.

Second, some products offer a different return or different features, depending on your health. These are products with an insurance element, such as pensions (Chapter 4), investment-type life insurance (Chapter 6) and annuities (Chapter 8).

YOUR BELIEFS

If you have strong ethical or religious beliefs, you may want to avoid some types of investments or actively seek out others. Chapter 3 includes sections about sharia-compliant products and ethical banking. Chapter 6 looks at ethical investment funds.

GROWTH OR INCOME?

Use the charts in this section as a guide to suitable savings and investments. Whatever your goal, these decisions essentially boil down to two types:

- **Growth.** Saving regularly or investing a single sum to build up a lump sum (either for use as a lump sum or to provide an income later on).
- **Income.** Investing a lump sum to provide an income now.

Pick the appropriate chart opposite and overleaf for guidance on the savings and investments that are most likely to be suitable.

Jargon buster

Sharia law The system of Islamic law. It covers many aspects of day-to-day life including, for example, prohibiting the giving or receiving of interest

 Chapters 3 to 9 give details about minimum and maximum investment limits and charges.

Investing for growth

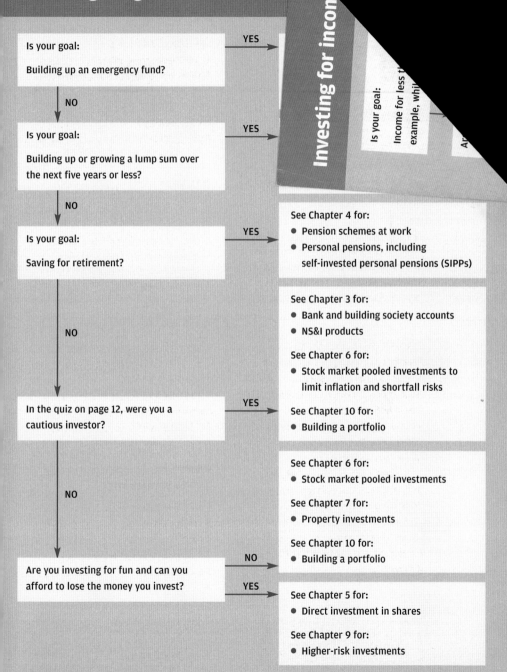

Investing for income

Is your goal:

Income for less t[...]
example, whi[...]

Ar[...]

Is your goal:

Building up an emergency fund? — **YES**

↓ **NO**

Is your goal:

Building up or growing a lump sum over the next five years or less? — **YES**

↓ **NO**

Is your goal:

Saving for retirement? — **YES**

See Chapter 4 for:
- Pension schemes at work
- Personal pensions, including self-invested personal pensions (SIPPs)

↓ **NO**

See Chapter 3 for:
- Bank and building society accounts
- NS&I products

See Chapter 6 for:
- Stock market pooled investments to limit inflation and shortfall risks

In the quiz on page 12, were you a cautious investor? — **YES**

See Chapter 10 for:
- Building a portfolio

↓ **NO**

See Chapter 6 for:
- Stock market pooled investments

See Chapter 7 for:
- Property investments

See Chapter 10 for:
- Building a portfolio

Are you investing for fun and can you afford to lose the money you invest? — **NO**

YES

See Chapter 5 for:
- Direct investment in shares

See Chapter 9 for:
- Higher-risk investments

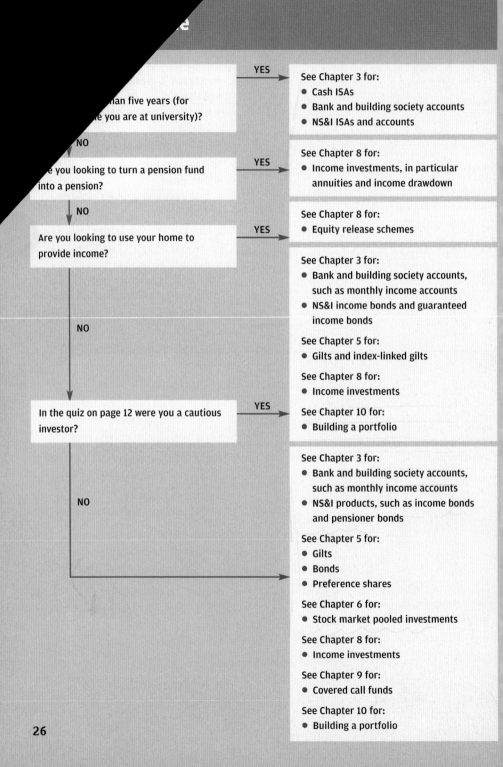

YES → See Chapter 3 for:
- Cash ISAs
- Bank and building society accounts
- NS&I ISAs and accounts

...an five years (for ...e you are at university)?

↓ NO

...e you looking to turn a pension fund into a pension?

YES → See Chapter 8 for:
- Income investments, in particular annuities and income drawdown

↓ NO

Are you looking to use your home to provide income?

YES → See Chapter 8 for:
- Equity release schemes

See Chapter 3 for:
- Bank and building society accounts, such as monthly income accounts
- NS&I income bonds and guaranteed income bonds

See Chapter 5 for:
- Gilts and index-linked gilts

See Chapter 8 for:
- Income investments

↓ NO

In the quiz on page 12 were you a cautious investor?

YES → See Chapter 10 for:
- Building a portfolio

See Chapter 3 for:
- Bank and building society accounts, such as monthly income accounts
- NS&I products, such as income bonds and pensioner bonds

See Chapter 5 for:
- Gilts
- Bonds
- Preference shares

See Chapter 6 for:
- Stock market pooled investments

See Chapter 8 for:
- Income investments

See Chapter 9 for:
- Covered call funds

See Chapter 10 for:
- Building a portfolio

NO

Tax, wrappers and wraps

Tax is fundamental to your choice of investment strategy. Tax allowances can give a big boost to your returns. In addition, the Government has several schemes to encourage saving. But don't chase tax benefits if they take you outside your risk-comfort zone.

How you are taxed

Deciding which savings and investments will be tax efficient for you depends not just on the tax treatment of the product, but crucially on your personal tax position too.

Choosing investments without considering your tax position is like throwing darts wearing a blindfold. You might throw your arrows in roughly the right direction, but you are unlikely to hit the triple 20. There are two main taxes you need to consider:

- **Income tax** on interest, dividends or other income (see below), and
- **Capital gains tax** on profits from investing (see pages 31–3).

Depending on your investment goals, you might also want to consider inheritance tax (IHT) (see page 34), which is a tax on what you leave when you die and, in some cases, gifts you make in your lifetime.

INCOME TAX

Income is any flow of money you get. For tax purposes, this is divided into three types:

- **Non-savings income.** This includes earnings from a job, profits from self-employment, pensions and rent from property.
- **Savings income.** Interest from savings accounts and products, including bank and building society accounts, most NS&I products, interest from gilts, and so on.
- **Dividend income.** This means dividends from shares and distributions from share-based investments.

Some income is tax free but most is taxable. This doesn't mean you pay tax on every last penny of your taxable income because some things you spend money on qualify for tax relief and everyone has a yearly tax-free allowance. You can get tax relief on some expenses (called 'outgoings'), for example, contributions to an occupational pension scheme. This, in effect, increases the amount of taxable income you can have each tax year before you start to pay tax.

The table opposite shows the main income tax allowance for 2008–9. It varies according to your age. The extra

For details of how savings income and dividend income are taxed, go to pages 35–42. See page 36 for tax-free savings and investments.

Main income tax allowance in 2008-9 [1]

Your age	Personal allowance
Under 65	£5,435
65 to 74	£9,030 [2]
75 and over	£9,180 [2]

[1] If you are blind or partially sighted, you might also get blind person's allowance of £1,800
[2] Reduced by £1 for every £2 of income over £21,800, but the allowance is not reduced to below £5,435.

amount for people aged 65 and over is often called 'age allowance' and it is reduced by £1 for every £2 of your income above a given level (£21,800 in 2008-9). For example, if you are aged 66 and your income is £22,800, your age allowance would be reduced by £500 to £8,530. The allowance for older people is never reduced below the basic amount (£5,435 in 2008-9).

How much tax?

From 2008-9 onwards, there are two main income tax rates: 20 per cent and 40 per cent, though some or all of your income from savings and investments may be taxed at 10 per cent.

Jargon buster

Tax relief at source A payment that qualifies for tax relief is treated as a net-of-tax amount. Tax relief is then added. For example, if you pay £80 into a personal pension, the pension provider claims £20 tax relief from Her Majesty's Revenue & Customs (HMRC) and adds it to your scheme

To work out the tax that is due, your personal allowance and the tax bands (see the table below) are set first against your non-savings income. They are next set against your savings income and lastly against any dividend income. The case study, overleaf, shows how this works.

Tax bands in 2008-9

Band of taxable income		Tax rate on		
		Non-savings income	Savings income	Dividend income
Starting-rate band	First £2,320	20%	10%	10%
Basic-rate band	Next £33,680	20%	20%	10%
Higher-rate band	Anything over £36,000	40%	40%	32.5%

29

That's not quite the end of the story because married couple's allowance (available only where one or both of the couple was born before 6 April 1935) and relief for some higher-risk investments (see Chapter 9) are given as a reduction in the tax bill.

> **❝Unless your other income is very low, you cannot benefit from the 10 per cent rate on savings income.❞**

Case Study Sam

In 2008-9, Sam earns £30,000, gets £90 interest from a cash ISA and has gross interest of £300 from a savings account. He pays £1,500 into his employer's pension scheme. The ISA interest is tax free. The tax bill on the rest of his income is worked out as follows:

	Non-savings income		Savings income	
Gross income	£30,000		£300	
Less occupational pension contribution	£1,500		not applicable	
Total income	£28,500		£300	
Less personal allowance	£5,435		£0	
Taxable income	£23,065	Tax	£300	Tax
Starting-rate band	£2,320	at 20% = £464	£0	at 10% = £0
Basic-rate band	£20,745	at 20% = £4,149	£300	at 20% = £60
Higher-rate band	£0	at 40% = £0	£0	at 40% = £0

Note that Sam's earnings use up the whole of the starting-rate band, so there is none of it left to set against his savings income. This means he cannot benefit from the 10 per cent starting rate for savings. All his income is taxed at 20 per cent, giving a total tax bill of £464 + £4,149 + £60 = £4,673.

For more detail about the tax system, including married couple's allowance, see the *Which? Essential Guide Tax Handbook 2008/9.*

Extra basic-rate band

The standard upper limit for the basic-rate band for 2008–9 is £36,000 but is increased if you have made:

- Contributions to a personal pension.
- Donations to charity using Gift Aid.

Both of these ways of spending your money qualify for tax relief. Tax relief at the basic rate is given 'at source'. If you are a higher-rate taxpayer, the gross amount of your pension contributions and Gift Aid donations is added to the standard £36,000 to give you a larger-than-normal basic-rate band. This ensures you get higher-rate tax relief on these expenses.

> **❝ Tax-free gains include profits from selling your home and some collectables. ❞**

CAPITAL GAINS TAX (CGT)

A capital gain is the increase in the value of something during the period you have owned it. So it could be the profit you make when you sell something for a higher price than you paid for it. Equally, it could be the increase in value of something you give away or were given in the first place.

Some capital gains are tax free (see page 41 for some examples). The rest are taxable, but most people don't pay any capital gains tax (CGT) because everyone has a yearly tax-free allowance (£9,600 in 2008–9).

Until recently, you could also reduce the likelihood of having any taxable gains by claiming **indexation allowance** and **taper relief**, but these have both been abolished for sales and other disposals you make on or after 6 April 2008.

Taper relief was especially favourable if you were disposing of business assets, which were defined to include some investments such as shares quoted on

---

Be aware that, if you are close to a tax threshold, the income you get from your savings or investments might take you into a different tax band and you'll need to take this into account when making your investment decisions.

Jargon buster

Indexation allowance Ensured you did not pay CGT on gains due purely to inflation over the period 1982–98. It was abolished from 6 April 2008

Taper relief Reduced the amount of CGT you paid according to how long you had held an asset, with higher relief for business assets. It was abolished from 6 April 2008

Any taxable gains?

Step 1

Start with the final value of the item. This is the sale proceeds if you sold it or its market value if you gave it away.

Step 2

Deduct the initial value. This is the price you paid for the item or its market value when you were given it. If you have owned it since before 31 March 1982, it is the market value on that date.

Step 3

Deduct any allowable expenses. These include buying and selling costs, such as dealing charges, stamp duty, valuation and advertising; and the cost of improvements that enhance the value, such as having a painting cleaned.

Step 4

What is left is the chargeable gain (if you are left with a positive number) or allowable loss (if you are left with a negative number).

Step 5

Add together all your chargeable gains for the tax year and subtract any allowable losses made in the same tax year. If the losses reduce your gains to zero, there is no tax to pay and any unused losses can be carried forward indefinitely to use in a future tax year.

Step 6

Deduct any allowable losses brought forward from earlier years. Only deduct enough to reduce your chargeable gains for the year to the amount of the tax-free allowance (see next step). Continue to carry forward any unused losses.

Step 7

Deduct your annual allowance (£9,600 in 2008–9). Any amount that is left is your taxable gain for the year.

the Alternative Investment Market (AIM) and shares you have received through an employee share scheme at work. Since the abolition of the relief, gains on these investments are taxed more heavily than previously. (However, disposals of part or all of your own business may qualify for a new entrepreneurs' relief that reduces the effective rate of CGT on the first £1 million of gains you make over your lifetime from such disposals.)

To work out whether you have any tax to pay, follow the seven steps in the chart, opposite.

How much tax?

For sales or gifts you make from 6 April 2008 onwards, taxable gains are taxed at a single, flat rate of 18 per cent.

❝ Most people don't pay capital gains tax because everyone has a yearly tax-free allowance. ❞

Case Study   Meera

Meera sells some shares in 2008-9 for £22,000. They originally cost her £8,000 and she can claim buying and selling costs of £50. She does not have any losses this tax year, but has £5,000 of losses made in earlier years. She works out her taxable gain as follows:

Step 1   Final value is £22,000.

Step 2   Deducting the initial value of £8,000 leaves £14,000.

Step 3   She can deduct allowable expenses of £50.

Step 4   This leaves a chargeable gain of £13,950.

Step 5   She has no allowable losses this year.

Step 6   Out of the £5,000 of carried-forward losses, she uses £4,350 to reduce her chargeable gain to £13,950 - £4,350 = £9,600. She can continue to carry forward the remaining £5,000 - £4,350 = £650 of losses.

Step 7   The whole remaining gain is covered by her annual allowance of £9,600. This means there is no tax to pay.

To find an accountant, solicitor or tax adviser, see the Useful addresses on pages 212-16. For more information about IHT, see the *Which? Essential Guide* to *Giving and Inheriting*.

INHERITANCE TAX (IHT)

There are two aspects of IHT that might be particularly important to you: passing on your wealth tax efficiently and setting up trusts in your lifetime.

Passing on wealth

In general, anything you leave when you die in excess of a set allowance (£312,000 in 2008–9) may be taxed at 40 per cent. However, some bequests are tax free, for example, things that have been used in a business. The definition of business assets for the purpose of IHT includes investments in shares listed on the AIM (see page 99) and commercial woodland.

Setting up trusts

A trust is a legal device that lets you give away assets while placing conditions on how they are used. They are a popular way of making gifts, for example, to children. You may have to pay IHT at the time you set up a trust, the trust may have a tax charge every ten years and setting up trusts can affect the eventual tax bill on your estate.

> **!** IHT planning is a specialist area and often complex. It is outside the scope of this book. Consider getting professional advice from an accountant, solicitor or specialist tax adviser.

TAX AND CHILDREN

The UK tax system generally applies to all individuals, regardless of age. This means, for example, that all children, however young, have their own income tax personal allowance and most are non-taxpayers. Children also have their own capital gains tax allowance.

There are some rules to prevent parents from getting an advantage from their children's tax position. In particular, if a parent makes a gift to a child and the invested gift produces an income of more than £100 a year, all of the income (not just the excess over £100) is taxed as that of the parent.

Throughout this book, where other special tax rules apply to children, we point this out.

Case Study **Ian and Tess**

Ian is a basic-rate taxpayer. Over the years, he has been regularly putting money into a building society account for his daughter, Tess, who is now aged ten. She – like most children – is a non-taxpayer and in previous years there has been no tax on her interest. But, in 2008–9, gross interest of £120 is credited to the account. Because the interest comes to more than £100, the whole £120 counts as Ian's income and he must declare it to his tax office by 5 October following the end of the tax year in which the interest is credited. He pays tax on the interest of 20% x £120 = £24.

How investments are taxed

Don't be swayed by the rates in advertisements. It's your after-tax return that counts so here is an overview of the main tax rules for a selection of common investments and what they mean for different taxpayers.

TAX-FREE SAVINGS AND INVESTMENTS

The return from some savings and investments is completely tax free. If you are a taxpayer, you'll get a higher return from an investment that is tax free than from a taxed investment offering the same gross rate. Higher-rate taxpayers have the most to gain from tax-free savings and investments (see the table, below).

" Higher-rate taxpayers have the most to gain from tax-free savings and investments. "

If you are a non-taxpayer, you do not get any benefit from the saving or investment being tax free. But the market for some tax-free products, such as cash ISAs, tends to be very competitive, so don't ignore tax-free products – they might still give you the best return. Personal pensions are a special case, where even non-taxpayers get tax relief (see page 71 and Chapter 4).

Quite a few investments offer a return that is partially tax free. In this section and throughout Chapters 3 to 9, we consider the extent to which these can be useful if you are a taxpayer.

Tax-free and taxed returns compared

If you can get a tax-free return of:	To match it, you would need a gross taxed return of this much:		
	Non-taxpayer	Basic-rate taxpayer	Higher-rate taxpayer
3%	3.00%	3.75%	5.00%
4%	4.00%	5.00%	6.67%
5%	5.00%	6.25%	8.33%
6%	6.00%	7.50%	10.00%
7%	7.00%	8.75%	11.67%
8%	8.00%	10.00%	13.33%
9%	9.00%	11.25%	15.00%

Tax-free savings and investments at a glance

Risk level	Completely tax free	Partly tax free
Lower risk	• NS&I index-linked savings certificates (Chapter 3) • NS&I savings certificates (Chapter 3) • NS&I children's bonus bonds (Chapter 3) • Cash ISA (Chapter 3) • Save-As-You-Earn account (Chapter 5) • Premium bonds (Chapter 3)	
	• Stocks and shares ISA investing in bonds or cash (Chapter 6) • Child trust fund (CTF) investing in bonds or cash (Chapter 6)	• Gilts (Chapter 5) • Most corporate bonds (Chapter 5)
	• Your own home (Chapter 7)	
		• Stocks and shares ISA investing in equities (Chapters 5 and 6) • CTF investing in equities (Chapter 6) • Friendly society tax-efficient plan (Chapter 6) • Pension schemes (Chapter 4)
Higher risk	• Venture capital trust (Chapter 9) • Some collectables (Chapter 9)	• Enterprise investment scheme (Chapter 9)

TAXABLE SAVINGS INCOME

Taxable savings income includes:

- The interest earned by most NS&I products, bank and building society accounts and credit union accounts.
- Interest from gilts and corporate bonds.
- Distributions paid from some types of investment fund that hold cash, gilts and/or bonds.

You receive this income either with tax already deducted or gross.

Savings income with tax deducted

The interest you get has already had tax at 20 per cent deducted. This is the way most bank and building society interest is paid. It's convenient if you are a basic-rate taxpayer because the tax deducted exactly matches your liability with nothing to reclaim and no extra tax to pay.

If you are a non-taxpayer, you can reclaim all the tax that has been deducted. You do this through your tax office, using form R40. In the case of bank and building society interest, non-taxpayers can usually register to receive interest without any tax deducted. (This is not always possible if you hold an account jointly with someone who is a taxpayer.) Register by completing form R85 from the account provider.

Starting-rate taxpayers can reclaim half the tax deducted, using form R40.

If you are a higher-rate taxpayer, you have further tax to pay. To find the extra tax due in 2008–9, follow these steps:

- **Step 1** Gross up the net interest using the formula:
  Gross interest = Net interest / (100% – 20%)
  = Net interest / 0.8
- **Step 2** Multiply the gross interest by 20% (which is the same as 0.2)

Alternatively, use the ready reckoner below to check how much interest you will have after all tax has been reclaimed or paid.

Case Study George

George is a higher-rate taxpayer. In 2008-9, he gets £500 interest from a building society account. This is the net amount after tax has already been deducted. He grosses it up as follows: £500 / (100% – 20%) = £625. Multiplying this by 20 per cent gives £125, which is the extra tax he has to pay. His after-tax interest is £500 – £125 = £375.

Alternatively, using the ready reckoner below, he sees he will have £75 interest after tax for each £100 of interest he receives. Therefore, £500 interest received becomes 5 x £75 = £375 after all the tax has been paid.

Interest ready reckoner

Interest you receive with tax already deducted	Non-taxpayer Amount you'll have after reclaiming all the tax	Starting-rate taxpayer Amount you'll have after reclaiming half the tax	Basic-rate taxpayer Amount you'll have. No tax to reclaim or pay	Higher-rate taxpayer Amount you'll have after paying extra tax
£1	£1.25	£1.13	£1.00	£0.75
£10	£12.50	£11.25	£10.00	£7.50
£100	£125.00	£112.50	£100.00	£75.00
£1,000	£1,250.00	£1,125.00	£1,000.00	£750.00

 To claim a refund of tax paid on interest, get form R40 from your tax office or visit www.hmrc.gov.uk/individuals/fgcat-claimingarepayment.shtml. To register for gross interest, get form R85 from the account provider.

In recent years, HMRC has been cracking down on people who do not declare income from offshore bank accounts. If you don't declare this income, you risk back-taxes, interest charges, fines and possible imprisonment.

Savings income paid gross

You receive gross interest from, for example, some NS&I products (such as NS&I income bonds), offshore bank accounts, gilts (usually) and corporate bonds. Taxpayers must declare this income and pay tax on it.

DIVIDEND INCOME

Dividend income includes dividends from shares and distributions from most share-based investment funds.

Dividends are effectively paid with tax at 10 per cent already deducted and you get a tax credit for that amount. You cannot reclaim the tax, even if you are a non-taxpayer. Basic-rate taxpayers have no further tax to pay.

If you are a higher-rate taxpayer, you do have additional tax to pay. To work out the extra tax due in 2008–9, follow these steps:

- **Step 1** Gross up the net dividend income using the formula:
  Gross dividend = Net dividend / (100% − 10%)
  = Net dividend / 0.9
- **Step 2** Multiply the gross dividend by 22.5% (or 0.225)

Foreign dividends

For 2008–9, dividends from foreign companies are taxed in the same way as UK dividends (in other words, treated as having a 10 per cent tax credit), provided you own no more than 10 per cent of the shares of the company concerned. From 2009–10, the 10 per cent restriction ceases.

LIFE INSURANCE

The taxation of investment-type life insurance is complex and often misunderstood. In many cases, there is no tax for you personally to pay on the gain you make from a life insurance investment, but that does not mean it is tax free.

Investment-type life insurance lets you invest in one or more underlying funds of investments through the framework of a life policy. You can think of the life insurance as being a wrapper around the investments, with the wrapper determining how they are treated for tax purposes. Normally, the life company must pay corporation tax on any income made by the investment funds and also on any gains. You can't claim back any of the tax paid by the company, even if you personally have unused CGT or other allowances.

The pay out from a life insurance policy is called a 'gain' and means the profit you make over and above the total premiums you have paid. Despite being called a 'gain', the pay out comes under the income tax rather than CGT rules. Because the gain has already been taxed in the company's hands, any basic-rate income tax in your hands is waived. But you might have to pay higher-rate tax and, if applicable, you could lose age allowance (see page 29), but only if the insurance is a 'non-qualifying policy' (see below).

Qualifying policies

There is no personal tax on a gain from a 'qualifying' life insurance policy. Most regular-premium life insurance investments, such as endowment policies linked to mortgages, are qualifying policies. A qualifying policy is one that meets certain conditions, in particular:

- Premiums must be paid yearly or more frequently.
- You must keep the policy going for at least ten years or three-quarters of the original policy term, whichever is less.

If the conditions are not met – for example, you cash in the policy after just a few years – the policy is treated instead as a non-qualifying one.

Non-qualifying policies

Policies where you invest a single lump sum (a 'single premium') and regular-premium policies that do not meet the conditions described above are non-qualifying policies.

Usually the gain from a non-qualifying policy counts as part of your income for the year you receive it when working out your tax bill and, if applicable, age allowance. There is no basic-rate tax

to pay but higher-rate tax could be due at the difference between the higher and basic rate (which is 20 per cent in 2008–9), though you might get 'top-slicing relief' (see box, below).

Top-slicing relief

As explained above, there is no basic rate tax for you to pay on the gain from a life insurance policy because the company has already paid some tax. But, if you are a higher-rate taxpayer, you may have to pay extra tax at the difference between the higher and basic rates (40 – 20 = 20 per cent in 2008-9). If adding the gain from a life insurance policy to your income for the year takes you from the basic-rate tax band into the higher-rate band, you are automatically given 'top-slicing relief' if this will reduce the tax due. The relief bases the tax bill on the average of the gain over the length of time the policy has run.

For example, suppose in 2008-9 you have £500 of your basic-rate band left and make a gain of £5,000 on a policy that has run for five years. Adding the £5,000 to your other income for the year would mean that £4,500 of the gain was taxed, giving an additional tax bill of (40% – 20%) x £4,500 = £900.

Top-slicing relief would rework the tax bill as described in the following three steps:

- Divide the gain by the policy term: £5,000 / 5 = £1,000. Add £1,000 to your other income for the year and work out tax on the £1,000.
- Half would be covered by your basic-rate band and £500 would be taxed at the higher rate, giving a bill on the £1,000 slice of (40% – 20%) x £500 = £100.
- Multiply the tax on the £500 slice by the policy term to find the final tax bill: £100 x 5 = £500. Top-slicing relief has reduced the tax bill by £900 – £500 = £400.

Rasheed invests £10,000 in a single-premium life insurance bond. Each year for ten years, he draws off £400. This is within the 5 per cent rule, so there is no tax implication at the time.

The policy ends in June 2008 when Rasheed is 67 and pays out £12,000. Rasheed's total gain from the policy is £12,000 + (10 x £400) – £10,000 = £6,000.

Rasheed is a basic-rate taxpayer with other income in 2008-9 of £21,000. There is no higher-rate tax for Rasheed to pay on the life insurance gain, but the gain is added to his other income to work out how much age allowance (see page 29) he gets. His total income of £27,000 exceeds the age-allowance income limit of £21,800 by £5,200. This means his age allowance is reduced by £5,200 / 2 = £2,600. So instead of getting the full £9,030, he gets £9,030 – £2,600 = £6,430. This means an extra £2,600 of his income is taxed at the basic rate, adding 20% x £2,600 = £520 to his tax bill for the year.

For a maximum of 20 years, you can draw out an amount up to 5 per cent of the premiums you have paid without the gain counting as part of your income for that year. Instead, any tax on these payments is deferred until the year in which the policy finally comes to an end. If you draw less than 5 per cent in any year, the unused part can be carried forward to increase the amount you can draw out in subsequent years.

Offshore policies

If you invest in a policy with an offshore life company, the tax treatment is different. The company is outside the scope of the UK tax system, so does not pay UK taxes on the income and gains from its investment funds. Typically, offshore life companies are in tax havens, chosen to avoid any tax at all on their investment funds. Offshore policies are nearly always non-qualifying and taxed as shown above right.

- Since no tax has been paid by the company, as a UK resident you do not get any waiver of basic-rate tax.
- Instead, all taxpayers are liable for tax at their top rate on a pay out.
- However, you can still draw out 5 per cent of the premiums paid each year while deferring any tax to the year when the policy comes to an end.

Top-slicing relief is still given when working out any higher-rate tax.

GAINS ON SHARE-BASED INVESTMENTS

If you buy some shares or, say, unit trusts on one day and sell them later, you work out whether you have made a capital gain or loss using the normal rules described on page 32. But if you have bought the same shares in the same company on several different dates, how do you know which shares you have sold? The CGT rules spell this out. You match your sale to your purchases in the following order:

1 Shares acquired on the same day.
2 Shares acquired at any time in the next 30 days.
3 Shares acquired before the day you sold them. All these shares form a pool and you work out your capital gain or loss by working out the initial value (see page 32) as the average for all the shares in the pool.

The rules used to be more complicated, but became simpler with the abolition of indexation allowance (see page 31) from 6 April 2008.

GAINS ON COLLECTABLES

Special rules apply to capital gains tax (CGT) on 'tangible moveable property', which is tax jargon for things like paintings, furniture, books, jewellery and other personal possessions. These special CGT rules can make collectables a particularly tax-efficient choice of investment.

Tax free and tax limited

Sale or other disposal of the following items is always tax free:

- **Wasting assets with a predictable useful life** of 50 years or less (even if the actual life turns out to be longer), for example, wine.
- **Personal possessions with a predictable life** that is longer than 50 years, such as antiques and paintings, but a sale

price (or market value if given away) of less than £6,000.

- **British money,** including sovereigns dated after 1837.
- **Private cars,** including vintage and classic cars.

If you make a loss on a long-life personal possession sold for less than £6,000, the loss is worked out as if the item had been sold for £6,000 not the actual sale price.

Where a long-life personal possession is sold for £6,000 or more, there is a cap on the chargeable gain of five-thirds of the sale price less £6,000. Losses are worked out in the normal way, as described on page 32.

If you own an asset jointly with someone else, the £6,000 limit then applies separately to each person's share of the asset.

** Special CGT rules can make collectables a particularly tax-efficient choice of investment. **

Treatment of sets

Tax avoidance rules aim to stop you working the above rules to your advantage by splitting up a set and selling each item separately. HMRC define a set as:

- **Items that are essentially similar and complementary,** for example, a set of chessmen, and
- **Their value is greater when sold together** than separately.

41

Bill bought a pair of silver candlesticks for £2,500. He arranges to sell them to a dealer for £10,000, which will give him a capital gain of £7,500. But he splits the sale into two transactions: one candlestick for £5,000 on 5 April 2008 and the second for £5,000 on 6 April 2008. HMRC do not accept that the £6,000 limit applies to each sale independently (in which case the gains would automatically be tax free). Instead, using the special rules described on page 41, they work out Bill's gain as follows:

Final value	£10,000
Actual gain	£7,500
Gain limited to	(£10,000 − £6,000) x 5 / 3 = £6,667

However, the £6,667 gain is split in two with half (£3,334) being taxed in the 2007-8 tax year and the other half (£3,333) in 2008-9.

> **❝If you don't get a tax return or form P810, declare any gains or income by 5 October.❞**

Pay as you earn (PAYE) Method of collecting tax direct from your earnings or pension income

If you split a set and sell bits of it separately in several sales to the same person or people who are connected with each other (for example, business partners or relatives), HMRC will treat all the sales as a single transaction for the purpose of working off the £6,000 limit. But if the sales straddle two tax years, the gain will still be apportioned between the two years, giving you the benefit of two annual allowances.

TELLING THE REVENUE

If you get a tax return or a tax review form (P810) each year, give the details asked for about any income and capital gains you have had from your savings and investments.

If you don't get a tax return or form P810, you still have to declare any income or gains if there is tax due on them. You must do this within six months of the end of the tax year in which you made the income or gains. So, for income and gains received in 2008–9, you must tell your tax office by 5 October 2009. Your tax office will then most likely send you a tax return to complete.

You will pay any tax due either by instalments through the self-assessment system or by deductions from any earnings or pension through the Pay As You Earn (**PAYE**) system.

For more information about paying tax through self-assessment or **PAYE**, see the *Which? Essential Guide Tax Handbook 2008/9* or www.hmrc.gov.uk.

Tax-efficient wrappers

Wrappers are not investments but affect the tax treatment of the investments you put inside them. Investing through these wrappers can save you hundreds or even thousands of pounds of tax each year.

The Government wants people to save, for example, so they have an emergency fund, for retirement and so that children develop the savings habit. To encourage these sorts of saving, the Government has set up various schemes that offer tax incentives. There are three main schemes to consider:

- Individual savings accounts (ISAs)
- Child trust funds (CTFs)
- Pensions, including self-invested personal pensions (SIPPs).

The schemes are not themselves investments. Think of them, instead, as wrappers that go around the underlying investments. So, if you are going to choose any of the investments anyway, it will often make sense to save or invest through one of these tax-efficient wrappers.

INDIVIDUAL SAVINGS ACCOUNTS (ISAS)

ISAs were introduced in 1998, replacing two earlier government schemes – tax-efficient special savings account (TESSAs) and personal equity plans (PEPs). There are two types of ISA to be aware of:

- **Cash ISAs,** investing in savings accounts with banks, building societies and NS&I.
- **Stocks-and-shares ISAs,** investing in stock market investments, such as, gilts, bonds, shares and investment funds investing in these.

 The Government also offers tax incentives to encourage you to invest in small and growing companies. For details, see Chapter 9, which looks at higher-risk investments.

The tax benefits

The return from a cash ISA is completely tax free. Where a stocks-and-shares ISA is invested in a real estate investment trust (REIT) (see Chapter 7) or investments that produce interest, such as gilts and corporate bonds, the return is also tax free.

The income from shares and share-based investments held through an ISA is taxed at 10 per cent. There is no further tax on this income and any capital gains

are tax free. Given that a basic-rate taxpayer holding these investments direct would pay 10 per cent tax on the income and would typically have enough annual allowance to make their gains tax free, taxpayers whose top rate is the basic rate or less usually do not gain any tax advantage from investing through a share-based ISA. But there is an administrative advantage because you do not report income and gains from ISAs on your tax return.

Transferring your ISAs

You can switch an ISA you have taken out this year to a different manager, but only if you switch the whole ISA. Where you have ISAs from earlier years, you can switch the whole or part of them to one or more new managers.

A stocks-and-shares ISA can only be transferred to another stocks-and-shares ISA. You can transfer a cash ISA to another cash ISA or, from 6 April 2008, a stocks-and-shares ISA.

TESSAs and PEPs

The deadline for converting a TESSA to a cash ISA is now past and all old TESSAs have matured and ceased.

Since 1998, you could not add to your old PEPs but you could keep them going. From 6 April 2008, all remaining PEPs are automatically being converted to stocks-and-shares ISAs.

CHILD TRUST FUNDS (CTFs)

CTFs have been introduced for every child born from 1 September 2002. Each CTF is opened using a voucher from the Government at birth for £250 (or £500 for a child whose family is on a low income). A further £250 or £500 is paid in by the Government when the child reaches age seven. Family, friends and other people can add to a child's CTF as well.

The CTF remains invested until the child reaches age 18, when he or she can use the money in any way he or she likes. At 18, the CTF can be rolled over into an ISA if the young person wants to carry on saving tax efficiently.

You can choose whether to invest your child's CTF on a:

- **Savings basis** in an account with a bank, building society or credit union.
- **Stocks and shares basis** in, for example, gilts, corporate bonds, shares and investment funds investing in these.
- **Stakeholder basis.** The money is invested initially on a stocks and shares basis and, from around the age of 13 years, shifted gradually into safer investments.

The tax benefits

CTFs are taxed in the same way as ISAs. This means any interest from the savings and investments in the CTF is tax free. Share-based income is taxed at 10 per cent. Any capital gains are tax free.

Yearly investment limit

In addition to the government vouchers, parents, friends and others can collectively add £1,200 a year to each child's CTF.

Since children have their own income tax and CGT allowances, they are likely to be non-taxpayers anyway, so the tax benefits of a CTF can be a bit of an illusion. But bear in mind that the income from parental gifts is taxed as that of the parent if it comes to more than £100 (see page 34). This means CTFs can be a tax-efficient way for parents to build up their children's nest eggs.

SELF-INVESTED PERSONAL PENSIONS (SIPPs)

The Government offers a variety of tax breaks to encourage people to save for retirement. With many pension schemes, you have only a limited choice, if any, about how the pension fund is invested. But a SIPP gives you very wide freedom to choose what savings and investments you put inside the wrapper. You can include, for example:

- Savings-type accounts.
- Gilts, corporate bonds, shares and investment funds investing in these.
- Unquoted shares.
- Some types of investment property either held directly or through a fund.

Martin wants to get the maximum tax relief he can each year on his pension contributions. In 2008-9, his earnings are £60,000 and he pays higher-rate tax on £18,565 of this. He works out that a contribution to his SIPP of up to £14,852 will qualify for 40 per cent tax relief. This is how he worked it out:

- A gross contribution up to £18,565 will qualify for higher-rate relief since this relief is given by extending his basic-rate band by the amount of the gross contribution (see page 31).
- Basic-rate relief of 20 per cent is given at source, so Martin should make a net contribution of (100% - 20%) x £18,565 = £14,852.
- The SIPP provider claims the basic-rate relief of 20% x £18,565 = £3,713 and adds it to Martin's scheme.
- None of Martin's income for the year is taxed at the higher rate, which saves him £3,713 in higher-rate tax.
- This means £18,565 goes into Martin's SIPP at a total cost to him of £18,565 - £3,713 - £3,713 = £11,139.

Tax benefits

SIPPs benefit from a range of tax rules:

- **Contributions** qualify for income tax relief at source at the basic rate. Even non-taxpayers get this relief. Higher-rate taxpayers get additional relief through an increase in their basic-rate band (see page 31).
- **Pension fund investments.** Income from share-based investments is taxed at 10 per cent, but other income and capital gains are tax free.
- **Tax-free lump sum.** At 'retirement', you can usually take a quarter of your pension fund as a tax-free lump sum.
- **The pension** is taxable, but your top tax rate in retirement may be lower than your tax rate while working. In that case, tax on your pension is likely to be lower than the tax relief you have had while your pension has been building up.

Yearly investment limit

From 6 April 2006, there were major changes in the rules for pension schemes. As a result, most people can pay as much as they want into their pension scheme.

Each year, you can get tax relief on pension contributions up to:

- At the very least, £3,600, or
- If greater, the value of the whole of your UK earnings.

Other limits may restrict the contributions of the seriously wealthy (see Chapter 4).

For more about cash ISAs and savings CTFs, see Chapter 3. Chapter 4 looks in detail at pension schemes, including SIPPs. See Chapter 6 for more about share-based ISAs and CTFs.

Ten tax tips

Follow these tips to boost your returns.

1   **Cash ISAs.** If you are building up savings, aim to use your full cash ISA each year (Chapter 3). In 2008–9, you can save £3,600 this way. At 6 per cent interest, a basic-rate taxpayer would save £43 tax a year, a higher-rate taxpayer £86.

2   **Pensions.** For retirement, save through a pension scheme (Chapter 4). With a personal pension, whatever your tax position, for every £1 you pay in, HMRC adds another 25p. Higher-rate taxpayers get extra tax relief.

3   **Higher-rate taxpayer?** If you invest in the stock market, use your stocks-and-shares ISA allowance (Chapter 6). In 2008–9, you can invest up to £7,200 through this wrapper (less anything you've put into a cash ISA). On each £1 of dividend income, you'll save 25p tax and gains will be tax free.

4   **Losing age allowance?** Switch to tax-free investments, such as NS&I savings certificates and cash ISAs (Chapter 3) or investments giving capital gains rather than income (Chapters 5 to 7). Each £1 of income you switch saves you 30p in tax (see page 29).

5   **Giving to your children.** If income from your children's investments would be taxed as yours (see page 34), use a CTF (see page 45) or NS&I children's bonus bonds (Chapter 3). Each £1 of income no longer taxed as yours, saves you 20p if you are a basic-rate taxpayer and 40p if you are a higher-rate taxpayer.

6   **Basic-rate taxpayer with unused CGT allowance?** Think twice before choosing investment-type life insurance (see pages 39–40). The insurance company pays tax on the returns that you can't reclaim. If you invest in, say, unit trusts (Chapter 6), you could effectively save 18p tax on each £1 of capital gain.

7   **Non-taxpayer?** Reclaim tax already deducted from any savings income you receive. Better still, register for gross interest (see page 37). For each £1 of net interest you get, reclaim 25p.

8   **Enjoy art and antiques?** Collectables can be a tax free (see page 41). On each £1 of gain, you can save 18p tax compared with a taxable investment.

9   **Calling all taxpayers.** Don't overlook tax-free savings, such as NS&I savings certificates and premium bonds (Chapter 3). Higher-rate taxpayers gain most, with every £1 of tax-free income saving them 40p in tax.

10   **Invest for capital gains.** If you pay tax on your income but have unused capital gains tax allowance, think about switching to investments that produce growth rather than income (Chapters 5 to 7). Each £1 of income you switch could save you 20p if you are a basic-rate taxpayer, 40p if you pay at the higher rate.

Wrap accounts

The internet is driving the creation of one-stop shops for savings and investments. Most people's finances are a mish-mash of different products with different providers and a filing cabinet full of annual statements and other paperwork. Wrap accounts aim to bring order to this chaos and may also deliver hard cash benefits too.

IT'S A WRAP

A wrap account holds all your savings and investments in one place. Within the wrap, you can have different wrappers, such as ISAs, SIPPs and life insurance, as well as direct holdings.

You can buy, sell and manage all of these savings and investments through the wrap account. The wrap can also show valuations for other assets and liabilities, such as your home and a mortgage.

The pros and cons of wrap accounts

Pros

- You are able to see your whole personal balance sheet in one place. This makes it easier to target your goals and assess your overall level of risk.
- You can check on your savings and investments online at any time rather than waiting for annual statements.
- The convenience of a big choice of savings and investments in one place.
- Less administration because you can buy, sell, make transfers, get valuations and so on through just one provider and using a single set of procedures.
- Fast transactions because you give your instructions online.
- Potential cost savings because the wrap provider, who is buying and selling in bulk on behalf of all its customers, should be able to negotiate lower charges for the underlying investments.

Cons

- The wrap provider needs to be paid, so this adds an extra level of charges to your savings and investments.

 So far, there are only a handful of wrap account providers but their number is likely to grow. To find out what's on offer, type 'wrap account' into an internet search engine, such as Google.

Savings

Savings, such as bank and building society accounts and NS&I, are the bedrock of everyone's financial planning. They are ideal for short-term goals and, for the longer term, can help you tailor your overall portfolio to your chosen level of risk.

Your financial plan

Savings, in other words, deposit-based investments, are important because they are products with low capital risk. This makes them good for short-term goals and creating the right balance of risk across all your investments.

SOURCES AND USES

Deposit-based investments are offered mainly by banks, building societies, NS&I and credit unions. Some investment funds (see Chapter 6) invest in deposits. Deposits are the most suitable choice for:

- **Money you may need back at short notice,** for example, an emergency fund.
- **Savings you are building up over a short period** (less than five years). For example, money for a holiday or to pay for a wedding.
- **Money you will need back on a set date** that is within the next five years. With a long-term goal (such as, retirement), it will usually make sense to invest in stock market investments at first, but once you are within five years or so of your goal, consider switching to safer investments to guard against a fall in the value of your savings.
- **Reducing the level of risk in your portfolio as a whole.** See Chapter 10.

HOW DEPOSITS WORK

When you put money into a building society account or other deposit, you are, in effect, lending your money to that institution. The institution typically lends your money to other people so that, for example, they can start up businesses or buy homes. But some of the money is kept in reserves, so that those depositors who want their money back at any point in time can be repaid. (Savings institutions work on the basis that not everyone will want their money back at the same time.)

There is an underlying promise that you will get your original money (your 'capital') back in full. The institution pays for the privilege of using your money by paying you interest or, in the case of sharia-compliant products, a share of the profits that your money generates (see page 57).

There are various deposit-based investments designed to suit different needs. Examples are given opposite.

 To shop around for best-buy savings accounts, use a price-comparison website, such as www.switchwithwhich.co.uk, www.fsa.gov.uk/tables or www.moneyfacts.co.uk or the tables published in *Which?* or newspapers.

- **Instant or easy access accounts.**
You can get your money back without
restriction or penalty at any time
you choose.
- **Notice accounts.** You have to tell the
institution in advance (say, 30, 60, 90
or 120 days) that you want to
withdraw your money. You may be
able to get your money back sooner
but on loss of some interest.
- **Term accounts.** You invest your money
for a set period. Usually you cannot
have your money back sooner.

As a general rule, the greater the
restrictions on getting your money back,
the higher the interest you should get.
For example, you would expect notice
and term accounts to pay more than
easy access accounts and a 120-day
notice account should, in theory, pay
higher interest than a 30-day notice
account. Within a single bank or building
society, that rule will probably hold across
the range of products that it offers. But
across the market as a whole, you can
often find, say, easy access accounts that
offer a higher rate than most notice
accounts. This is because different

institutions are competing for different
types of customer. So it always pays to
shop around for the best deal.

RISK

Your capital may be safe with deposits,
but it does not mean this way of saving
is risk free.

Capital risk

What all deposit-based investments have
in common is that the provider promises
to return your capital in full. Whether or
not a deposit is low risk depends on the
quality of the promise. Safest of all are
NS&I, which are issued by the
Government and the risk of default is
considered non-existent.

It's against the law for a bank or
similar institution to do business in the
UK without being authorised by the FSA.
Deposits with FSA-authorised institutions
are covered by the Financial Services
Compensation Scheme (FSCS) (see table,
below). The FSCS steps in where the
provider has become insolvent and
cannot pay all the money it owes.

The limit in the table applies per
person, so if you hold an account jointly

Financial Services Compensation Scheme: protection for deposits [1]

Amount of deposit	Level of protection
First £35,000	100%
Anything above £35,000	No protection

[1] Protection applies per person and would apply collectively to all accounts they have with a failed institution.
At the time of writing, these deposit protection arrangements were under review and the Government had indicated
that they might be improved.

with someone else, you can both recover up to £35,000 (in other words £70,000 between you). The limit applies once only to all the accounts you have with the failed institution and any money that you owe to the institution, such as an outstanding personal loan, would be deducted.

" The AER is the best way to compare the return from different accounts. "

Understanding interest rates

Comparing returns

As well as the headline rate of interest, advertisements and marketing literature for deposits must show the annual equivalent rate (AER). This is the true interest rate that you get over a year (assuming the interest rate does not change, if it is variable) and is the best way to compare the return from different accounts.

The AER takes into account not just the amount of interest you get but also when the interest is credited to your account or paid out. For example, suppose two accounts have a headline rate of 6 per cent but one credits you with 0.5 per cent interest every month and the other credits the whole 6 per cent in a single sum at the end of the year. The table opposite compares how your savings would grow. You can see that having interest credited earlier and more frequently increases your overall return. This is reflected in the AER, which for the first account is 6.17 per cent but only 6 per cent AER for the second.

Accounts compared

The table shows how £1,000 would grow if invested in two accounts, both with a 6 per cent headline rate. Account 1 credits interest monthly. Account 2 credits interest at the end of the year.

" Having interest credited earlier and more frequently increases your overall return. "

 To check whether a financial institution is authorised by the FSA, see www.fsa.gov.uk/register/home.do.

Interest-rate risk

Different deposit-type investments pay different types of interest, for example:

- **Variable rate.** The interest rate rises and falls in line with the general level of rates in the economy as a whole.

- **Tracker rate.** A special type of variable rate where it is guaranteed to move directly in line with, say, the Bank of England base rate or the institution's own base rate.

- **Fixed rate.** A rate of interest that is fixed for a set period from the time you invest.

	Account 1	Account 2
Headline rate	6%	6%
Interest paid	Monthly	Yearly
AER	6.17%	6%

Month	Account 1	Account 2
	£1,000	£1,000
1	£1,005	£1,000
2	£1,010	£1,000
3	£1,015	£1,000
4	£1,020	£1,000
5	£1,025	£1,000
6	£1,030	£1,000
7	£1,036	£1,000
8	£1,041	£1,000
9	£1,046	£1,000
10	£1,051	£1,000
11	£1,056	£1,000
12	£1,062	£1,060
24	£1,127	£1,124
36	£1,197	£1,191
48	£1,270	£1,262
60	£1,349	£1,338

Gross and net

The AER is always the gross (before-tax) return you can get. In addition to a gross headline rate, advertisements and marketing literature might also show a net rate. The advertisement must make it clear on what basis the net rate is shown. It will usually be the rate net of tax at the basic rate.

Bonus rates

To tempt new investors, many accounts offer extra interest for the first few months when you open an account. After that, the interest reverts to a lower rate. The AER shows the overall interest rate for the first year and takes account of both the bonus and the subsequent reduction.

See page 57 for information about sharia-compliant and ethical savings that may be a better choice if you have strong beliefs.

With a variable or tracker rate, you accept the risk that the return you get will fall if general interest rates fall. This can be a particular problem if you are relying on the interest to provide you with income.

A fixed rate lets you lock into the current level of interest rates. It can be a good choice if you expect interest rates generally to fall in future. However, you lose out if general interest rates rise. Although you may be able to withdraw your money early from a fixed rate deal, there is likely to be a penalty charge, which you would need to weigh against the extra return you hoped to get by switching out of the deal.

Guaranteed equity products link the interest you get to stock market performance. Although your capital is not at risk, your return is exposed to stock market risk (see page 62 for details).

Inflation risk and shortfall risk

As discussed in Chapter 1, when you choose deposit-based investments, the price you pay for low capital risk is increased shortfall risk and, in most cases, inflation risk. These make deposits unsuitable for long-term goals, unless combined with other higher-risk investments. Index-linked NS&I certificates are unusual because they protect you from inflation risk (see page 60).

TAX

Except where the return from a deposit-type investment is tax free, it is taxed as savings income (see Chapter 2).

HOW MUCH YOU CAN INVEST

Some deposits have a minimum and/or maximum investment limit. Many have tiered interest rates, so that you earn a higher rate, the larger your balance.

ACCESS TO YOUR MONEY

Many accounts come with a cash card, letting you make withdrawals at cash machines. With phone and internet accounts, you often invest and make withdrawals only through another account that you designate, usually your current account. Some accounts let you make withdrawals through branches.

❝ A fixed rate can be a good choice if you expect interest rates generally to fall in future. ❞

Easy access savings

The following products can be suitable if you need instant access to your money. All the accounts let you get your money back instantly or within a few days. You choose when and how much to pay in, so these are suitable for regular saving, lump sum investment and ad hoc amounts.

BANK AND BUILDING SOCIETY EASY ACCESS ACCOUNTS

Description The simplest type of savings account. You choose when and how often to invest and can withdraw your money at any time without notice or penalty. Useful for your emergency fund and any short-term savings. It is a competitive market with some high rates offered. Best returns usually on internet and phone accounts. Bank branch-based accounts typically offer particularly low returns.

Return Interest, variable. Often tiered (higher rates on larger balances).

Tax Taxed as savings income, paid net (see page 36).

Minimum/maximum investment Often none.

BANK AND BUILDING SOCIETY CHILDREN'S ACCOUNTS

Description Easy access accounts designed for children. There may be free gifts on opening and sometimes magazines or club membership. The child can make his or her own deposits and withdrawals from age seven. This is useful for teaching your child how to manage money and save. Access is usually through branches, but a few accounts come with a cash card.

Return Interest, variable.

Tax Taxed as savings income, paid net (see page 36). Your child is likely to be a non-taxpayer, so register to receive gross interest (see page 37).

Minimum/maximum investment Usually none.

Emergency fund

Usually you should put your emergency fund in an easy access account. But if you could draw on another source of money in an emergency - for example, by paying for repairs with your credit card or borrowing from family - you could instead have your emergency fund somewhere where you have to give a few days' notice to get it back. This would be worth doing if it means you can get a higher return on your savings.

Think about combining your emergency fund with other short-term savings. The larger combined sum may mean you can get a higher return (for example, in an account with tiered rates - in other words, higher rates on larger balances).

NS&I EASY ACCESS ACCOUNT

Description Alternative to an easy access account from a bank or building society, but NS&I interest rates are usually lower than you can get elsewhere. The account comes with a cash card. You can make withdrawals up to £300 a day at cash machines and post offices.

Return Interest, variable.

Tax Taxable as savings income (see page 38), but interest paid gross.

Minimum/maximum investment
Minimum £100. Maximum £2 million per person.

NS&I INVESTMENT ACCOUNT

Description Alternative to an easy access account from a bank or building society, but the interest rates on this account are normally much lower than you can get elsewhere. You can pay money in at post offices or by direct debit. Withdrawals are sent by post so, in practice, it takes a few days to get your money back.

Return Interest, variable.

Tax Taxable as savings income (see page 38), but interest paid gross.

Minimum/maximum investment
Minimum £20. Maximum £100,000 per account (whether a sole or joint account).

CREDIT UNION ACCOUNTS

Description Credit unions are community banks owned by their savers and borrowers. Members are linked by a common bond, for example, they all live in the same area or work for the same employer. Many aim to provide affordable lending to low-income households and encourage the savings habit. Some work-based schemes offer more competitive savings accounts and deduct your savings direct from your pay.

Return Interest (often called a 'dividend') paid yearly, variable. The maximum rate is 8 per cent a year, but 2–3 per cent is more typical.

Tax Taxed as savings income, but paid gross (see page 38).

Minimum/maximum investment None.

CASH ISAs

Description Tax-free accounts from banks, building societies and NS&I. Many are easy access accounts, but there are a few notice accounts too. Highest rates tend to be for internet and phone accounts.

Return Interest, usually variable. A few accounts offer a fixed interest rate. One offers an inflation-linked return.

Tax Tax free.

Minimum/maximum investment
Minimum is often £10 or £20. Minimum for NS&I Direct ISA is £1,000. Maximum is £3,600 a year. In addition, you may be able to add money transferred from other ISAs you have (see page 44). But the ISAs offering the best returns often do not accept transfers.

To compare most of the cash ISAs on the market, use the FSA's comparative tables at www.fsa.gov.uk/tables.

Sharia-compliant and ethical savings

There is some opportunity to match your savings accounts to your ethical or religious beliefs. These accounts do not necessarily offer the best returns on the market, so you may need to sacrifice some return for your principles.

Mudaraba savings accounts

Under Islamic law, interest (Riba) is banned. To earn a return fairly you must share in the risks of the person using your money. With a Mudaraba savings account, you rely on the bank to invest your money wisely and you and the bank share any profits that are made.

The bank takes care to invest the money in accordance with sharia law, avoiding, for example, investments in businesses involved with alcohol, gambling, pornography or pork.

Bear in mind that you do not have to be a Muslim to share Islamic savings values and sharia-compliant savings accounts are open to everyone.

Ethical savings

Banks and to a lesser extent building societies may lend money to a very wide range of companies and other organisations that may be engaged in all types of business. Increasingly, investors are concerned that their money should not be used to fund unethical activities – such as the arms trade, exploitation of child labour in the third world or destruction of forests – and want to see their money put to good use, such as tackling climate change and improving human rights.

A few providers of savings products do actively take an ethical stance. These are:

- Ecology Building Society. This building society will use your money only to finance sustainable development, for example:
  - energy efficient housing
  - renovation of derelict buildings
  - lending to small-scale ecological businesses.
- Triodos Bank. The bank funds only ventures and businesses that are beneficial to people or the environment, such as:
  - organic farming
  - charities
  - fair-trade companies.
  (Triodos only offers notice accounts.)
- Co-operative Bank and its internet arm, Smile. Uses money in accordance with an ethical policy based on its customers' ethical choices. For example, the bank supports human rights, fair trade, sustainability and animal welfare.

Many smaller building societies still lend mainly for home purchase rather than to companies and so they can be considered to be ethically neutral.

 At the time of writing, only the Islamic Bank of Britain (www.islamic-bank.com) was offering sharia-compliant savings accounts in the UK.

Savings for growth

Many savings products can be used to build up a lump sum. Whether you are saving for something special or growing your money for no particular purpose, the deposit-type products in this section could be the answer.

EASY ACCESS ACCOUNTS AND ISAS

If you are looking for accounts that offer a variable rate of interest, you will not necessarily get a better return by turning to notice and term accounts. The market for easy access accounts, including easy access ISAs, is so competitive that you can often get just as good a rate without any restrictions on your money. For details of easy access accounts, see pages 55–7.

BANK AND BUILDING SOCIETY NOTICE ACCOUNTS

Description You invest regularly, a lump sum or ad hoc amounts. To withdraw money without penalty, you need to give advance notice. Most accounts let you withdraw your money immediately, but you then lose interest corresponding to the amount that would have been earned

> **❝ A deposit-type product can be used to build up a lump sum for something special. ❞**

over the notice period. Different accounts have different notice periods, for example 7, 30, 60, 90 or 120 days. The longer the notice period, the higher the interest rate you should expect to get.

Return Interest, variable.

Tax Usually taxed as savings income (see page 36), paid net. Some notice accounts come within an ISA wrapper (see page 43), in which case the return is tax free.

Minimum/maximum investment With some accounts no minimum; with others, say, £1,000, £5,000 or £10,000. No maximum (except ISAs).

BANK AND BUILDING SOCIETY TERM ACCOUNTS

Description These are often called 'bonds'. You invest a lump sum for a period that is fixed at the outset – say, from one year up to five years. Sometimes, you can't get your money back early. Usually you can, but lose, say, 90 or 120 days' interest.

Return Normally fixed for the term, occasionally variable.

Tax Taxed as savings income (see page 36), paid net. You are liable for tax on the interest when it is credited to your account, not when you cash it in. For example, if interest is credited once a year and you are a higher-rate taxpayer, you will have extra tax to pay each year.

Minimum/maximum investment
Sometimes no minimum; more often £500, £1,000 or more. Any maximum is typically high, for example, £1 million.

BANK AND BUILDING SOCIETY ESCALATOR BONDS

These are a variation on the term account. You get a fixed rate that increases for each year you hold the bond. In other respects, these bonds work like term accounts (see left).

BANK AND BUILDING SOCIETY REGULAR SAVINGS ACCOUNTS

Description You commit to paying in a regular amount each month. The commitment might last only for a set period – say, one year – or could be indefinite. There are often restrictions on withdrawals, for example, a maximum of two per year. If you miss any (or more than a stated number) of the regular payments or exceed the maximum

---

Over-50s accounts

Some bank and building society accounts and bonds are open only to people aged 50 or over. They don't necessarily offer a better deal than accounts available to everyone, so shop around before you decide.

---

number of withdrawals, usually the account reverts to a lower rate of interest. Sometimes you have to take out another product (say, a current account or bond) with the provider to be eligible for this type of account.

Return Interest, usually variable but occasionally fixed. The rate is often much higher than you can get on less restricted accounts.

Tax Taxed as savings income (see page 36), paid net.

Minimum/maximum investment
Minimum is usually £10 or £20 a month. Maximum is typically £200, £250, £500 or £1,000.

NS&I FIXED INTEREST SAVINGS CERTIFICATES

Description You invest a lump sum for a fixed term. (In October 2007, you had a choice of either two or five years.) You can get your money back early, but then get a lower return. If you cash in during the first year, you forfeit all the interest. When a certificate reaches the end of its term, you can let it automatically roll-over for a further term, switch to a different NS&I certificate or cash it in. Withdrawals are posted so allow a few days.

Return Lump sum at end of term or earlier encashment. Certificates work like escalator bonds (see left) paying you a higher fixed rate for each year you hold the certificate. You get the advertised fixed return provided you hold the certificate for its full term.

Tax Tax free.

Minimum/maximum investment
Minimum £100. Maximum £15,000

per issue of new money plus any amount you are reinvesting from maturing certificates.

NS&I INDEX-LINKED SAVINGS CERTIFICATES

Description As for NS&I fixed interest savings certificates (see page 59), except that in October 2007 you have a choice of either a three- or five-year term and the return is inflation-proofed.

Return Lump sum at end of term or earlier encashment. Certificates pay a fixed rate of interest, which increases for each year of the term, plus an amount equal to inflation (see opposite).

Tax Tax free.

Minimum/maximum investment Minimum £100. Maximum £15,000 per issue of new money plus any amount you are reinvesting from maturing certificates.

NS&I products versus banks and building societies

NS&I products are issued on behalf of the Government, which makes them super safe (see page 51), but most are in other respects directly comparable to the products offered by banks and building societies. A few NS&I products - index-linked savings certificates, children's bonus bonds and premium bonds - have no direct comparison.

NS&I product	Comparable bank and building society product	Key difference
Easy access account Investment account	Easy access accounts	
Direct ISA Mini cash ISA	Cash ISAs	
Fixed interest savings certificates Capital bonds	Escalator bonds	NS&I certificates are tax free
Fixed rate savings bonds used for growth	Term accounts	
Fixed rate savings bonds used for income Income bonds Pensioners guaranteed income bonds	Monthly income accounts Over-50s accounts	
Guaranteed equity bond	Guaranteed equity bonds	

How NS&I index-linked certificates might grow

The table shows how £10,000 invested in a five-year certificate in October 2007 might grow if future inflation runs at 2.5 per cent a year.

Year	Interest rate	Interest rate plus inflation	Value of certificate at end of year
1	0.95%	3.45%	£10,345
2	1.15%	3.65%	£10,723
3	1.35%	3.85%	£11,135
4	1.55%	4.05%	£11,586
5	1.76%	4.26%	£12,080

NS&I GUARANTEED GROWTH BONDS

Description You invest a lump sum for a fixed term. (In March 2008, you had a choice of one, three or five years.) You can get your capital back early but lose 90 days' interest. Withdrawals are posted, so allow a few days.

Return Fixed rate.

Tax Taxed as savings income (see page 36) and paid net of tax. Interest is taxable when it is credited to your account (not just at maturity) so higher-rate taxpayers have extra tax to pay each year. Non-taxpayers and starting rate taxpayers can reclaim all or part of the tax.

Minimum/maximum investment Minimum £500. Maximum £1 million in total of these bonds, NS&I guaranteed income bonds (see page 65) and fixed-rate savings bonds.

NS&I FIXED-RATE SAVINGS BONDS

These bonds are no longer available to new investors and were replaced from 23 February 2008 by NS&I guaranteed growth bonds (see left). The two types of bond are very similar. Existing fixed-rate savings bonds can continue until they mature.

NS&I CAPITAL BONDS

These bonds are no longer available to new investors. They allowed you to invest for a fixed return paid at the end of five years. Existing bonds can continue until they mature. They work like escalator bonds (see page 59), so if you cash in early you get less than the maximum return. If you cash in during the first year, you lose all the interest. Interest is credited gross and taxable each year as it is credited.

For an estimate of the current value of your NS&I index-linked savings certificates, use the calculator at www.nsandi.com/products/ilsc/calculator.jsp.

GUARANTEED EQUITY BONDS

Description These are offered by banks, building societies and NS&I. You invest a lump sum for a set term, typically two, three or five years. Your money earns interest that is paid out when the bond matures. Usually you cannot get your money back early. The aim of these bonds is to give you a return linked to the stock market, but without any risk to your capital. Don't confuse these deposit-type bonds with other stock market-linked bonds offered by insurance companies (see page 132).

Return Although the return is technically interest, it is calculated as a proportion of the increase in one or more stock market indices or a collection of specified shares (for example, 115 per cent of any growth in the FTSE 100 Index over the term). Alternatively, you might get a pre-set fixed return, provided one or more stock market indices rise by at least a pre-set amount (for example, 8 per cent a year, provided the FTSE 100 grows by 10 per cent or more). If the stock markets fall or do not rise by the pre-set amount, you get no interest at all, but you do still get your capital back in full. Bear in mind that if stock markets are rising, the return from these bonds is lower than the return you would get by investing direct in shares or share-based investments. This is because, although you are benefiting from a rise in share prices, you are not receiving any income from the underlying shares and this is usually a significant part of the overall return.

Tax Usually taxed as savings income (see page 36), paid net. Tax treatment varies (so check with the provider), but usually tax is due only when the bond matures. Some of these bonds are offered within a cash ISA wrapper in which case the return is tax free.

Minimum/maximum investment
Minimum can be £500 but more often in the range of £1,000 to £10,000. Maximum is £3,600 for ISA version. Any maximum for non-ISAs is generally high.

Case Study Gazala

In 2003, Gazala invested £10,000 in a three-year guaranteed equity bond, offering 80 per cent of any rise in the FTSE 100 Index over the three-year term. Share prices, as measured by the index rose 39 per cent and, on maturity, Gazala received £13,120, equivalent to a return of 9.5 per cent a year. However, with dividend income reinvested, a direct investment in share-based investments could have grown to £15,900 over the same period, a return of over 16 per cent per year.

 For ideas on investing in shares and share-based investments, see Chapters 5 and 6.

CHILD TRUST FUND (CTF) – SAVINGS BASIS

Description Savings account for a child born from 1 September 2002, which you can open with their CTF voucher. Family, friends and anyone else can add to the account. The child cannot withdraw the money until he or she reaches 18 years. (See page 45 for more details about CTFs.)

Return Variable.

Tax Tax free. Bear in mind that a child is usually a non-taxpayer anyway. However, these bonds can be useful if income would otherwise be taxed as that of the parent (see page 34).

Minimum/maximum investment Usually £1 but £10 with some accounts. Maximum is £1,200 a year (in addition to government vouchers).

A CTF is a long-term investment, so a savings account is unlikely to be the most suitable choice. Consider a stakeholder CTF or share-based CTF (see page 45).

> **❝ Bear in mind that a child is usually a non-taxpayer anyway. ❞**

NS&I CHILDREN'S BONUS BONDS

Description Anyone aged 16 or over can take out these bonds for anyone under 16. Until the child reaches 16, a parent usually manages the investment. From 16, the child can take over. You invest a lump sum for five years. At the end of the five-year term, the investment can be automatically rolled over for a further five years. This can carry on until the child reaches 21. Bonds are held in the name of the child and for their benefit, so you personally cannot get back money you have given this way. The child can get the money back early, but with a lower return. Bonds cashed in during the first year get no interest at all. Withdrawals are posted, so allow several days.

Return Lump sum at end of the term or earlier encashment. These bonds work like escalator bonds (see page 59), paying a higher fixed rate for each year the bond is held. The child gets the advertised fixed return provided the bond is held for each full five-year term.

Tax Tax free. Bear in mind that a child is usually a non-taxpayer anyway. However, these bonds can be useful if income would otherwise be taxed as that of the parent (see page 34).

Minimum/maximum investment Minimum £25. Maximum £3,000 per issue per child.

 For a list of CTF providers and accounts, go to www.childtrustfund.gov.uk.

Savings for income

Deposit-type investments can be used to provide income but watch out for inflation. Consider mixing these deposits with other investments so that your portfolio produces income and growth.

The main problem with drawing off the interest from a deposit as income is inflation. Your capital is not growing at all and so any level of inflation eats into its buying power (see the table, below). This also means that the buying power of the income it produces tends to fall as the years go by.

If you are investing for the long term, it makes sense to put at least some of your money into other investments that will produce some growth to counter the effects of inflation (see Chapter 10).

EASY ACCESS ACCOUNTS AND ISAS

These accounts are not specifically designed to provide an income, but there is nothing to stop you making regular withdrawals. They can be ideal, for example, for students investing their loan, any grants and parental top up until needed. (See pages 55 and 56 for details of easy access accounts and cash ISAs.)

How inflation can eat into your capital and income

The table shows the buying power of your capital and income at the end of each year assuming you earn 5 per cent a year interest and inflation averages 2.5 per cent a year.

Year	Buying power of your:	
	Capital	Monthly income
Start	£10,000	£42
1	£9,756	£41
2	£9,518	£40
3	£9,286	£39
4	£9,060	£38
5	£8,839	£37
10	£7,812	£33

BANK AND BUILDING SOCIETY MONTHLY INTEREST ACCOUNTS

Description You invest a lump sum and the interest is paid out regularly each month to the bank or other account you designate. The account runs indefinitely and you can add further money whenever you like. When you want your capital back, with some accounts access is instant, others are set up as notice accounts.

Return Variable.

Tax Taxed as savings income (see page 36), paid net.

Minimum/maximum investment Some accounts have no minimum. With others, minimum of, say, £1,000. No maximum.

NS&I GUARANTEED INCOME BONDS

Description You invest a lump sum and receive a monthly income during a fixed term. (In March 2008, you had a choice of one, three or five years.) You can get your capital back early but lose 90 days' interest. Withdrawals are posted so allow a few days.

Return Fixed monthly income.

Tax Taxed as savings income (see page 36) and paid net of tax. Higher-rate taxpayers have extra to pay. Non-taxpayers and starting-rate taxpayers can reclaim all or part of the tax.

Minimum/maximum investment Minimum £500. Maximum £1 million

in total of these bonds, NS&I guaranteed growth bonds (see page 61) and fixed-rate savings bonds.

NS&I INCOME BONDS

Description You invest a lump sum and receive a regular income paid into the bank or other account that you designate. The bond runs indefinitely and you can add further capital whenever you like. This is an easy access account so you can get your capital back without notice. Withdrawals are posted, so allow a few days.

Return Variable. Tiered, with higher rate on balances of £25,000 or more.

Tax Taxed as savings income (see page 37), paid gross.

Minimum/maximum investment Minimum £500. Maximum £1 million.

NS&I FIXED-RATE SAVINGS BONDS

These bonds are no longer available to new investors and were replaced from 23 February 2008 by NS&I guaranteed income bonds (see left). Existing bonds can continue until they mature.

NS&I PENSIONERS GUARANTEED INCOME BONDS

These bonds are no longer available to new investors. Existing bonds can continue until they mature.

 To check how much income you would get from an NS&I guaranteed income bond, use the NS&I calculator at www.nsandi.com/products/gib/calculator.jsp.

Other savings products

Premium bonds and Zopa are higher-risk alternatives to conventional savings. When it comes to premium bonds this may sound surprising, but not only are your savings vulnerable to inflation – there is also a risk of getting no return on your money.

PREMIUM BONDS

Description You invest a lump sum that buys one bond for each £1 invested. Instead of earning interest, your bonds take part in a monthly draw. You can take prizes as cash or opt to have them automatically reinvested to buy further premium bonds. You can get your original capital back at any time. Withdrawals are made by post, so allow a few days.

Return In October 2007, the prize fund was equivalent to 4 per cent a year of the total invested in premium bonds. This rate is variable. One bond had a 1 in 21,000 chance of winning any prize in a single draw and a 1 in 18 billion chance of a jackpot win. Prizes range from £50 to £1 million (see the table, left). If you held the maximum £30,000 of bonds, with average luck you could expect 17 prizes a year.

Tax Prizes are tax free.

Minimum/maximum investment Minimum £100. Maximum £30,000 including any reinvested prizes.

Premium bond prizes in October 2007	
Prize value	Number of prizes
£1 million	2
£100,000	20
£50,000	39
£25,000	80
£10,000	197
£5,000	395
£1,000	4,759
£500	14,277
£100	223,712
£50	1,455,999

Source: National Savings & Investments

> **❝One bond has a 1 in 18 billion chance of a jackpot win. ❞**

 For more information about premium bonds, see www.snandi.com/products/pb/index.jsp.

Premium bonds – just a lottery?

Premium bonds are an 'interest lottery'. You are not gambling with any of your original capital, but you are staking the interest you would otherwise have earned each month in the hope of winning a prize.

In October 2007, the prize fund was set at 4 per cent. Prizes are tax free, so that's equivalent to 5 per cent for a basic-rate taxpayer and 6.67 per cent for a higher-rate taxpayer. On that basis, assuming you could earn the prize-fund rate of return, premium bonds looked a reasonable choice for higher-rate taxpayers, but anyone who is paying tax at a lower rate could get a better return elsewhere.

Of course, the lure is the possibility of winning £1 million. If you invested the maximum £30,000 in premium bonds, your chance of winning the jackpot in any one draw in October 2007 was about 1 in 600,000. Suppose instead you invested the £30,000 in a building society account paying 6 per cent a year and drew out the interest each month. A higher-rate taxpayer would get £90 a month after tax. This could buy 90 Lotto tickets. Each Lotto ticket has a 1 in 14 million chance of winning the jackpot in any one draw, and 90 tickets boost your chance of the jackpot to about 1 in 155,000. A basic-rate taxpayer could buy 120 tickets and would have a 1 in 117,000 chance of the jackpot.

The Lotto odds are very long, but they are better than premium bonds. If your reason for buying premium bonds is the chance of a jackpot win, you would do better to invest in a savings account and use the interest to buy Lotto tickets instead.

ZOPA

Description Zopa is a social lending marketplace. It brings together people who want to borrow money and people who want to lend without any bank as middleman. As a lender, you say how much you are willing to lend, at what rate and for how long. Borrowers are risk-rated and you can choose at which risk levels you want to lend. There are no guarantees, but Zopa estimates that in its highest-risk category, the risk of default is about 1 in 20. To protect you further, your money is not all lent to one person. Your money can be split into chunks as small as £10, so a £1,000 investment

To check for unclaimed premium bond prizes, go to www.nsandi.com/products/pb/haveYouWon.jsp.

could be spread across 100 different borrowers. You get your money back as the loans are repaid (and in the meantime receive the interest). You cannot get your money back early.

Return The return you get depends on the rate you set (less Zopa's fee of 0.5 per cent), the extent to which your loans are taken up and the level of bad debts you experience. Zopa states that in 2007 the average lending rate after fees but before bad debts was 7 per cent. Until your money is lent out, it is held in a bank account where you earn interest.

Tax Interest is taxed as savings income (see page 37), paid gross.

Minimum/maximum Minimum £10. Maximum £25,000. (You can lend more but then need a consumer credit licence, which Zopa can help you get.)

A new asset class?

Some experts have suggested that social lending schemes, such as Zopa, are a new asset class (see Chapter 1) that can help you to diversify your investments. This is a controversial view. Zopa is essentially a deposit-type investment so seems to sit squarely within the cash asset class. The interest rates you can get through Zopa are likely to move up and down broadly in line with interest rates in the economy as a whole. On the other hand, Zopa gives you the opportunity to specialise in lending at higher risk for a higher return – something that is not possible through bank and building society savings.

❝ The return you get depends on the rate you set, the extent to which your loans are taken up and the level of bad debts. **❞**

 To find out more about Zopa, go to http://uk.zopa.com/ZopaWeb.

Pensions

Building up a pension is one of the most common reasons for saving. There are a variety of tax incentives to encourage you to save for retirement provided you use a pension scheme, which is a tax-efficient wrapper around your investments.

Pensions as an investment

Building up a pension is a large, long-term investment. Most people start work around the age of 20 and carry on into their sixties. This means that you have 40 years or more to build up a retirement income, making pension savings one of the longest-term goals of your life.

You might not be particularly aware of your pension savings, but nearly everyone who works is building up some **state pension**. In addition, many employees belong to an **occupational pension** scheme at work. In both these situations, the amount you are paying in is automatically deducted from your wages or salary and the pension you get arrives more or less automatically once you reach the appropriate age.

The picture is very different if you decide to top up your pension or you don't belong to an occupational scheme (for example, you are self-employed). You have to make decisions about how much to save, when, how often and where to invest. A pension scheme is not an investment in its own right. It is a

❝ You have to make decisions about how much to save, when, how often and where to invest. ❞

'wrapper' (see Chapter 2), which can contain investments from any of the asset classes looked at in Chapter 1, including equities, bonds, property and cash. A **pension fund** can end up being worth tens or hundreds of thousands of pounds.

TAX INCENTIVES

The tax incentives when you save through a pension scheme are:

- **Tax relief on contributions.** You get tax relief up to your top rate of tax. With some types of scheme, you get the relief even if you are a non-taxpayer (see box, opposite).
- **No tax on an employer's contributions.** With many types of fringe benefits that you get through work (such as a company car or medical insurance), you have to pay tax on the value of the benefit. But anything your employer pays towards your pension counts as a tax-free benefit.

 For a detailed guide to planning ahead for retirement, see the *Which? Essential Guide Pension Handbook.*

- **Tax relief on pension investments.** Your contributions (and any paid by your employer) are invested, typically, in shares, property, bonds, gilts and so on. Income from shares is taxed at 10 per cent, but the rest of the income from the investments and any capital gains are tax free.
- **Tax-free lump sum.** When you want to draw your pension, you can usually take a quarter of the investment fund that has built up as a tax-free lump sum.
- **Taxable pension, but ...** The rest of your investment must be drawn gradually as pension, which is taxable. However, most people pay less tax once they retire, because their income tends to

be lower and people aged 65 and over get a higher income-tax allowance (see page 29). This means that the total tax on your pension will quite likely be less than the total tax relief you had while your savings were building up.

Jargon buster

PAYE tax review form A simple form you may have to fill in every few years if you pay tax through PAYE to check that the correct amount of tax is still being deducted from your pay or pension

Personal pension A pension scheme that you arrange for yourself and that stays with you even if you change jobs

How you get tax relief on contributions

Pension contributions qualify for income tax relief (but not relief from national insurance contributions), which is given in different ways depending on the type of scheme.

Occupational scheme

Your contributions are deducted from your pay before income tax is worked out. This means you automatically get tax relief up to your top rate. But it also means you get no tax relief if your pay is too low for you to have to pay tax – in that case, you might do better to save through a personal pension, but need to weigh the tax relief gained against any loss of employer contributions.

Personal pension

You get 'tax relief at source'. This means that whatever you pay in is treated as a net contribution from which tax relief at the basic

rate has already been deducted. The pension provider claims the relief from HMRC and adds it to your scheme (see case study, overleaf). You get this relief even if you are a non-taxpayer. If you are a higher-rate taxpayer, you can claim extra relief through your tax return or PAYE tax review form. You can pay into a personal pension for someone else – for example, your partner or child. In that case, tax relief at source is still added to the scheme although you cannot claim any higher-rate relief. (But the scheme member can, if he or she is a higher-rate taxpayer.)

Retirement annuity contract

This is an old-style of personal pension that you would have started before 1 July 1988. Depending on the scheme provider's rules, you might pay gross contributions. In that case, you claim all the tax relief through your tax return or PAYE tax review form.

EMPLOYER'S CONTRIBUTIONS

A major advantage of saving for retirement through an occupational pension scheme is that your employer pays into the scheme on your behalf. In a non-contributory scheme, your employer bears the full cost of your pension savings. More often, your employer contributes, say, half to two-thirds of the cost (see page 79). Although there is nothing to stop your employer contributing to your personal pension, most employers choose not to.

ALTERNATIVES TO A PENSION SCHEME

Saving for retirement is a long-term goal, so any investments suitable for long-term saving would do. This includes, for example, shares (see Chapter 5), unit trusts and other investment funds (see Chapter 6) and property (see Chapter 7).

You can invest in these direct or through the pension scheme wrapper. Another option would be to invest in the same sorts of assets through a stocks-and-shares ISA – another wrapper (see page 43). The table opposite compares these three options. Pensions win on the tax breaks but lose on flexibility.

HOW MUCH YOU CAN SAVE

Technically, you can pay as much as you like into a pension scheme, but you get tax relief only on contributions made before the age of 75 and up to:

- £3,600 each tax year, or
- If larger, 100 per cent of your UK earnings for the tax year.

The limit applies to the total of your contributions to all the pension schemes you belong to or have. It does not include contributions paid for you by your employer but does include contributions paid on your behalf by anyone else (for example, your partner).

You may have to *pay* some tax if you are a large investor (meaning that you invest over £235,000 in 2008–9 or have total pension savings of more than £1.65 million). Ask your tax adviser for details.

See Chapter 8 for your options once you are ready to start your pension. See the *Which? Essential Guide Pension Handbook* for details of death benefits payable from pension schemes.

Pensions, ISAs and direct investments compared

Feature	Pension scheme	Stocks-and-shares ISA	Direct investment
Your employer may contribute	Yes, if occupational scheme; sometimes in other cases	No	No
Tax relief on money you pay in	Yes	No	No
Investment grows largely tax free	Yes	Yes	No
Tax free when you take money out	Usually up to 25% is tax free; rest must be drawn as taxable pension	Yes	Income usually taxable; gains usually taxable if more than annual allowance (see page 32)
Can withdraw money whenever you like	No; minimum age is 50, increasing to 55 in 2010	Yes	Yes, usually
Complete flexibility over how much you cash in and when	No	Yes	Yes, usually

PENSION VERSUS INHERITANCE

The Government is determined that pension savings will actually be used to provide retirement income and not to pass money on tax-efficiently to the next generation. There are various rules to bolster this intention.

First, you must start to draw a pension by the age of 75 at the latest. If you die before age 75 and before your pension has started, your scheme can usually pay out a tax-free lump sum to anyone you have nominated. But, on death after your pension has started, any lump sum you leave is taxed – at 35 per cent if you are under 75 and (unless left to charity) at up to 80 per cent if you are over 75.

HOW YOU INVEST

Sometimes, the people running the pension scheme choose which investments to put in your pension scheme wrapper. With many, you have at least some choice. Some – for example, SIPPs (see page 89) – leave the investment decisions entirely to you.

For an idea of how much pension your savings might generate, see www.pensioncalculator.org.uk.

Pensions and risk

Saving for retirement is fraught with risks. Final-salary occupational schemes protect you from most of the risks, so are a particularly valuable investment if you can join one. If not, there are tactics you can use to manage the risks.

SHORTFALL RISK

Trying to build up a pension using lower-risk-lower-return investments, such as building society accounts, could be very expensive indeed and would carry a big risk of your savings falling short of the amount you need for a comfortable retirement. To overcome shortfall risk, generally you need to choose share-based investments because they offer the potential for higher returns.

CAPITAL RISK

There are two aspects to capital risk: the risks inherent in the investments you choose; and the risk of your pension provider failing to deliver.

Investment risk

As with all long-term goals, suitable investments are likely to be share-based. So pension savings nearly always involve capital risk. But with some types of occupational scheme – for example, final

salary schemes – your employer, not you, bears the capital risk. With most others, you bear the risk and this can have a dramatic effect on your pension.

As you approach retirement, your investment stops being long term. From around ten years to go, you have a medium-term goal and, within five years of retiring, you have a short-term goal.

Therefore it makes sense gradually to switch your savings during that last ten years to lower-risk investments, such as bonds and cash. This locks in your past stock market gains and insulates you from any fall in share prices when you are close to retiring. Some investment funds – called 'lifestyle funds' – automatically make this shift for you (see Chapter 6).

Pension provider failure

State pensions and public sector occupational pension schemes are generally considered to be completely safe from failure. They are provided by the Government, which, if need be, can always resort to raising extra money through taxes in order to pay the promised pensions.

Other schemes are not so rock-solid as investors in Equitable Life and

❝ Pension savings nearly always involve capital risk, but it might be your employer who bears it. ❞

74

Pension compensation schemes

	Pension Protection Fund	Fraud Compensation Fund	Financial Services Compensation Scheme
Type of scheme it protects	Final-salary occupational schemes	Occupational schemes (all types)	Personal pensions
When might you be protected?	Your employer goes bust and the pension scheme cannot meet all the pension promises	Your employer goes bust (or is likely to) and the pension fund has been reduced because of dishonesty	The provider (or an adviser you relied on) has gone bust owing you money
How much might you get?	100% of your pension if already retired; otherwise 90% of your pension (up to a limit)	Could be up to 100% of what you are owed	Usually 100% of the first £2,000 and 90% of the remainder [1]

[1] in some cases, 100% of the first £30,000 and 90% of the next £20,000

members of the Maxwell pension funds or other failed final-salary schemes can testify. There are now various compensation schemes designed to at least partially protect your pension savings (see the table, above).

INFLATION RISK

Inflation attacks your savings while they are building up and your pension once it starts to be paid.

❝ Compensation schemes have been designed to at least partially protect your pension savings. ❞

To find out more about the Pension Protection Fund or Fraud Compensation Fund, contact www.pensionprotectionfund.org.uk. To find out more about the Financial Services Compensation Scheme, contact www.fscs.org.uk.

While your savings are building up

If you belong to a final salary occupational pension scheme, your savings are protected from inflation while they build up because your promised pension is a proportion of your pay at or near retirement. Provided your pay rises at least in line with price inflation, the starting value of your pension is also increasing.

If you leave a final salary scheme before reaching retirement, the link with your pay is broken. Although some, or all, of your promised pension may continue to be increased in the period between leaving the scheme and retiring, this might not be enough to protect you against inflation.

With most other pension schemes, including personal pensions, your savings are completely exposed to inflation. There are two main tactics for countering this:

- Increase the amount you save each year at least in line with inflation.
- Choose share-based investments. Although they involve higher capital risk, they also offer higher potential returns that may beat inflation.

Inflation once your pension starts

The buying power of any fixed income will fall year by year as prices rise and the income buys less (see page 18). Some pensions automatically protect your pension from being eroded in this way. For example, the state pension and many public sector pensions are automatically increased in line with inflation once they start to be paid.

Larger occupational schemes often make some increases but not necessarily enough to match inflation. With other schemes, including personal pensions, it is left up to you to decide whether or not to choose an inflation-proofed pension (see Chapter 8).

LONGEVITY RISK

This has two aspects. It's the personal risk of outliving your investments and being left with too little or nothing to live on. It's also the general risk that, if – as is happening now – everyone is tending to live longer, the cost of pensions increases.

The personal risk

In general, living long should be a cause for celebration, but it plays havoc with

People are living longer

Year in which age 65 is reached	Number of years an average person aged 65 is expected to live	
	Men	Women
1986	14.8	18.4
1996	17.3	20.1
2006	19.5	22.2
2016	20.6	23.1
2026	21.4	23.9
2036	22.3	24.8

Jargon buster

Lifetime annuity Investment where you give up a lump sum and in return get an income for life. Once purchased, you cannot change your mind and get your lump sum back

pension savings. The longer you live after retiring, the longer your pension must be paid out, so the more expensive your pension becomes.

In final-salary schemes, your employer promises to pay you a pension for as long as you live. This means your employer, not you, bears the longevity risk. However long you or anyone else lives, your pension carries on. But if everyone is living longer, the cost to the employer of paying these pensions increases. Not surprisingly then, many employers have been closing down their expensive final-salary schemes and this may affect you.

With most other types of scheme, you can protect yourself from the personal risk of living a very long time by buying a lifetime annuity (see pages 160–5). The lifetime annuity is a special type of investment that guarantees to pay you an income for however long you live.

The general risk

As the population as a whole is tending to live longer, the cost of buying an annuity has been going up. As the cost rises, you need to save more to get the same pension (or alternatively retire later).

In general, there is not much you can do to protect yourself from an increase in annuity costs between now and the time you reach retirement. All you can do is to keep checking whether you are on track for the retirement you want and adjust your savings if not. This will mean increasing your savings as the cost of annuities rises.

❝ You can protect yourself from the personal risk of living a very long time by buying a lifetime annuity. ❞

To check if you are on track for the retirement you want, try Money Trail, free from Age Concern: www.ageconcern.org.uk/moneytrail. For more information about how pension schemes work, see the *Which? Essential Guide Pension Handbook*.

Work-based pensions

Joining a pension scheme at work can be the best way to invest for a pension. Employers with five or more employees must offer some kind of pension arrangement through your workplace.

The pension arrangement that a employer must offer could be:

- **An occupational pension scheme** (see opposite).
- **A group personal pension.** This is a personal pension that you can join through work. Your employer chooses the provider and may have negotiated some special features, for example, lower charges. If your employer makes contributions on your behalf equal to at least 3 per cent of your pay, then your employer does not have to offer any other type of pension scheme. See page 86 for more information about personal pensions.
- **A stakeholder scheme.** This is a personal pension that meets set conditions, for example, a cap on charges and a low minimum contribution. Your employer does not have to contribute towards this at all (see page 88).

If you work for a very small employer, there might not be any pension scheme at work. In that case, you need to arrange your own pension savings (see page 86).

OCCUPATIONAL PENSION SCHEME

This is generally the best type of pension arrangement because your employer makes substantial payments into the scheme for you. Belonging to an occupational scheme is basically extra pay that is automatically diverted to your pension savings.

There are two main types of occupational pension scheme: defined benefit and defined contribution, which is more often called money purchase.

Defined benefit schemes

A defined benefit scheme is any scheme that promises you a pension at retirement worked out according to a set formula, as shown opposite.

 To find out about any pension scheme available through your workplace, talk to your human resources department.

- **Final salary scheme.** Your pension is a fraction of your pay at or near retirement multiplied by the number of years you have been in the scheme.
- **Career average scheme.** Your pension is a fraction of the average of your pay during the time you have been in the scheme.

In a defined benefit scheme, you are not involved in the investment decisions. You are promised a particular pension and it is up to your employer to ensure there is enough money available to meet the promise. Usually there is a pension fund where all the contributions are invested. The fund is valued every few years to check whether it is big enough to meet the pension promises. If not, the employer's contribution – and sometimes your own – increases. With many public sector schemes, there is no pension fund and taxpayers finance the pensions.

All defined benefit schemes protect you from investment risk. Final-salary schemes go even further. By linking your pension to your pay at retirement, they protect you from inflation while your savings are building up and from longevity risk. Public sector pensions increase with inflation once they start, making them particularly valuable.

Most defined benefit schemes are contributory (meaning that you have to pay some of the cost). Typically you pay around 5 per cent of your salary as contributions. Your employer will almost certainly be paying at least double that and often much more.

Case Study **Brian**

Brian currently earns £30,000 a year and belongs to a final salary pension scheme. It will give him a pension of 1/80th of his pay at retirement for each year he has been in the scheme. He expects to have 40 years membership. Based on his pay now, this would be a pension of $1 / 80 \times £30,000 \times 40 = £15,000$ a year. If his pay by retirement has increased (with inflation and promotions) to £100,000, his pension will also have increased to $1 / 80 \times £100,000 \times 40 = £50,000$.

❝ With a money purchase scheme, you don't know in advance how much pension you will get. **❞**

Money purchase schemes

The principles of a money purchase scheme are very simple: you pay money in, it grows and you use the proceeds to buy a pension.

All personal pensions (see page 86) are money purchase schemes. What makes an occupational money purchase scheme distinctive is:

- **Employer contributions.** Your employer contributes to the pension on your behalf. Typically, this might be around 5–7 per cent of your pay (which is less than would be contributed to a defined benefit scheme).

- **Investment decisions.** Your employer usually makes the main decisions about where the pension fund is invested. But often you will be offered some limited choice, for example, a selection of different investment funds.
- **Pension at retirement.** At retirement, you can shop around for your pension, but might also have the option of a pension provided by the scheme itself.

Unlike a defined benefit scheme, with a money purchase scheme, you don't know in advance how much pension you will get – in other words, you face shortfall risk. It depends, for example, on how well the invested contributions grow – you, not your employer bear all the capital and inflation risks while your savings build up. It also depends on how much the provider deducts in charges. The amount of pension you can buy will depend on the cost of annuities when you reach retirement, so you are exposed to the general effects of longevity risk. How all these risks turn out can have a very big impact on the pension you get.

The impact of charges

According to the Government, paying 1 per cent a year extra in charges could cut the pension of a man who saves for 43 years from age 25 by one-fifth.

Case Study | Dana and Jamila

All the figures in this case study have been adjusted for the impact of inflation and are given in today's money.

For 30 years, Dana paid into a money purchase pension scheme. Her pay averaged £30,000 a year and her own and her employer's contributions together came to £250 a month (£3,000 a year). By retirement, she had a pension fund of £117,000 with which she was able to buy a pension of £5,250.

Jamila also belonged to a money purchase scheme for 30 years with contributions of £3,000 (in today's money) paid in each year. Unfortunately, in the last couple of years before she retired, the stock market slumped and Jamila's pension fund was only £86,000. Although she got a slightly better annuity deal than Dana, her pension was still a lot less at £4,040 a year.

See Chapter 8 (pages 160-5) for information about annuities.

Case Study Mary and Phil

By retirement at age 65, Mary, who is aged 60 now, will have been in a final salary scheme for 16 years. Based on her current salary of £24,000, her pension would be 1/80 x £24,000 x 16 = £4,800 a year, which will increase with inflation once it starts to be paid.

Mary is looking at buying added years to boost her pension. The cost of each added year, which is based on her age and salary now, is a lump sum of £4,284. Each added year that she buys would increase her pension by 1/80 x £24,000 = £300 in the first year and this would be

increased in line with inflation in each subsequent year.

Mary's husband, Phil, earns £40,000 and belongs to an occupational pension scheme. He wants to save extra and is looking at the AVC scheme at work. It offers matched contributions: for every 1 per cent of his pay that Phil puts into the AVC scheme, his employer will add a contribution equal to 0.5 per cent (up to a maximum employer contribution of 2 per cent). For example, if Phil pays in £50 a month, his employer will add £25, taking the total contribution to £75.

TOPPING UP AN OCCUPATIONAL PENSION

Your employer might offer various arrangements at work for increasing your pension savings. Depending on the terms of each deal, these can be a good investment.

Added years

This is only an option with the type of defined benefit scheme where your pension is based on the number of years you have been in the scheme. You may be able to buy extra years. These feed

through the pension formula to increase the pension you get (and other benefits, such as the tax-free lump sum). This can be a good way to boost your pension, but added years are usually expensive.

Additional voluntary contribution (AVC) scheme

You pay extra contributions into a money purchase arrangement. The proceeds are then used to buy extra pension or other benefits when you retire. You might do better to save extra through your own personal pension (see page 86) if this would give you, say, a wider choice of investments and more flexibility over when you draw the benefits. But an AVC scheme at work can be worthwhile if your employer will match your contributions (see case study, above) or the charges for the AVC scheme are particularly low.

❝ An AVC scheme at work can be worthwhile if your employer will match your contributions. ❞

Salary sacrifice

You may be able to give up some of your pay in return for your employer paying extra contributions to your pension scheme. This has tax advantages for both you and your employer, but bear in mind a reduction in your salary can affect other payments based on it, such as sick pay or tax credits.

You pay income tax and national insurance contributions (NICs) on your salary. Your employer has to pay NICs on it too. But contributions that your employer makes to a pension scheme on your behalf are tax-free benefits for you and qualify for tax relief for your employer. So switching some of your overall pay package from salary to pension reduces your tax bill. Because your employer is also saving tax, he or she might even be willing to pass on some of the savings to you, boosting the benefit you get from sacrifice even further. Ask the human resources department at work if your employer operates a salary sacrifice scheme.

Case Study   Fynn

Fynn earns £50,000 a year gross. After income tax and national insurance, he takes home £35,468. He is considering giving up £3,000 gross pay through a salary sacrifice scheme at work in return for an increase of £3,000 in his employer's contribution to his pension scheme. If he goes ahead, Fynn's gross pay will fall to £47,000 but his take home pay will fall by only £1,770 to £33,698 because his tax and national insurance have also fallen. So Fynn gets £3,000 extra paid into the pension scheme at a cost to him of just £1,770.

"Giving up some pay in return for your employer paying extra to your pension scheme has tax advantages."

New national pension scheme

The Government estimates that around 7 million people (about one-fifth of the working population) are not saving enough for retirement. Lack of pension savings is particularly a problem for women and low- to middle-earners.

To encourage more people to save for retirement, the Government is establishing a new national pension savings scheme. This will effectively make an occupational money purchase scheme available to every employee from 2012 onwards. The main features of the scheme are summarised in the box, below.

❝ A new scheme will be available to every employee from 2012. ❞

HOW THE SCHEME WILL WORK

At the time of writing, the Government was still considering the details of how the scheme will work, but the broad outline has been decided.

Automatic enrolment

If you are an employee, aged between 22 and state pension age and earning more than £5,000 a year, you will be automatically enrolled into your employer's occupational pension scheme, if there is one, or into the new national scheme.

Main features of the national pension savings scheme

- Money purchase scheme.
- Low charges.
- Automatic enrolment.
- Right to opt out and information to help you decide.
- Employer contribution equal to 3 per cent of your pay.
- Your contribution: 4 per cent of your pay up to a maximum contribution of £3,600 a year.
- Tax relief on your contribution: worth about 1 per cent of your pay.
- You have your own personal account with the scheme.
- Your account stays with you when you change jobs.

You can opt out of the national scheme if you want to. In that case, you need to consider how you will manage in retirement. If your current earnings are low and expected to remain so, you might not be able to save enough for retirement to take you above the level at which you would qualify for state benefits for pensioners on low incomes. In that case, any pension savings you make could be wasted and so opting out might be sensible. In other cases, if you opt out of the national scheme, you should usually consider making some alternative savings for retirement, for example, through a personal pension (see page 86).

If you are self-employed, you can voluntarily join the scheme, but you will not get the benefit of any employer contribution (see below).

Contributions

Assuming you stay in the scheme, you and your employer must pay contributions of at least a minimum amount. This will be 4 per cent and 3 per cent, respectively, of your earnings between certain limits (expected to be between about £5,000 and £33,500). Your contributions will qualify for basic rate tax relief, which will increase the amount going into your account by a further 1 per cent. (Higher-rate tax payers will be able to claim extra relief.)

The maximum contribution you can make will be capped at £3,600 a year (to be increased each year in line with earnings inflation). Your contributions to the scheme will be deducted automatically from your pay and passed on by your employer.

Investments

The national scheme will be run by a centralised body (whose name had not yet been decided at the time of writing). You will deal with that body when you have queries or receive statements and so on. In general, the centralised body will organise the investment of the pension fund, but you will be able to choose between several different investment funds if you want to. The choice is likely to include some funds that will be suitable for people with ethical or religious concerns.

Your money will go into a default fund if you don't want to make any investment choices. This will probably be a lifestyle fund (see page 132).

Advice

The Government is exploring ways to set up a national advice network to help people make financial decisions, such as whether or not to belong to the new national pension savings scheme.

Jargon buster

Means-tested state benefits State benefits that you can get only if your income and savings are low, for example, pension credit, council tax benefit and housing benefit

The new national scheme – a good investment?

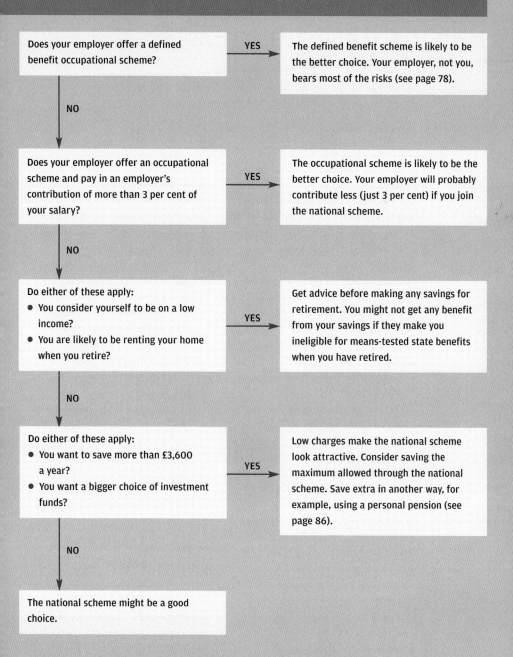

Does your employer offer a defined benefit occupational scheme?

YES → The defined benefit scheme is likely to be the better choice. Your employer, not you, bears most of the risks (see page 78).

NO ↓

Does your employer offer an occupational scheme and pay in an employer's contribution of more than 3 per cent of your salary?

YES → The occupational scheme is likely to be the better choice. Your employer will probably contribute less (just 3 per cent) if you join the national scheme.

NO ↓

Do either of these apply:
- You consider yourself to be on a low income?
- You are likely to be renting your home when you retire?

YES → Get advice before making any savings for retirement. You might not get any benefit from your savings if they make you ineligible for means-tested state benefits when you have retired.

NO ↓

Do either of these apply:
- You want to save more than £3,600 a year?
- You want a bigger choice of investment funds?

YES → Low charges make the national scheme look attractive. Consider saving the maximum allowed through the national scheme. Save extra in another way, for example, using a personal pension (see page 86).

NO ↓

The national scheme might be a good choice.

Personal pensions

These are the main option for anyone who cannot join an occupational scheme or wants to save extra. Investment choice and charges are important factors when choosing a personal pension.

Personal pensions are pension schemes that you can take out independently of your work and that stay with you even if you move from job to job. They are always money purchase schemes, so you cannot know in advance what pension you will get. That depends on:

- The amount paid in through contributions.
- The charges deducted by the provider.
- How well the invested contributions grow.
- The cost of annuities at the time you want to start drawing your pension.

Because these schemes are personal to you, it is largely up to you how you invest your savings. But your choice of investments will depend to some extent on the type of personal pension you choose. The table opposite summarises the main types of scheme.

> **“** Personal pensions are always money purchase schemes, so you cannot know in advance what pension you will get. **”**

 To compare different providers' personal pensions (including stakeholder schemes), see www.fsa.gov.uk/tables.

Types of personal pension

	Personal pension (standard)	Group personal pension (see page 78)	Stakeholder scheme	Self-invested personal pension (SIPP)
Providers	Mainly insurance companies	Mainly insurance companies	Mainly insurance companies	For example, fund management companies, insurance companies, fund supermarkets, stockbrokers, IFAs
Who chooses the provider?	You	Your employer	You or, if offered through your workplace, your employer	You
Usual investment choice	Choice of investment funds (see Chapter 6)	Choice of investment funds (see Chapter 6)	Choice of investment funds (see Chapter 6), but limited with some schemes	Investment funds, shares, gilts and bonds, commercial property, other (see page 90 and Chapters 5 to 7)
Who chooses the investments?	You	You	You, but if you don't choose, default is a lifestyle fund (see page 132)	You
Charges	May be lower or higher than for stakeholder schemes	Your employer might negotiate special terms, such as low charges	Must meet certain conditions (see page 88), including a cap on charges	May be charges for the SIPP wrapper as well as the investments inside, so some SIPPs are expensive (see page 89)

STAKEHOLDER PENSION SCHEMES

To use the name 'stakeholder', a personal pension must comply with a set of conditions. The aim is to ensure that the scheme offers a straightforward, value-for-money deal. The main conditions are:

- **Charges.** For schemes taken out from 6 April 2005, charges must be no more than 1.5 per cent a year of the value of your pension fund for the first ten years and 1 per cent a year thereafter. (For schemes started before 6 April 2005, the limit is 1 per cent a year throughout.) There can be no other charges.
- **Contributions.** The minimum contribution can be no higher than £20. It's up to you when and how often you pay.
- **Transfers.** You must be able to transfer your investment to another scheme at any time without penalty.

- **Investment simplicity.** You don't have to choose how your money is invested. If you make no choice, your money goes into a default investment. From 6 April 2005, the default is a lifestyle fund (see page 132).

SELF-INVESTED PERSONAL PENSIONS (SIPPs)

SIPPs are personal pensions where you control how your money is invested. You can either make the decisions completely by yourself or you might opt to get financial advice (see Chapter 10).

SIPPs have been around for a long time and were traditionally expensive schemes aimed only at very wealthy investors. In 2006, the Government brought in new, more liberal rules for all pension schemes. Initially, it looked as if SIPPs would be able to invest in virtually any investment you cared to name, including buy-to-let properties, antiques and fine wines. This sparked enormous interest in SIPPs from

---

Stakeholder schemes – a good choice?

A stakeholder scheme will not always be the most suitable choice (for example, you might pay lower charges and have more choice with some personal pensions), but it offers a transparent, reasonable value deal. This makes it a good baseline against which to compare any other personal pension. For example, if the personal pension you are looking at costs more, ask yourself what extra features (for example, wider investment choice) the personal pension has to justify the extra charges.

 To compare the different stakeholder pension schemes available, use the FSA comparative tables at www.fsa.gov.uk/tables.

Watch out for charges

A SIPP may come with some or all of the charges below. Some off-the-peg SIPPs have no set-up charge or annual fee, but make their money from commission on the investment funds you choose. The most common SIPP charges are:

- **SIPP set-up fee.** This ranges from nil to, say, £300 + VAT.
- **Annual SIPP administration charge.** Ranges from nil to, say, £500 + VAT or 0.5 per cent of the value of your fund.
- **Dealing charges** when you buy and sell shares, gilts and bonds (see Chapter 5).
- **Property purchase administration fee.** Say, £400 to £750 + VAT.
- **Transfers in from other pension schemes.** Ranges from nil to, say, £750 + VAT.
- **Transfers out to other pension schemes.** Ranges from nil to, say, £150 + VAT.
- **Buying an annuity.** Up to, say, £150 + VAT.

investors with more modest wealth. But, fearing tax abuse, the Government made a major u-turn and imposed penalty tax charges on some types of investments. This makes it uneconomic to use a SIPP to invest in:

- **Residential property.** This includes your home, any second home in the UK or abroad, buy-to-let properties, beach huts and timeshares. It does not include (so you could invest in) student halls of residence, children's homes, care homes, hospitals and prisons. (See Chapter 7 for more information.)
- **Tangible moveable property.** This is the Government's term for physical items that you can touch. It includes, for example, antiques, jewellery, fine wines, paintings, boats, cars, stamps and books.

The tax penalties do not apply if you invest through what the Government calls a genuinely 'diverse commercial vehicle'. This would include, for example, a real estate investment trust (REIT) investing in residential property (see Chapter 7).

Despite the Government's u-turn, the interest in SIPPs has remained and the market for them has become very competitive, driving prices down. As a result, there are now two types of SIPP emerging: bespoke SIPPs that offer a wide range of investments and services

❝ Don't pay extra for services or flexibility that you will never use. ❞

 To find out what SIPPs are on offer, see occasional surveys in specialist magazines such as *Money Management* or use an internet search engine. If you need help, consult an IFA.

and tend still to be expensive; and cheap, off-the-peg SIPPs that offer a more limited investment range (or charge heavily for adding others). The key then to choosing a SIPP is to be very clear about what you want and choose a SIPP that meets just those needs. Don't pay extra for services or flexibility that you will never use.

SIPP investments

SIPPs are offered by a wide range of providers, such as stockbrokers, some IFAs, fund supermarkets and wrap account providers.

Depending on the SIPP you choose, you may be able to invest in some or all of the investments in the box, below.

SIPPs do not limit you to the investments of a single provider. Typically they let you choose from all the providers on the market or at least a very big selection. For example, a SIPP will usually let you choose from hundreds of different investment funds.

❝ Typically, SIPPs let you choose from a very big selection of providers on the market - if not all of them. ❞

Investments you may be able to put in your SIPP

Type of investment
- **Deposit accounts***. These are accounts that pay you interest similar to the investments described in Chapter 2.
- **Gilts and corporate bonds* (see Chapter 5).**
- **Investment trusts* (see Chapter 6).**
- **Real estate investment trusts (REITs)* (see Chapter 7).**
- **Unit trusts and open-ended investment companies (OEICs)* (see Chapter 6).**
- **Insurance company investment funds (see Chapter 6).**
- **UK quoted shares***. Shares quoted on the London Stock Exchange, including the Alternative Investment Market (see Chapter 5).
- **Traded endowment policies (see Chapter 6).**
- **Unquoted shares. For example, shares in a family company (see Chapter 5).**
- **Commercial property. For example, a building used by your business if you have your own company.**
- **Futures and options (see Chapter 9).**

* Likely to be available with cheaper off-the-peg SIPPs

Stock market direct

Shares, gilts and bonds are the building blocks of any investment portfolio. Spreading your money across a range of different shares and other assets reduces risk and creates an engine for investment growth or income.

Shares: the basics

An understanding of shares is essential whether you invest direct or through the funds described in Chapter 6. As a shareholder you are not simply an investor; you are part-owner of a business.

Imagine you are a local builder running your own company. The risks of the business fall on your shoulders but you also reap the profits. Now imagine yourself as one of thousands of shareholders in BP, Marks & Spencer, Unilever or the pre-nationalised Northern Rock. As a shareholder, you are a part-owner of the company. The businesses are bigger, but you still reap the rewards and bear the risks just as you would with a smaller firm. The main difference is that, as a small shareholder in a large company, you have very little involvement with or influence over the running of the business.

The main reason for investing in shares is that, for long-term goals (say, ten years or more), history suggests that shares will nearly always outperform safer investments, such as building society accounts. By taking on the risks of business ownership, you share in the profits when the business does well. When you hold a spread of shares in

> **❝** For long-term goals, history suggests that shares will nearly always outperform safer investments. **❞**

many different companies, you effectively share in the growth of the economy.

THE REWARDS

The return from holding shares may come in two forms: dividends and capital gain.

Dividends

Dividends are regular income, usually paid every six months. This is the way the company pays out profits from the business to its shareholders.

Not all companies pay dividends. New, growing and smaller companies may be ploughing their profits, if any, back into the business and have nothing left over for shareholders. Large, established companies are more likely to pay out dividends. The more profitable the company, the larger the dividends might be.

The company has already paid tax on its profits, so dividends come with a 10 per cent tax credit. This exactly meets

---

Asset class

Shares make up the asset class called 'equities' (see pages 19 and 21). The class can be divided into different sub-groups, for example, UK equities and overseas equities.

What are stock market investments?

Companies and governments cannot always generate enough money of their own to manage their affairs as they wish. So they look for outside finance.

How companies and governments raise money

This may be in the form of:

- **Loans.** For example, a bank loan. The company, say, pays the bank interest and on or before some agreed date repays the money it has borrowed. An alternative is to raise a loan in the form of a bond. In that case, the original lender does not have to keep the loan but can sell it to someone else. When a company raises money in this way, it is called a corporate bond. Bonds issued by the Government are called gilts. Local authorities and other organisations also issue bonds.
- **Shares.** A different way to raise money is to sell part of the business to someone else. Companies do this by issuing shares to outsiders. In return for their cash, the outsiders are given a chance to receive part of the profits if the company does well. Shares usually have no repayment date and would be pretty unattractive to outsiders if there was no way for them to get their money back. So the original purchaser can sell their shares on to other people.

This ability to sell corporate bonds, gilts, shares and so on to other investors creates a market of buyers and sellers. Any investment that can be bought and sold on such a market is a stock market investment.

Regardless of the terms of the original loan or original share sale, once a stock market investment is sold on, the market creates the resale price. If there is a lot of demand for a particular bond or share, its price will tend to rise. If there are more sellers than buyers, its price will generally fall. In other words, stock market investments nearly always involve capital risk.

In general, it's up to you whether or not you accept the risks of these investments and there's no compensation if you lose money. An exception may be where you have followed the advice of a professional adviser (see Chapter 10).

Risks and rewards for investors

REWARDS FOR THE INVESTOR

Limited, may be fixed → Unfixed, potentially high

Bank and other loans	Bonds/gilts	Shares

Lower → Higher

RISKS FOR THE INVESTOR

the tax liability of basic-rate taxpayers. You can't reclaim the tax if you are a non-taxpayer and higher-rate taxpayers may have further tax to pay.

Capital gain

If you can sell the shares at a higher price than you paid, you may have to pay capital gains tax on any gain.

If you sell the shares for less than you paid, you make a capital loss and may be able to claim tax relief on the loss.

Many factors influence the price of a company's shares. For example, how the company's profits (and so dividend pay outs) are expected to grow in future; and whether the company is likely to be a takeover target (which might cause a bidding war for its shares).

❝ Large, established companies are more likely to pay out dividends. ❞

Tax-efficient shareholdings

If you hold shares through a tax-efficient wrapper, such as a stocks-and-shares ISA, SIPP or a CTF, dividends are taxed just at 10 per cent with no higher-rate tax and gains are tax free.

THE RISKS

The main risk when you hold shares is capital risk – in other words, the risk that you will lose your original investment or gains that you have previously built up. This can happen because the share price falls or, at the worst, because a company you have invested in goes bust.

You can manage these risks by holding a spread of different shares and even different investments. Holding the shares of a single company is high risk but holding a broad spread of different shares can be a very sound investment strategy and makes sense if your reason for holding shares is to achieve some long-term goal, such as building up a pension.

If you are investing in shares for fun and the hope of making a quick profit, you are likely to actively seek the risks that holding a few selected shares entails. This is because risk is basically symmetrical. The risk of making large losses goes hand in hand with the chance of making large gains.

Different sectors

If you choose companies that are all in the same sector, your whole investment is at risk if that sector is hit by bad events – for example, the 2007 credit squeeze that sent all bank stocks plunging. It makes sense to choose shares from a range of sectors, for

 For more about how dividends and capital gains are taxed, see Chapter 2. See Chapter 10 for more information about building a diversified portfolio. See Chapter 6 for investing in shares through investment funds.

example, banks, insurance, property, mining, retailers, pharmaceuticals, electricals, and so on.

Some sectors and companies (called 'defensive stocks') are particularly resilient in an economic downturn. For example, electricity and water suppliers tend to hold their value because they are providing essential services that industrial and domestic consumers can't easily cut back on.

Different countries

Many new share investors feel most comfortable choosing the shares of companies based in their home country. But, if you stick just to UK companies, you are vulnerable if the UK economy goes into recession. Investing across a range of different countries spreads your risks and gives you the opportunity to profit from growing economies, such as China and India. This does not necessarily mean going beyond the UK stock markets. Many foreign companies are listed on the London Stock Exchange and many UK-based companies are, in fact, multinationals, deriving a large chunk of their profits from operations overseas.

If you invest in overseas business, there is an additional risk from changing exchange rates. This affects you directly if you buy currency in order to buy shares on an overseas stock market and then convert your dividends and gains back into sterling. It affects you indirectly if you invest in UK-quoted shares but the company operates abroad and is converting its profits back into sterling.

Case Study Yan

Yan decided to invest £5,000 in some shares quoted on the New York Stock Exchange. The exchange rate was $1.85 to the pound, so (for the purpose of simplicity in this example, ignoring any commission and charges), Yan's £5,000 converted to $9,250. The share price was $2, so (again, ignoring dealing charges), Yan bought 4,625 shares.

A year or so later, the shares had increased to $3 per share – a 50 per cent increase. Yan sold them, realising $13,875. By then, the exchange rate had changed to $2 to the pound. So converting his money back to sterling, he had £6,938. This gave him a 39 per cent profit on his original investment. He did not get the full benefit of the 50 per cent share price rise because of the adverse exchange rate movement. If charges are taken into account, his profit was lower still.

Different assets

Finally, given how global businesses and the economy are these days, it is quite possible that events in one part of the world have a domino effect on the rest of the world. However well diversified your holdings, all your shares might be hit. To protect against this, you could spread your money across different asset classes with only a portion invested in equities (shares) and the rest in, for example, cash, bonds and property.

THE PAPERWORK

For tax purposes, you need to keep the paperwork you get when you buy shares for many years and, when you sell, you may need to fill in a tax return (see page 42). You can avoid these problems if you invest through an ISA or SIPP.

Shares: a mixed bag

The risks and your potential return vary with the type of shares you choose. Shares are issued by all sorts of companies and they can offer different types, so there is a rich diversity of investments available for the equity investor.

DIFFERENT SHARES

Most common are ordinary shares, but there are other types that offer the investor different features.

Ordinary shares

Ordinary shareholders are the owners of the company. You have no special privileges, in particular:

- **There is no guarantee** that you will get any dividends.
- **If dividends are usually paid,** there is no guarantee that you will get a particular amount.
- **If the company goes bust,** you are last in line of all the people waiting to be paid (such as the pension scheme, HMRC, the workers, the banks, and so on) and probably will not get back any money at all.

As you can see, ordinary shareholders bear more risk than other types of shareholder. To persuade you to take these extra risks, when the company is doing well, ordinary shareholders get the lion's share of the profits paid out by the company once it has met all its other obligations.

Most ordinary shares are 'voting shares'. This means that you, along with all the other shareholders, have the right to vote on matters relating to the company, such as whether a dividend should be paid, what fees the directors should get and whether to agree to a takeover. Usually, you get one vote for each share you hold.

Preference shares

Preference shares are a halfway house between ordinary shares and corporate bonds (see page 114). Preference shareholders do not usually have any ownership rights over the company but, as the name suggests, they have some special privileges. These vary depending on the terms and conditions for the particular shares, but typically include:

- Dividends, if they are paid at all, of a set amount.
- Preference shareholders get their

“When the company is doing well, ordinary shareholders get the lion's share of the profits.”

dividend before anything is paid out to ordinary shareholders.

- If a dividend is missed, with **cumulative preference shares**, the missed amounts are made good once the company has sufficient profits. 'Non-cumulative' preference shares do not replace any missed dividends.
- Some, called **redeemable preference shares**, have a set date on which the company buys back your shares at a set price.
- If the company goes bust, preference shareholders – although near the end of the line for any pay out – do get any money back before the ordinary shareholders.

These privileges generally make preference shares less risky than ordinary shares. That's why the rewards are more limited, with dividends usually only up to a set amount and nothing extra even in a bumper year. (However 'participating' preference shares do get extra payouts.)

Usually preference shareholders do not have any voting rights.

DIFFERENT MARKETS

Most shares are designed to go on indefinitely, so, when you want to sell, you have to find someone else who is willing to buy. You buy shares either when they are newly issued from the company or from an existing holder who wants to sell. It is usually easy to buy and sell shares, provided they are traded in a large, formal market place.

Listed shares

To make it easy to find buyers and sellers, many companies opt to have their shares listed on a formal stock exchange, such as the London Stock Exchange.

To have its shares listed on the Exchange's main market, a company must be reasonably large (with a **market capitalisation** of at least £700,000) and have been trading for at least three years. You can trade shares in everything from relatively new **growth companies** to mature multinationals. The largest 100 companies on the main market are the constituents of the **FTSE 100 Index**. The Exchange ensures there is a ready market in all these shares.

The shares of many foreign companies are listed on the London Stock Exchange. But you can also buy and sell foreign shares through overseas stock markets, such as the New York Stock Exchange, the Deutsche Börse or the Hong Kong Stock Exchange.

PLUS Markets plc is a rival to the London Stock Exchange. Any company that has been approved for listing by the FSA or an equivalent regulator in another European Union country is eligible to join

London Stock Exchange companies

In October 2007, there were more than 1,100 companies listed on the London Stock Exchange main market with a combined value of more than £2 trillion. Over 70 per cent of these companies had a market capitalisation of £50 million or more. The companies come from over 40 different industry sectors, including, for example, oil and gas, banks, general retailers, pharmaceuticals, real estate and mining.

PLUS. The PLUS-listed market lets you trade in many of the shares listed on the London Stock Exchange main market as well as companies that have chosen to be listed only on PLUS.

Unlisted shares

These are shares that are not listed on a recognised stock exchange. Some are traded on stock markets, such as the:

- Alternative Investment Market (AIM). This is a junior market run by the London Stock Exchange. Companies that do not have sufficient size or track record to be listed on the main market may opt to be traded on AIM instead. But AIM includes some well-established companies too
- PLUS-quoted market run by PLUS Markets. This is aimed at young companies.

Unlisted shares tend to be in smaller companies with growth prospects. They are generally more risky investments than the companies listed on the main

Jargon buster

FTSE 100 An index that is calculated as a weighted average of the share prices of the 100 largest companies quoted on the London Stock Exchange. It is often used as a measure of the performance of the stock market as a whole

Growth company A company, usually fairly new, that is expected to grow significantly in future

Hedge fund An investment fund that can use a much wider range of investment techniques than other funds, enabling it, for example, to make money when stock markets are falling (see Chapter 9)

Market capitalisation A way of valuing a company by multiplying the number of ordinary shares it has issued by the current share price

Recognised stock exchange A UK or overseas market for trading in shares which is on a list kept by HMRC. To be on the list, a UK exchange must be regulated by the FSA and, an overseas exchange, by an equivalent regulator in its home country

> ❝Unlisted shares are generally more risky than the companies listed on the main markets.❞

Ethical investing

The stock market index company, FTSE, produces an index called FTSE4Good, of companies that invest in a socially responsible way. For details, see www.ftse.com/Indices/FTSEGood_Index_Series/index.jsp.

markets. Typically, they pay no dividends – they might not even be making any profits yet.

The government offers tax incentives to encourage investors to back UK-based unlisted and unquoted trading companies – see Chapter 9 for details.

Unquoted shares

Some unlisted shares – for example, new start-ups and small family-owned companies – are not quoted on any stock market. This makes them very difficult to value. They are also hard to sell because

there is no easy way to find a buyer. For these reasons, unquoted shares are an extremely high-risk choice for outside investors. (See Chapter 9 for more information.)

SHARE REORGANISATIONS

A company may make changes that affect your shareholding, for example:

- **Scrip or bonus issue.** The company issues free additional shares to existing shareholders. The share price adjusts so the value of your shareholding is broadly unchanged.
- **Share split.** For example, each share priced at 500p is replaced by five shares and the share price adjusts to 100p. The value of your shareholding should not change.
- **Share consolidation.** For example, every five shares priced at 10p are replaced by a single share and the share price adjusts to 50p. The value of your shareholding should be broadly unchanged.
- **Rights issue.** The company raises new money by selling additional shares. They are offered first to existing shareholders. You choose whether to buy some or all of the shares offered. The share price will also change, which means that the value of your holding will usually alter.

> **❝ Unquoted shares are hard to sell because there is no easy way to find a buyer. ❞**

 For more information about the London Stock Exchange, see www.londonstockexchange.com. For information about PLUS Markets, go to www.plusmarketsgroup.com.

Buying and selling shares

If you want to buy or sell shares, you need to use a stockbroker. This can be a firm you deal with face-to-face at a local branch or office, but more often you will use an internet, phone or postal service. Some banks and building societies offer a stockbroking service, but are usually not the cheapest option.

TYPES OF SERVICE

Stockbrokers offer three levels of service, depending on how much support you want. They are:

- **Execution-only.** The broker just carries out your buying and selling instructions. This is the cheapest service, especially if you trade online. With many internet-based services, you deal directly with the stock market using the broker's software and your transaction is carried out within seconds. You pay for an execution-only service through a charge each time you buy or sell. Often the charge will be a flat fee that could be as low as £10 to £12.
- **Advisory.** The broker discusses your investment goals and offers advice about suitable purchases and sales. The broker may be proactive, contacting you to suggest good buying and selling opportunities. Alternatively, the broker might just respond to your specific queries. Either way, the final investment decisions are yours. You pay for an advisory service through a charge each time you deal. Typically, the charge will be a percentage of the value of the shares you are buying or selling, say 1.7 per cent, subject to a minimum of, say, £15.
- **Discretionary.** You explain your investment goals and the broker takes over managing your share portfolio to meet those goals, making the investment decisions for you. This is the most expensive service and suitable only if you have a reasonably large amount to invest (starting at about £20,000 but more often in the region of £100,000). You will pay a variety of charges, for example, a

To find a stockbroker, use the London Stock Exchange Locate a broker service at www.londonstockexchange.com/en-gb/pricesnews/education/resources/broker/ or contact the Association of Private Client Investment Managers and Stockbrokers (APCIMS) at www.apcims.co.uk.

percentage each year of the value of your portfolio plus dealing charges each time the broker buys and sells shares on your behalf.

NOMINEE ACCOUNTS

With a nominee account, your broker is the legal holder of your shares but holds them on your behalf. In general, company information and voting rights go to the legal owner, your broker. However, under new laws, which came into force in October 2007, you can ask your broker to nominate you as its proxy so that you can attend shareholder meetings, speak at those meetings and vote. You can also ask to be sent company information, though increasingly a company's report and accounts and other shareholder information are openly available on the company's website.

Why you might need a nominee account

When you buy and sell shares, you usually have to deliver the money or shares within three working days. This is a very tight timescale and hard to meet if you are sending paper share certificates or cheques through the post. You have two options:

- **Delayed settlement.** You can arrange with the broker to pay or provide the

shares within, for example, five or ten days. You pay extra for this.
- **Electronic dealing.** You pay the money or transfer your shares electronically.

Increasingly, electronic dealing is the norm. Since the passing of new legislation in 2006, the Government has the power to make this the only option but has said it will consult before doing this. Already, shares held through ISAs are always traded electronically.

To deal electronically you must hold your shares electronically and you need either your own account with the electronic **settlement system**, called CREST, or to hold your shares in a nominee account with your broker who then organises sales and purchases through its own CREST account. Most investors opt for a nominee account. If you prefer to have your own CREST account, ask your broker for details.

To learn more about the CREST system, ask your broker or see www.euroclear.co.uk.

DEALING OPTIONS

Most people deal by phone or internet. If you choose postal dealing, the service is more limited.

By phone or internet

Whether buying or selling, you give your instructions, specifying either the number of shares involved or the total value of the transaction. There are various different types of instruction (called orders) that you can give your broker. For example, your broker might accept some or all of the following:

- **At best.** This is the standard transaction. Your instructions are carried out straightaway and you get the highest price available if selling or pay the lowest price available if buying.
- **Limit order.** You specify the lowest price you are willing to sell at or the highest price at which you are willing to buy. Your order stays on the system for a maximum period that the broker allows, say, up to 30 or 90 days. If, within that period, the share price reaches the limit you have set, your order goes ahead. If the share price fails to reach your limit, your order lapses. With a limit order, your broker might be able to get the share price you want but not the quantity. In that case, the broker may buy or sell part of the shares as you ordered and carry out the rest of the deal in one or more further transactions. Each transaction incurs charges, so to avoid this, you could use a kill-or-fill order.

- **Kill-or-fill.** An instruction to buy or sell a given quantity of shares immediately at a particular price (or better). If that's not possible, the deal is cancelled.
- **Stop-loss.** An instruction to automatically sell your shares if their price falls to (or below) a set level within a specified period (say 30 or 90 days). You would use this to limit the amount of money that you can lose or to lock in profits you have already made.

Case Study Julia

Julia wants to buy 1,000 shares in Marks & Spencer. The current price of 605p per share is more than she wants to pay. So she puts in a limit order to buy 1,000 shares at 575p (or less) if they fall to that price within the next 90 days.

Earlier in the year, Julia was worried about shares she held in Barratt Developments. She had bought them a few years ago at 500p and, at their peak, they were worth over 1,250p. With volatile stock markets and a downturn in the housing market forecast, she was worried she might lose all the profits she had made. In August 2007, she placed a stop-loss order to sell her full holding of 1,000 shares if the share price fell to 750p or less within the next 90 days. In October, the order was triggered.

- **Stop-buy.** An instruction to automatically buy specific shares if their price rises to (or above) a set price within a specified period (say 30 or 90 days). You might want to use this, for example, to make sure you are on board if a share suddenly breaks out of its current level and starts to rise rapidly.

By post

When dealing by post, your instructions take a while to arrive and you don't know at what share price you will deal. If you are buying, you can specify the number of shares you want to buy or the total you want to pay. If you are selling, you specify the number of shares you want to sell or the amount you want to raise. The broker simply deals at best within those instructions. With some postal broking services, there are further delays because the broker bundles together trades for many different investors to deal in bulk every few days.

DEALING COSTS

Each time you buy or sell shares there are various charges to pay (see the example of a contract note, overleaf). This can make frequent dealing expensive, especially if you are buying or selling only small amounts. After each transaction, you'll get a contract note that summarises your deal and itemises the charges. Keep all your contract notes – you may need them for capital gains tax purposes (see page 108).

A further charge is the difference (called the spread) between the higher price at which you can buy a share (the offer price) and the lower price at which you can sell (the bid price). This charge is built into the prices at which you buy and sell so does not appear as a separate entry on a contract note and effectively pays the firms (called market-makers) that ensure it is possible for you to buy and sell at any time.

The spread is usually small for the frequently traded shares in a large company, for example, just a $1/2$p or so. It is much larger for small and infrequently traded shares (for example, 10 per cent of the **mid-price**). The spread means that if you sold some shares and immediately bought them back, you would make a loss. The larger the spread, the greater this charge.

Jargon buster

Offer price (also called the ask price) The (higher) price you pay when buying shares

Bid price The (price) you get when you sell shares

Mid-price The point halfway between the bid and offer price for a share

Spread The difference between the bid and offer prices

66 A further charge is the spread. The larger the spread, the greater this charge. **99**

A typical contract note

Stock name and details The name of the company and type of shares – in this case, ordinary shares. The '25p' is the face value of the shares. The face value is relevant to the way shareholders' money is shown in the company's accounts, but otherwise is not relevant to investors and bears no relation to the share price.

Account: Julia Paresh
Account no: 123456

XYZ Brokers
Customer services 0870 000 0000
email: info@xyz.co.uk

19 November 2007

CONTRACT NOTE AND TAX INVOICE

Account type: DEALING
Trade date & time: 19/11/2007 15:38
Settlement date: 22/11/2007
Transaction reference: 1234567890

You have bought:

Stock name	Stock details	Quantity	Price	Consideration
Marks & Spen Gp	Ord sh 25p	1,000	5.7495	5749.50
			Commission	12.50
			PTM levy	0.00
			Stamp duty	28.75
			TOTAL	5790.75

Bargain condition: ex-dividend

Consideration The name given to the amount you pay for the shares when buying or get for them when selling. It equals the quantity multiplied by the price.

Commission What the broker charges for carrying out your instructions. Typically, say, 1.7 per cent of the consideration subject to a minimum of £15. But many execution-only services charge less – say, a flat-rate of £10 or, as in this case, £12.50.

If you buy shares **ex-dividend**, a dividend is due to be paid within the next few weeks but the seller not you will receive it. If you buy cum-dividend, you get the next dividend payment.

PTM levy A charge to fund the work of the Panel on Takeovers and Mergers, which makes sure that takeover bids and mergers are carried out in a fair and orderly way. The charge is £1 on sales and purchases with a consideration above £10,000. There is no charge on smaller transactions, such as this one.

Stamp duty A tax paid to the government on shares purchases (but not sales). It is 0.5 per cent of the consideration. If you are using a paper share certificate rather than electronic dealing, from 2008-9 stamp duty on purchases up to £1,000 is waived (saving you £5).

To check how much stamp duty you might pay when you buy shares, use the HMRC calculator at http://sdcalculator.inlandrevenue.gov.uk.

OTHER WAYS TO BUY SHARES

You may be able to buy shares in the company you work for through an employee share scheme at work. In general, any perks you get with your job count as part of your earnings and are taxed, but several types of employee share schemes have tax advantages. Two of the most popular employee shares schemes are outlined below.

There is normally no income tax on any free or discounted shares you get through an employee shares scheme approved by HMRC (as there is on most pay and fringe benefits from your job). You may have to pay capital gains tax when you sell the shares, but only if your gains each year come to more than the yearly allowance (£9,600 in 2008–9) (see Chapter 2). If you have substantial gains, consider selling your shares in several tranches so that you stay within the allowance.

Shares received through a share incentive plan or SAYE scheme can, within 90 days, be transferred to a stocks-and-shares ISA or self-invested pension plan (SIPP) without any tax on the transfer. In that case, when you eventually sell, the gains will be tax free.

Share incentive plan (SIP)

You can get shares in your employer's company in up to four different ways:

- **Free shares.** Your employer can give you up to £3,000-worth of shares each tax year. He or she can choose to set performance targets in your work that you must meet in order to qualify.
- **Partnership shares.** You can buy shares worth up to £1,500 each tax year (or 10 per cent of your salary if this is less).
- **Matching shares.** Your employer can give you free shares in proportion to the partnership shares you buy. The maximum number of matching shares is two for each partnership share.
- **Dividend shares.** You can use dividends you get from the shares in the scheme to buy more shares (up to a maximum of £1,500 per tax year).

The shares are held in a **trust fund** for you and, provided you keep the shares in the trust for five years (three years for the dividend shares), you get full relief from income tax and national insurance on them. If you withdraw your shares earlier, you lose some or all of the tax relief and you might lose your free and matching shares.

There is no CGT on any growth in the value of the shares during the period they are kept within the plan.

Approved Save As You Earn (SAYE) scheme

You save a set amount each month, between £5 and £250, for three or five years. Your savings are normally deducted direct from your pay by your employer. You can opt to leave the money in a five-year account invested for a further two years. At the end of the term, a tax-free bonus is added to your savings at a rate set by the Government.

At the end of the term, you can use the savings to buy shares in your employer's company. The price of the shares is fixed at the time you start to save and can be up to 20 per cent less than the actual share price at that time. If the share price has risen in the meantime, you could have a handsome capital gain if you sell the shares. You don't have to take up the option to buy the shares – you can just withdraw the savings if you prefer.

If you sell the shares, your gain for CGT purposes is generally the price at which you sell them less the amount of savings with bonus that you used to buy the shares. The gain is taxable under the normal CGT rules (see page 32), so you might want to sell only part of your holding at any one time if that helps to keep your gains below your yearly tax-free allowance (£9,600 in 2008–9). Alternatively, within 90 days of exercising your option, transfer the shares to an ISA or SIPP or other personal pension. (The amount transferred must be within the normal investment or contribution limits –

Eggs in one basket

Shares you get through an employee share scheme can be worth a lot relative to other investments you hold. Bear in mind that with your job and a large part of your savings linked to a single company, you are very vulnerable if the company were to run into difficulties. Once you have your employee shares, consider selling some to buy a wider range of investments.

see page 43 for ISAs and page 72 for pension schemes.) The transfer does not count as a disposal and so does not trigger any CGT bill and gains from a subsequent sale within the ISA or pension scheme will be tax free.

For more information about employee shares schemes, see the HMRC website at www.hmrc.gov.uk/shareschemes.

OTHER WAYS TO SELL SHARES

Some companies (especially those that have many small shareholders as a result of **privatisation** or **demutualisation**) offer their existing shareholders a cut-price share-dealing service – contact the company for details.

You might decide that, instead of holding shares direct, you would rather invest in shares through an investment fund (see Chapter 6). Many investment fund managers operate share exchange schemes so that you can swap your direct shareholdings for an investment in their fund – ask the fund for details.

Jargon buster

Demutualisation The process of converting a business, such as a building society or some insurers, that is owned by its customers or members into a more widely owned company. This usually involves giving the customers or members shares in the new company

Privatisation The process of turning a state-owned business into a more widely owned company; for example, by selling shares to the general public

Trust fund A legal arrangement where someone holds investments or other property not for their own use but for the benefit of someone else

Reading the financial pages

Newspapers give you some basic information that can help you keep track of shares. Not every listed company chooses to have its details published in newspapers. For more comprehensive information on all listed companies, the internet is the best resource.

A typical newspaper listing

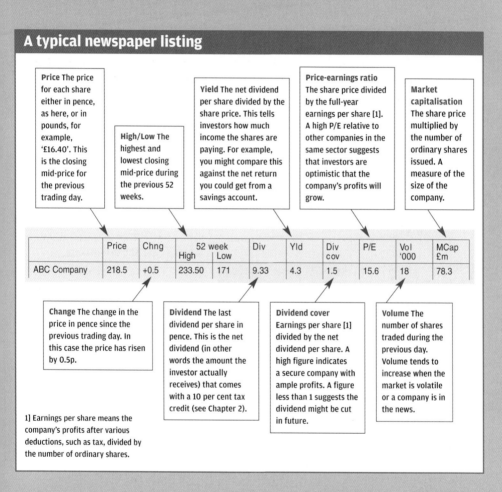

Price The price for each share either in pence, as here, or in pounds, for example, '£16.40'. This is the closing mid-price for the previous trading day.

High/Low The highest and lowest closing mid-price during the previous 52 weeks.

Yield The net dividend per share divided by the share price. This tells investors how much income the shares are paying. For example, you might compare this against the net return you could get from a savings account.

Price-earnings ratio The share price divided by the full-year earnings per share [1]. A high P/E relative to other companies in the same sector suggests that investors are optimistic that the company's profits will grow.

Market capitalisation The share price multiplied by the number of ordinary shares issued. A measure of the size of the company.

	Price	Chng	52 week High	Low	Div	Yld	Div cov	P/E	Vol '000	MCap £m
ABC Company	218.5	+0.5	233.50	171	9.33	4.3	1.5	15.6	18	78.3

Change The change in the price in pence since the previous trading day. In this case the price has risen by 0.5p.

Dividend The last dividend per share in pence. This is the net dividend (in other words the amount the investor actually receives) that comes with a 10 per cent tax credit (see Chapter 2).

Dividend cover Earnings per share [1] divided by the net dividend per share. A high figure indicates a secure company with ample profits. A figure less than 1 suggests the dividend might be cut in future.

Volume The number of shares traded during the previous day. Volume tends to increase when the market is volatile or a company is in the news.

1] Earnings per share means the company's profits after various deductions, such as tax, divided by the number of ordinary shares.

For online share information, see, for example, the Investor Centre section of the London Stock Exchange website www.londonstockexchange.com.

Tax and shares

If you buy shares of the same type in the same company on several different occasions at different prices, later on how do you know which shares you are selling? There are some special capital gains tax (CGT) share identification rules to help you work this out.

THE SHARE IDENTIFICATION RULES

Chapter 2 describes how dividends are taxed and the general rules for working out CGT when you sell or give away your shares. Where you have identical shares bought on different dates at different prices, you need to know what initial value (see page 32) to use in your calculations. The share identification rules sort this out. They apply to shares and to holdings in investment funds, such as unit trusts (see Chapter 6).

When you sell some shares, you match them to your purchases in the following order:

- Shares bought the same day.
- Shares bought within the next 30 days. This a tax avoidance measure designed to stop bed and breakfasting (see box).
- Shares bought earlier. All the shares are pooled together and the price at which you bought them is deemed to be the weighted average for the pool.

The rules used to be much more complicated but were simplified from 6 April 2008.

You need to know the price at which you originally bought your shares, and any subsequent share reorganisations (see page 99). So make sure you keep all contract notes and other paperwork.

Bed and breakfasting

This is the practice of selling some shares and immediately buying them back. You might want to do this to realise a loss to set against other gains or to realise a gain so you can use your yearly CGT allowance. But, in its basic form, the technique does not work because the law says the shares you sell must be matched to shares you buy back within the next 30 days rather than the earlier purchase that produced the gain or loss. Where a gain is involved, you can make the technique work if you sell the shares but, instead of buying them back in your own name, you buy them back within an ISA (called bed-and-ISA). Another variation that works is to sell the shares and, instead of you buying them back, your husband, wife or civil partner immediately buys the same shares (bed-and-spouse). If a loss is involved, anti-avoidance rules might catch you – get tax advice before you sell.

Case Study Emma

Emma has 3,000 shares in ABC plc, which she bought at a price of 50p per share. They now stand at £2.50 a share and so are worth £7,500. She thinks they will continue to grow so wants to carry on holding them. But she would also like to realise the gain on the shares now because she has unused tax-free allowance that would make the gain tax free:

- Ideally, she would like to sell the shares today and buy them back tomorrow. If she could do this, she would make a capital gain of 3,000 x (£2.50 – £0.50) = £6,000 that would be tax-free because it is well within her tax-free allowance for the year and, having bought the shares back at £2.50, this would be the new initial value for working out CGT on any subsequent sale.

- But the tax avoidance rules stop her doing this. They say that the 3,000 shares she sells at £2.50 must be matched with the 3,000 shares she buys the next day at £2.50. Her gain on these shares is 3,000 x (£2.50 – £2.50) = £0 and she is still holding 3,000 shares that have an initial value of 50p each.

- Emma can make her scheme work if she sells the shares as planned and next day buys 3,000 shares at £2.50 through an ISA instead of in her own name. The sale in her own name is not matched to the purchase next day by the ISA manager.

“ Tax avoidance measures stop bed and breakfasting. But you can buy back shares within an ISA (bed-and-ISA). ”

For advice about tax, contact a member of the Chartered Institute of Taxation www.tax.org.uk. For general tax information, see the *Which? Essential Guide Tax Handbook 2008/9*.

Gilts and bonds

Gilts and corporate bonds are often referred to collectively as 'fixed-interest' investments. This is because, in their standard form, they pay you a regular stream of interest payments at a set amount over a fixed term. But there are variations.

THE RISKS

Gilts and bonds can be especially useful for investors seeking income, but can be useful too if you are a growth investor looking to spread your money across a range of asset classes. Bonds are generally medium-risk investments offering a moderate return. The main risks with them are:

- **Inflation risk.** Rising prices reduce the value of the fixed-interest payments. Index-linked gilts (see page 113) tackle this problem.
- **Interest-rate risk.** After you have bought, interest rates might rise, so that you could have got a bigger income elsewhere. You can switch but then expose yourself to capital risk. Depending on the soundness of the company issuing a bond, there is a risk that it might not make the interest payments as promised.
- **Capital risk.** If you hold a gilt or bond until the end of its term, you know exactly how much money you will get back. But if you sell on the stock market before then, you cannot predict what price you will get. Depending on the soundness of the company issuing

a bond, there is a risk that it might not pay back investors' money at the end of the term.

GILTS

When you buy gilts, you are lending money to the Government. The Government is considered very sound and highly unlikely to default on its interest payments or bond repayments – hence the name 'gilts' or 'gilt-edged' for its bonds.

The return from gilts

The return takes two forms:

- **Income** in the form of the interest the gilt pays out. This is taxed as savings income (see Chapter 2). It is usually paid gross, but you can arrange to have it paid with tax at the basic rate already deducted.

Asset class

Gilts and corporate bonds are the main constituents of the asset class called 'bonds' (see Chapter 1).

Anatomy of a gilt

Each gilt has a name, for example, Treasury 4% 2016, and can be described in terms of some basic features that are captured in its name as shown here.

Coupon This is the fixed interest you get in a year expressed as a percentage of the nominal value (£100). Interest is usually paid twice a year in two equal amounts. In this case, you get 4 per cent a year - if you hold £100 nominal of the gilt, you'll receive £2 every six months.

Redemption date This is the date on which the gilt will be repaid, in this case, on a set date in 2016 (in fact 7 September 2016 - you can find out the exact date from www.dmo.gov.uk or your broker). A few gilts have no redemption date at all - they go on indefinitely and are called irredeemables. The amount you get when the gilt is repaid is called the redemption value. Gilts have a basic unit of £100 - called the nominal value or par value - and you get back £100 for each £100 held (but see index-linked gilts on page 113). You can buy and sell gilts in any amount including a part-unit down to 1p.

A gilt, for example: Treasury 4% 2016

Treasury Just a name with no particular significance. Other names used are Exchequer, Conversion, War Loan and Consul.

- **Capital gain or loss** when the gilt is redeemed or you sell it before then on the stock market. Gains are tax free and you cannot claim any relief for losses.

When you buy a gilt, the price you are quoted is an amount for each £100 nominal of stock. For example, you might pay £95 for £100 nominal. Where the **market price** is lower than the **nominal value**, you will definitely make a capital gain if you hold the stock until redemption. If the market price is higher than the nominal value, you will make a capital loss if you hold until redemption – you might be prepared to accept the loss

if the gilt will pay you a competitive income in the meantime.

The price at which you buy determines the return you will get from the gilt. The return is usually expressed in two ways:

- **Interest yield (also called running yield or income yield).** This is the coupon as a percentage of the clean market price (see Accrued income, overleaf). It gives a measure of the income you will get.
- **Redemption yield.** This is the coupon plus the capital gain or loss at redemption expressed as a percentage of the clean market price. It gives a measure of the total return you will get if you hold the gilt to redemption.

If you buy a gilt and hold it until redemption, the return you get is fixed and guaranteed from the date you buy. If you plan to sell a gilt before it reaches redemption, you cannot know in advance what price you will get, so the return is then neither fixed nor guaranteed.

Accrued income

If you buy a gilt a week or so before the next interest payment is due, you buy the gilt ex-dividend. The seller, not you, gets the next dividend payment. The rest of the time, you buy gilts cum-dividend, and you get the next dividend. This cum-dividend price you pay is really made up of a payment for the gilt itself plus a payment for the part of the next interest payment that has built up so far (called the accrued income). The prices you see quoted in newspapers and online will usually be the price excluding any of the accrued interest – called the clean market price.

If all your holdings of gilts and corporate bonds come to more than £5,000 nominal, for tax purposes the price you receive when you sell a gilt and the first interest payment you receive when you buy a gilt are adjusted so that you pay the correct amount of income tax on the accrued income included in the gilt price. The adjustments are complicated and the scheme does not apply if all your fixed interest investments come to £5,000 nominal or less.

Buying and selling gilts

You can buy and sell gilts through a stockbroker (see page 100). Dealing charges are often slightly lower than those for shares.

Alternatively, you can trade through a special government scheme run for the Debt Management Office (DMO) by Computershare Ltd. The DMO Purchase and Sale Service offers a postal execution-only service and is usually cheaper for small transactions (see table, opposite, for the charges). The main drawback is that, being a postal service, you cannot specify the exact price at which you will buy or sell. Before you use the DMO service you must register

Cost of buying and selling gilts through the DMO Service

Deal type	Commission rate	Minimum charge
Purchase costs up to £5,000	0.7%	£12.50
Purchase costs over £5,000	£35 plus 0.375% of the amount in excess of £5,000	£35
Sale proceeds up to £5,000	0.7%	None
Sale proceeds over £5,000	£35 plus 0.375% of the amount in excess of £5,000	£35

Source: Debt Management Office. Reproduced under the terms of the Click-Use Licence.

and be accepted into its Approved Investors Group. This sounds daunting but is just the DMO's equivalent of the money laundering checks that any broker or bank makes.

An additional cost is the spread between the higher offer price (also called the ask price) at which you buy gilts and the lower bid price at which you sell.

Index-linked gilts

These are a variation on the normal gilt described left. They work in basically the same way, but, in order to protect the buying power of your investment from the effects of inflation, the following adjustments are automatically made:

- **Coupon.** Each six-monthly interest payment is increased in line with inflation since the gilt was issued.

- **Redemption value.** Instead of getting £100 at redemption for each £100 of nominal stock, you get £100 increased in line with inflation since the gilt was issued.

Inflation is measured using changes in the RPI (see page 17) for eight or (with more recently issued stocks) three months before the payment date.

Islamic bonds (sukuk)

In 2007, the Government started a consultation on the feasibility of issuing Islamic bonds (called sukuk). Islamic law forbids receiving or charging interest. Holders of sukuk become owners of some underlying asset and share in profits made from that asset. Assets that could underlie UK government sukuk might be, for example, a building or infrastructure (such as a toll road).

For detailed information about gilts, see *UK Government Securities: A Guide to Gilts* published by the Debt Management Office www.dmo.gov.uk. For information about the DMO Purchase and Sale Service, contact Computershare Investor Services at www.comptershare.com.

BONDS

Essentially bonds issued by companies, local authorities and other organisations work in the same way as gilts. Most pay interest set at a fixed rate as a percentage of the bond's nominal value. Usually there is a date when the bond is redeemed and the nominal value paid back. The running yield and redemption yield are worked out as for gilts (see page 111).

Extra risks and rewards

The main difference between bonds and gilts is risk. Unlike gilts, there is no certainty that a company, say, will honour its obligation to make the interest and capital repayments. To compensate you for this risk, corporate and other similar bonds generally offer a higher return than gilts.

The precise risk varies with the soundness of the company or other organisation. Specialist rating agencies give guidance on how safe a bond is thought to be. They each use their own systems, but the highest rating is usually AAA. But even bonds from well-established companies, such as Barings Bank, sometimes go belly up.

Variations

Some bonds have no redemption date. To get your money back, you have to sell in the stock market, so you cannot be sure in advance what overall return you will get. Most common of these are permanent interest-bearing shares (PIBS) issued by building societies and perpetual sub-bonds (PSBs), which are the equivalent issued by demutualised building societies.

Convertibles

These are bonds that give you the option on one or more set dates in the future to exchange your bonds for shares in the company at a share price set at the time the bonds are issued. You don't have to take up the option in which case your investment carries on in the normal way until the bond is redeemed or you sell it.

Whether or not it is worth exercising your option depends on the share price at the conversion date(s). The price at which a convertible bond trades in the stock market will reflect not just the return from its conventional bond terms but also investors' views about whether the bond will offer a profitable way to acquire the company's shares.

Buying and selling bonds

You buy and sell bonds through a stockbroker (see page 100).

Deep-discount bonds (also known as junk bonds)

These pay no interest at all. They are issued at a price well below their nominal value and the return, if any, comes from the substantial gain at redemption (or earlier sale in the stock market). These are often high-risk investments issued by companies that cannot afford to pay interest now and are banking on their growth prospects to attract you.

Investment funds

Investment funds give you a stake in ready-made portfolios run by professional fund managers and they can be suitable for virtually any financial goal. Most can be put inside tax-efficient wrappers, such as ISAs and SIPPs. The catch? Extra charges and the challenge of picking the best funds.

Fund versus direct investment

Investment funds are portfolios of shares, bonds or similar investments run by professional fund managers. You invest by taking a small stake in the fund along with many other investors. Funds are structured in a variety of ways with different charging, risk and tax implications.

THE ADVANTAGES

There are several advantages from investing through funds, especially if you are a relatively small investor.

Affordable risk-spreading

As Chapter 5 discussed, holding shares in a single company or just a few is risky. To get the risks down to a manageable level, you need to hold a spread of shares from different sectors and maybe even different countries. Academics suggest that around ten different, well-chosen shares could be enough to achieve a good balance of risk. Dealing charges make buying small quantities of shares uneconomic, so you should probably be looking at a minimum investment of, say, £1,000 for each shareholding. This means that, as an absolute minimum, you should be investing £10,000.

> ❝ With many investment funds, you can invest as little as £250 as a lump sum or £25 a month. ❞

Asset class

There are investment funds covering every type of asset class. See page 127 for details of the different funds available. See Chapter 7 for property investment funds and Chapter 9 for hedge funds.

With many investment funds, you can invest as little as £250 as a lump sum or £25 a month on a regular basis, and take a stake in a portfolio investing in not just ten different shares, but typically 50–100 of them.

Decisions made for you

When you invest direct in the stock market, you choose which shares or bonds to buy or sell and when. This may involve you in a lot of research as you try to decide which companies offer the best prospects.

When you invest through a fund, the fund manager does the research, and decides which investments to buy and sell and when. Your only decision is which investment funds will best help you meet your goals.

Less paperwork

Investing direct in the stock market is a very hands-on experience. If you directly hold your own portfolio of shares, you have to give a broker instructions each time you buy and sell some shares. Also, unless you use a nominee account (see page 101), you have to deal with communications from the companies you invest in and may have to take other decisions, such as whether to agree to a takeover or to buy extra shares if the company is trying to raise further cash from existing shareholders. Every time you alter the make-up of your portfolio, you have a fresh batch of paperwork to file away and may have to report your deals to the tax authorities.

But most of the communications and decisions disappear if you invest through an investment fund. The manager handles it all. The only paperwork you have to keep and may need to report concerns your dealings with the investment fund itself, not the underlying investments within the fund.

Bulk buys

Your money is pooled with that of many other investors, so the fund manager is able to buy and sell the underlying

investments in large quantities. As a result, the manager will pay cheaper wholesale prices than the charges you pay.

Stress-free overseas investments

The UK stock markets are well established and well regulated. You are dealing with people in your own language and probably have a good idea of how to find things out and what to do if there's a problem. The process can be much more difficult and confusing if you buy or sell shares quoted on stock markets in other countries. When you invest through a fund, the fund manager deals with all that.

THE DRAWBACKS

However, the advantages of investing through funds come at a price – fund managers need to be paid, you have less control over your investments and no guarantee that the fund managers will produce good returns.

> **‟Fund managers need to be paid and ultimately it's you who pays through a variety of different charges. ”**

 To find out more about the charges incurred in investment funds, see pages 120–5.

Charges

In general, fund managers are not cheap, nor are the marketing and sales processes that some types of investment fund use. Ultimately, it's you who pays through a variety of different charges, some made direct to the investment fund and others deducted from the value of your holding.

Less control

You can choose the investment fund, but you have no control over the specific shares and bonds that it holds. If you like to back your own hunches and enjoy the thrills and spills of watching your own choice, investment funds are possibly not for you.

Are the managers any good?

A major reason for investing through a fund is so that you can place investment decisions in the hands of skilled professionals. There are broadly two types of fund:

- **Actively managed.** The fund managers choose what goes into the fund and the timing of purchases and sales. The aim is to deliver fund performance that is better than the general stock market.
- **Passively managed.** The investments in the fund are chosen to replicate the stock market as a whole. The aim is to track stock market performance (and so these funds are called tracker funds). This strategy involves less intervention by the fund manager and less trading, so charges are normally lower than for an active fund.

The philosophy behind passive management is that fund managers cannot consistently beat the market, so there is no point in paying extra for active management. Research by, for example, WM Company, tends to back this up. For example, its 2004 comparison of unit trusts investing in UK companies against a stock market index found that over a 20-year period only one-fifth of active fund managers beat the market.

❝Research found that over a 20-year period only one-fifth of active fund managers beat the market.❞

Types of investment fund

All investment funds pool your money with lots of other investors to give you a stake in a ready-made portfolio. But they come in a variety of types, which have some key differences, especially when it comes to tax treatment and risk, as outlined in this section, culminating in the table on page 126.

UNIT TRUSTS

Trustees hold the investments in the fund on behalf of the investors.

Your investment

You buy units in the fund. The unit trust creates and cancels units as investors come and go, so the value of your units directly reflects the value of the underlying investments in the fund.

You can buy and sell units through the unit trust management company or an intermediary, such as a **discount broker**, fund supermarket, IFA or stockbroker. The minimum investment varies between, say, £250 and £1,500 for lump sums and, say, £50 to £100 for regular monthly saving.

The return

The return may be in two forms:

- **Distributions (income).** If the unit trust is invested in shares, these are dividend distributions paid with 10 per cent tax already deducted. The tax cannot be reclaimed. If the unit trust is invested largely in gilts and/or bonds, you get an interest distribution. This has tax at 20 per cent (in 2008–9) deducted, which can be reclaimed. In either case, higher-rate taxpayers have extra tax to pay unless the unit trust is held through a tax-efficient wrapper, such as an ISA or SIPP.

The wrapper

You can buy the following investments direct or, if you prefer, through a wrapper, such as a stocks-and-shares ISA, SIPP or CTF: unit trusts; OEICs; investment trusts; exchange-traded funds (ETFs). Buy direct and, depending on your personal tax situation, you may have tax to pay on any income or gains you make. Buy through an ISA, SIPP or CTF and you get the tax advantages of that wrapper (see Chapters 2 and 4).

If you invest in insurance funds, these come ready wrapped in an insurance policy. A UK-based insurer pays tax on the return from the investments before you get it. You cannot reclaim the tax and, for most taxpayers, investing this way is not tax-efficient. This does not apply to offshore funds held with a non-UK insurer. Some UK insurance-based funds come ready-wrapped in a tax-efficient wrapper, for example, personal pension schemes and tax-efficient friendly society plans, and some can be held through an ISA.

- **Capital gain (or loss).** You make a gain, if you sell your units at a higher price than you paid (see Chapter 2 for how gains are taxed). Gains made within an ISA, SIPP or CTF are tax free.

You can buy different types of unit when you invest. Distribution or income units can pay out an income. Alternatively, you can opt for the income to be automatically used to buy further units. Either way, you are taxed on the income as it arises. With accumulation units, there are no income pay outs. Any income made by the investments in the fund is automatically reinvested, increasing the unit price.

Unit trust charges

You buy units at a higher price – the offer price – than the bid price at which you could immediately sell them back. The spread between these two prices is typically around 5 per cent and includes an initial charge, which covers the costs of setting up and selling you the investment. Some unit trusts are single-priced, in which case the initial charge is quoted separately and added to what you pay. The initial charge may be reduced or waived if you buy through a discount broker or fund supermarket. Tracker funds often have no initial charge.

An annual management charge (AMC) covers the cost of the professional fund

manager and is a percentage of the value of your investment. In an actively managed fund, the AMC is typically around 1.5 per cent a year. In a tracker fund, it is usually 1 per cent or less.

Some unit trusts have an exit charge. This is most common where there is no initial charge. The exit charge aims to recoup the costs of selling you the investment if you cash in within, say, the first five years.

OPEN-ENDED INVESTMENT COMPANIES (OEICs)

The trust structure used by unit trusts is unfamiliar to investors in the rest of Europe, where it is more common for investment funds to be run by companies. To widen the international appeal of UK investment funds, OEICs were created. They are also called investment companies with variable capital (ICVCs). You invest by buying shares in the company.

The terms 'open-ended' and 'variable capital' refer to the fact that the company creates and cancels shares as investors

 For more information about unit trusts and OEICs, contact the Investment Management Association at www.investmentuk.org.

come and go. This means the value of your investment always directly reflects the value of the underlying investments in the fund.

From an investor's point of view, OEICs are very similar to unit trusts. The main difference is that OEIC shares are always bought and sold at a single price. So, instead of having a bid-offer spread (which is just a type of charge), with an OEIC this charge is shown separately and clearly labelled as a charge. You pay the same, but the charge is more transparent.

EXCHANGE-TRADED FUNDS (ETFs)

ETFs are shares traded on the stock exchange that represent an underlying investment fund. They are all tracker funds – in other words, each fund is set up to mimic the performance of a particular investment index, such as the FTSE 100. But, increasingly, new indices are being developed to widen the range of ETFs. For example, you can invest in ETFs that track commodities and there are plans to introduce ETFs linked to indices of sharia-compliant investments.

Your investment

You invest by buying shares in the ETF through a stockbroker in the same way that you would buy any other shares (see page 100). The only difference is that no stamp duty is charged on the purchase of ETF shares. The ETF creates and cancels shares according to the demand from investors. This ensures that the price of the shares directly reflects the value of the underlying investments.

Dealing charges generally make small investments in shares uneconomic. So ETFs are mainly suitable for investors with a lump sum of, say, £1,000 or more to invest.

The return

The return can be in two forms:

- **Dividends (income).** These are paid with 10 per cent tax already deducted, which cannot be reclaimed. Unless the shares are held through a tax-efficient wrapper, such as an ISA or SIPP, higher-rate taxpayers have extra tax to pay. (See Chapter 2 for more about the taxation of dividends.)
- **Capital gain (or loss).** You make a gain if you sell your shares at a higher price than you paid (see Chapter 2 for how gains are taxed). Gains made within an ISA or SIPP are tax free.

ETF charges

You have the normal dealing charges for buying and selling shares (see page 104).

There is a spread between the higher offer (ask) price at which you buy and the lower bid price at which you sell. This is usually fairly small, for example,

To find out more about ETFs, visit the London Stock Exchange website at www.londonstockexchange.com (follow the links to Investor Centre then Education).

Investment funds

between 0.1 and 0.5 per cent of the offer price. There is no other initial charge.

The annual management charge is usually 0.5 per cent or less, making ETFs cheaper than most investment funds.

INVESTMENT TRUSTS

Companies that are traded on the stock exchange whose business is running an investment fund.

Your investment

You invest by buying shares in the company. Unlike the funds looked at so far, an investment trust is a 'close-ended fund', which means that a set number of shares have been issued. If there is heavy demand, the investment trust does not issue extra shares. Instead the share price tends to rise. Similarly if a lot of investors want to sell, the share price tends to fall. The result is that the value of your shares only indirectly reflects the value of the underlying investments in the fund.

You can buy and sell the shares direct from the investment trust management company or through a stockbroker. When you use a broker, normal share dealing

Net asset value

The net asset value (NAV) of a share or unit is the value of the investments in the fund divided by the number of shares or units. For example, if a fund is worth £100 million and there are 50 million units or shares issued, the NAV is £2 per unit or share.

The price of units in a unit trust and shares in an OEIC or ETF is its NAV. This is because the fund management company issues and cancels units in line with the demand from investors. If there are more buyers than sellers, the management company creates extra units to match the extra money being invested in the fund. If there are more sellers than buyers, units are cancelled in line with the decrease in the money invested in the fund.

The price of an investment trust is not necessarily (or usually) equal to its NAV,

because the number of shares is fixed and does not adjust with demand from investors - instead the share price adjusts. If there are more buyers than sellers of the shares, the market price will tend to rise (even without any change in the value of the underlying investment fund). If there are more sellers than buyers, the share price will tend to fall. In the example above, the share price on the stock market might be, say, 190p per share. This is lower than the NAV of £2 per share, so the shares are said to be trading at a discount. If the share price was higher than the NAV, the shares would be trading at a premium. When the share price is trading at a discount it does not necessarily mean you have a bargain since the share price might never rise to match the NAV.

charges apply (see page 103), including stamp duty on purchases. Charges make small investments – say, less than £1,000 – uneconomic. If you deal through the management company, charges are often lower. The management company usually offers a regular savings scheme with a minimum investment of, say, £25 or £50 a month and will typically accept lump sums from £250 upwards.

The return

Unlike unit trusts, OEICs and ETFs, investment trusts can borrow money to boost the amount invested in their funds. This can magnify the gains and the losses for investors – an effect called gearing (see box, overleaf). It makes investments trusts generally a higher-risk investment than other types of investment fund, but also increases the chance of making higher returns. The return can be in the form of:

- **Dividends (income)** with 10 per cent tax already deducted, which cannot be reclaimed. Unless the shares are held through a tax-efficient wrapper, such as an ISA or SIPP, higher-rate taxpayers have extra tax to pay (see Chapter 2 for more about the taxation of dividends).
- **Capital gain (or loss).** You make a gain, if you sell your shares at a higher price than you paid (see Chapter 2 for how gains are taxed). Gains made within an ISA or SIPP are tax free.

Split capital investment trusts are investment trusts with a set life that offer investors a choice of different shares that deliver different returns. There will be at least two types of shares:

- **Income shares.** These receive all the income from the investment trust during its life. When the trust is wound up at the end of its life, the income shareholders typically get back a set amount or token amount depending on the rules for the particular shares.
- **Capital shares.** These receive no income and all the return is in the form of capital shared out when the trust is wound up.

Some split capital trusts issue zero-dividend preference shares, which receive no income and take priority over other shareholders in receiving a capital sum when the trust is wound up.

Investment trust charges

You have the normal dealing charges for buying and selling shares (see page 103), though these may be reduced if you buy and sell through the management company.

 For more information about investment trusts, contact The Association of Investment Companies at www.theaic.co.uk.

There is a spread between the higher offer (ask) price at which you buy and the lower bid price at which you sell. This will generally be small for a large, frequently traded investment trust, but higher for shares that are traded infrequently. There is no other initial charge.

The annual management charge is usually less than 1 per cent. Other charges are deducted direct from the fund.

INSURANCE-BASED FUNDS

These are investment funds run by insurance companies that you invest in by taking out an **investment-type life insurance** policy or personal pension.

Your investment

The money you pay into the insurance policy or pension plan is used to buy units in one or more investment funds. Minimum premiums vary depending on the type of insurance policy or pension involved. For example, around £500 for a growth bond, £5,000 for a bond

producing income and £20 a month for a regular premium policy.

You take out the life insurance or pension either direct with the insurer or through an intermediary, such as an IFA. You might take out a personal pension through your workplace and, if you belong to a money purchase occupational pension scheme, you will often also be able to choose which investment funds you invest in.

The return

Investment-type life insurance can be used to provide a lump sum pay out after a set term or a regular stream of pay outs to give you an income. In either case, the pay outs always count as income for tax purposes (Chapter 2 explains how the pay outs are taxed).

The important point to bear in mind with insurance-based funds is that normally the insurer has already been taxed on the return from the investment funds before it is paid out to you. You are essentially given a credit for the tax already paid. But, in most cases, the tax paid by the insurer will be greater than the tax you personally would have paid on the gross pay out from another type of investment fund.

However, this does not apply to the return from funds held through a pension scheme, tax-efficient friendly society plan or stocks-and-shares ISA. In these cases, the insurer does not pay tax on the return from the fund (other than 10 per cent on income from shares), so they can be a sensible tax choice.

Gearing

In the context of investment trusts, gearing means borrowing to invest. It has the effect of increasing gains and also losses. For example, suppose investors have together put £10 million into an investment fund and it grows by 10 per cent. The investors have made £1 million. Now suppose the invested money had in fact been £5 million from investors and £5 million of borrowing. Ignoring the cost of borrowing, the investors have now made £1 million on an investment of £5 million - a return of 20 per cent.

Charges

You might pay some or all of the following charges:

- **Policy or administration fee.** This is deducted from your premium or pension contribution before it is invested.
- **Unit allocation.** The percentage of the remaining premium that will be used to buy units in an investment fund. If the percentage is less than 100, this is another charge. For example, a 96 per cent allocation would mean 96 per cent of your money (less any policy fee) was being invested and 100 – 96 = 4 per cent being taken as a charge. If it is more than 100, you are, in effect, getting a rebate of part of the policy or administration fee. For example, suppose you invest £1,000 and £25 is taken as a policy fee. If the unit allocation is 102 per cent, then 102% x £975 = £994.50 is invested, so the net effect is a charge of £1,000 – £994.50 = £5.50.
- **Bid-offer spread.** You may have to buy units at a higher offer price than the bid price you would get if you cashed them in straightaway. This is exactly the same as the bid-offer spreads already considered when looking at shares in Chapter 5 (see page 103) and unit trusts in this chapter (see page 120). A typical spread would be 5 per cent. But with some funds the bid-offer spread is zero.
- **Annual management charge (AMC).** A percentage of the value of your investment – usually between 0.5 and 1.75 per cent.

(see page 103) ... (see page 120)

Switching funds

When you switch from one investment fund to another, this usually counts as a disposal for tax purposes and could trigger a capital gains tax bill. You will also usually incur a fresh set of initial and dealing charges. But switches between funds when you invest through a life insurance policy or pension scheme are not disposals for tax purposes. The insurer may also waive some or all of the charges.

- **Capital units.** The name given to units that have a higher-than-normal AMC, for example, an extra 0.5 to 1.0 per cent. You might have to hold capital units for the first few years.
- **Switching fee.** You may be able to switch from one investment fund to another without charge. Alternatively, just the first few switches a year might be free.
- **Surrender charge.** A reduction in the pay out if you withdraw your money before the end of the policy term or during the early years.

Jargon buster

Friendly society tax-efficient plan Investment-type life insurance policy from a friendly society that produces a largely tax-free return. But the maximum you can invest is very low at just £270 a year

Investment-type life insurance A life insurance policy that builds up a cash-in value and so is often used mainly as an investment rather than for providing life cover. Examples include endowment policies and whole-life policies (designed to run for as long as you live but which can be cashed in during your lifetime)

Investment funds compared

	Unit trusts and OEICs	Exchange-traded funds (ETFs)	Investment trusts	Insurance-based funds held tax-efficiently [1]	Other insurance-based funds
How you invest	Buy units	Buy shares on stock market	Buy shares on stock market	Take out pension scheme or insurance policy	Take out insurance policy
Relationship between price and net asset value [2]	Direct	Direct	Indirect	Direct	Direct
Investment style	Active or passive	Passive	Active or passive	Active or passive	Active or passive
Fund and product charges	Moderate, usually low for tracker funds	Low	Moderate, usually low for tracker funds	Often high	Often high
Minimum investment	From, say, £50 a month of £250 as a lump sum	None [3]	None if you buy through a broker [3]. From, say, £50 a month of £250 as a lump sum if you buy through manager's scheme	From, say, £20 a month of £500 as a lump sum, sometimes less	From, say, £20 a month of £500 as a lump sum
You pay dealing charges	No	Yes	Yes	No	No
Switching may trigger a tax bill	Yes	Yes	Yes	No	No
Tax (unless held in ISA, SIPP or CTF)	Income tax on income, CGT on gains	Income tax on income, CGT on gains	Income tax on income, CGT on gains	Return from ISA or friendly society plan is largely tax free (see Chapter 4 for tax and pension schemes)	Insurer has already paid tax on return. You cannot reclaim this and might have higher-rate tax to pay

[1] For example, through a pension scheme, tax-efficient friendly society plan, stocks-and-shares ISA or CTF
[2] Net asset value is the value of the investments in the fund divided by the total number of share or units issued
[3] But dealing charges when buying through a stockbroker mean small investments may be uneconomic. Aim to invest, say, £1,000 as a minimum

Choice of funds

Whatever your investment goals, there is almost certainly an investment fund or a mix-and-match of several funds that will suit your purpose. Some of the main options available are described below.

CASH ASSET CLASS

Useful if your main aim is to avoid capital risk and you are investing for less than five years. You might also mix with funds from other asset classes to manage your overall risk level.

Traditional money market fund

An alternative to the bank and building society investments described in Chapter 3, these funds aim to preserve your original capital and earn a high level of interest. By pooling your money with many other investors, the fund manager has large enough sums to invest on the wholesale money markets used, for example, by banks when they lend to each other. These generally offer consistently higher returns than you can get in the high street. Usually you have instant access to your money.

Enhanced money market fund

Similar to traditional money market funds, but these invest in a wider range of deposit-type investments, including some where the money is tied up for a bit longer and/or the underlying investments

are a little more risky. The aim is to earn a higher return, but this makes these funds a bit more risky than the traditional funds.

BOND ASSET CLASS

Bond funds are often particularly useful if you are investing for income. You might mix them with funds from other asset classes in order to manage your overall level of risk and return.

 Note that although you can invest direct in gilts and bonds to get a fixed and guaranteed return (see Chapter 5), when you invest in a bond fund, the return is not fixed, so you could therefore lose some or all of your capital.

❝ Bond funds are useful if you are investing for income. ❞

Fixed income: UK gilts

Most of the fund is invested in gilts and most of the remainder in other low-risk, government-backed investments.

Fixed income: index-linked

Most of the fund is invested in index-linked gilts, which is useful if you want to protect your capital and income from inflation.

Fixed income: bonds

Funds that invest most of the money in corporate bonds and preference shares (see Chapter 5). UK funds hold bonds denominated in sterling (or, if foreign currency bonds are held, arrangements are made to offset any movement in exchange rates). Global funds hold bonds from different countries.

Equity and bond income

A mix of bonds and shares designed to produce a high level of income.

PROPERTY ASSET CLASS

Property produces rental income, so can be particularly useful for income investors. When property markets are rising, there is also the chance of capital growth.

Property fund

Invests in the shares of listed property companies and/or direct in commercial properties, such as office blocks and shopping centres. Property can be hard to sell quickly, so, when you want your money back, some property funds are allowed to delay repayment by up to six months or even longer. In general, the fund managers have already paid tax on income from renting out properties that you cannot reclaim, but this is due to change for some unit trusts and OEICs from April 2008 (see Chapter 7).

Real estate investment trust (REIT)

A REIT is an investment trust, listed on the stock market, which invests in commercial and/or residential property. Instead of being taxed as an investor in a fund, you are taxed as if you were holding the underlying properties direct (see Chapter 7). From 2008–9, this tax treatment is extended to OEICs that invest in property and meet the required rules.

EQUITY ASSET CLASS

Equities are the backbone of most long-term growth strategies. Some equity funds are particularly useful for providing income and you might also consider income shares in a split capital investment trust (see page 123).

UK equity income

Invested mainly in the shares of UK-listed companies and aiming to provide some growth and a fairly high level of income (which you can reinvest if you are investing for growth).

UK all companies

These funds invest mainly in a wide range of companies listed on the UK stock exchange. In effect you are investing in the UK economy. The main objective is capital growth. Some invest only in larger or medium-sized companies, others invest across a wider spectrum.

“Equities are the backbone of most long-term growth strategies. ”

UK smaller companies

These funds also invest in a wide range of companies listed on the UK stock exchange, but in this case focusing just on smaller companies. This is more risky than the UK all companies sector and, instead of investing in the UK economy as a whole, you are backing the newer, smaller companies that have the potential to grow and maybe to give you higher returns.

Global growth

Invests in the shares of companies from many different countries with a main objective of capital growth.

Individual countries or continents

You have a wide choice of funds investing in the shares of companies in, for example, Europe, North America, Japan and Asia. Some specialise in smaller companies; others invest across the board. In general, investing in a single geographical area abroad is more risky than investing either in the UK (which does not involve any foreign currency risk) or in a global fund that spreads your money across a wide range of different geographical areas.

Ethical fund

Usually invests either in UK companies, particular geographical areas such as the USA or Asia, or on a global basis, but restricted to shares in companies that meet certain criteria, such as no involvement in the arms trade or gambling or actively promoting good working practices (see box, overleaf). Ethical Research Investment Services (EIRIS) estimates that around half a million private investors invest over £6 billion in ethical funds.

> **❝ Around half a million private investors invest over £6 billion in ethical funds. ❞**

Currency risk

In general, if you choose a fund investing in cash, bonds or equities abroad, you have an added layer of risk because changes in exchange rates can affect the value of your investment (see the case study on page 95). However, some funds adopt deliberate strategies (called hedging) to offset changes in exchange rates. Used this way, hedging is like taking out insurance – so essentially the fund has insurance to make good any losses through exchange rate changes, thereby removing this layer of risk. For more about hedging techniques, see Chapter 9. The fund's literature or your financial adviser should be able to tell you if a fund does this.

To learn more about ethical investing, contact the research body, Ethical Investment Research Services (EIRIS) at www.eiris.org or specialist IFA, Ethical Investors Group, at www.ethicalinvestors.co.uk.

Ethical investing

Ethical investing means making investment decisions that are consistent with your social, environmental or ethical beliefs. Ethical investing originated with religious groups, such as Methodists wishing to avoid giving support to the gambling and alcohol industries, but is now widely adopted by people of all religions and people who are not religious too.

There are three approaches to ethical investment:

- **Screening**. This involves selecting companies according to positive criteria, such as good employment practices and energy efficiency. It also involves avoiding companies according to negative criteria, such as involvement in the arms trade, tobacco or pornography. There are well over 50 ethical investment funds open to private investors that screen using a variety of different criteria.

- **Preference** (also called 'best in class'). This starts with the decision to invest in a particular sector, for example, oil. You then choose the most ethical or socially responsible company within that sector.

- **Engagement**. You invest in a company that does not behave as ethically or responsibly as you would like and use your shareholder powers to raise and vote on issues to improve that company's behaviour.

Bear in mind that ordinary ethical funds are unlikely to fully comply with sharia law. For example, ethical funds may be invested in banks (which involve Riba – the receiving and paying of interest) or supermarkets that sell non-halal products.

Therefore, if you are a Muslim, you may want to look instead at dedicated Islamic investment funds. An IFA can help you do this.

Tracker fund

Funds that are designed to give you returns that match the performance of a particular stock market index or other investment index. For example, it might track the UK FTSE 100 or FTSE 250 or an equivalent stock market index for another country. Tracker funds are passive funds (see page 118) and usually have lower charges than other investment funds. The fund does not necessarily hold every share in the chosen index. It may just hold a selection of investments that have been statistically found to closely mimic the index.

❝ Tracker funds usually have lower charges than other investment funds. ❞

Particular sectors

Funds that invest in particular sectors, for example, soft commodities (such as wheat, sugar), metals, mining, energy, technology media and telecommunications (TMT), healthcare or biotechnology. They are more risky than funds that invest across a wide range of different sectors.

Particular strategies

Funds that focus on, for example, emerging markets (developing countries experiencing or expected to experience strong economic growth, such as some eastern European countries, China and India), or defensive stocks (shares in companies that tend to carry on performing during an economic recession, such as utility companies and food retailers). The risk-reward level involved varies, depending on the particular strategy being adopted.

MIXED ASSET CLASSES

These funds all aim to save you the trouble of deciding how to allocate your money across the different asset classes.

Asset allocation/managed funds

Invest in a range of assets, including cash, bonds, property and equities. The manager switches the balance between the asset classes according to the aims of the fund and stock market conditions. Different funds have different aims, for example, cautious managed funds for low-risk investors, balanced for medium-risk investors and aggressive or active for those comfortable with higher risks.

With-profits funds

These are insurance-based funds (that you invest in via an insurance policy or pension scheme). They give you a return largely based on the performance of a wide range of investments, including bonds, property and equities. Your return is in the form of reversionary bonuses (paid each year) and a terminal bonus (paid when the insurance policy matures). It is the insurance company that decides whether to pay a bonus and the amount you get. Once added, the bonuses cannot normally be taken away, so your investment should not normally fall in value. In order to try to maintain a steady stream of bonuses, the insurer smoothes the returns by keeping back some of the profits from good years to boost the bonuses paid in years when investment returns are poor. If you withdraw your money before the end of the policy term or chosen retirement date, the insurer may claw back some of the reversionary bonuses through a special charge called a **market value reduction (MVR)** and you will usually miss out on the terminal bonus.

Jargon buster

Market value reduction (MVR) A charge to claw back some of the reversionary bonuses that have been credited to your with-profits policy, if you cash it in early. It is usually levied only when stock markets have been falling

Lifestyle funds

These are designed for specific long-term investment goals, such as saving for a pension or building up a lump sum at age 18 through a CTF. In the early years of the investment, the fund is invested totally in equities. In the last five to ten years of reaching your chosen pension age, or within the last five years of reaching 18, the fund automatically and progressively switches you into the safer asset classes, bonds and cash, in order to lock in your earlier gains and protect you from the effects of a last-minute fall on the stock market.

Multimanager/fund of funds

An investment fund that holds a selection of investment funds. The idea is that the fund manager takes on the tricky task of choosing particular investment funds for you. The downside is that there are two levels of managers to be paid, so overall expect to pay more in charges.

Protected/guaranteed funds

These funds do not mix assets for you, but they aim to give you some of the stock market growth of equities while protecting you from capital risk. A guaranteed fund promises, over, say, a three-month period, to return your capital in full and give you a return linked to the growth in a stock market index.If the index does not rise, you just get your capital back and no more. More common are protected funds. For example, a 90-per-cent fund will promise to return 90 per cent of your original capital plus a return linked to a stock market index. This limits your maximum loss over a three-month period to 10 per cent of your original investment.

Guaranteed equity bonds

Similarly, some insurers offer guaranteed equity bonds that offer the chance of stock market gains with a degree of protection against capital risk. Typically, you invest for a set period of several years and get a return, which is a proportion of the growth in a stock market index. If the stock market falls, you get back your capital in full provided the fall is not too large. But, if the market falls by more than a specified amount (say, 35 per cent), you lose some or even all of your original capital. These bonds can be used for growth or income – see page 171 for an income example. To assess the likelihood and possible extent of any loss, it is important to read the terms and conditions very carefully.

" Lifestyle funds automatically switch you into safer asset classes to lock in gains. "

Comparing funds

The success of your investment will depend on investment performance, charges and tax. Most important of these is performance, but there is no foolproof way of picking the winners.

There are literally thousands of investment funds to choose from, so how can you narrow down the choice? Your aim, of course, is to pick the funds that will give you the best return. Unfortunately, there is no way to do this with any certainty, but there are some broad guidelines you can follow, described below and overleaf.

THE BASICS

You need to take into account tax treatment and the level of risk inherent in the fund.

Be aware of tax

With income tax rates up to 40 per cent and capital gains tax (CGT) at 18 per cent, you do not want to pay tax on your investments unnecessarily. See the table overleaf to keep HMRC share to a minimum.

Be aware of risk and return

As discussed in Chapter 1, experts suggest that the degree to which you spread your money across the different classes – your asset allocation – accounts for more than 90 per cent of the variation in return you get from different funds and is more important than the

particular investment funds you pick within each class.

Bear in mind that if you are investing for the long term (ten years or more), you are likely to get the best return by having a high proportion of your money invested in equities and possibly property, so focus on the investment funds on page 128 to 132. For short- and medium-term goals, you should generally have proportionately more in the cash and bond classes (see pages 127–8). Adjust these basic approaches to take account of your personal approach to risk, according to whether you are a cautious, balanced or adventurous investor (see Chapter 1).

Within each asset class, you have a choice of sectors. Especially when it comes to equities, the choice is very wide. If you are a cautious or balanced investor, broadly based funds, such as UK all companies, UK equity income and global growth, are likely to be more suitable than the higher risk funds that specialise in particular geographical areas or individual sectors.

If you do not want to choose your own balance between the different asset classes, consider funds that make the choice for you (see pages 131–2) or get advice from an IFA.

Investing tax efficiently

Tax efficiency	Way of investing
MOST EFFICIENT	**SIPPs and other pension schemes** If you are happy to take the eventual proceeds partly as income and partly as a tax-free lump sum, this is the most tax-efficient way to invest in funds. Tax relief on contributions boosts your investment substantially and there are further tax advantages (Chapter 4).
	ISAs This is the next most tax-efficient way to invest in funds, provided: • You are a taxpayer choosing funds that invest in cash, gilts, bonds or REITs. • You are a higher-rate taxpayer, in which case investing this way in share-based funds will also be tax efficient. • You are any type of taxpayer who normally uses their yearly CGT allowance. Investing in any type of fund through an ISA will shelter you from CGT.
	Direct investment Your return after all taxes have been paid is likely to be highest if you choose a unit trust, OEIC, investment trust or ETF.
LEAST EFFICIENT	**Insurance funds** Because of the non-reclaimable tax paid by the insurance company, even on capital gains, this is usually the least tax-efficient way to invest in funds.

Offshore funds

If you invest in a fund based offshore, you will normally pay income tax rather than capital gains tax (CGT) on any gain you mke when you sell your units or shares in the fund. But, with a distributor fund (which has to pay out at least 85 per cent of its income to investors), you pay income tax on the income and CGT on any gains when you sell. From 2008–9, this treatment is extended to 'reporting funds', which can reinvest the inome but must report it and you must pay income tax on this income in the year it is reported.

PERFORMANCE

Having decided which asset classes and broad fund types to invest in, there is still a wide choice of individual funds. Moreover, past performance data show a big variation between the best and worst performers. For example, if you had invested £1,000 in a UK equity fund for ten years up to November 2007, it would have been worth over £3,500 if you had chosen the best fund but less than £1,500 if you had chosen the worst.

It would be very nice if you could pick the funds that are going to perform best in future. Unfortunately, there is no way of doing this. It's tempting to choose the funds that have performed best in the past. But research by the FSA found that there was no correlation between good past performance and future good performance, especially over the long term. The FSA research did, however, find there is a weak relationship between poor past performance and future poor performance, so there is some justification for avoiding the worst performers.

Bear in mind too the surveys (see page 118) that suggest active fund managers do not consistently beat the stock market. This suggests that, having picked your sector, you might just as well pick a tracker fund as any other.

❝ A high-charging fund has to work harder for the same return. ❞

CHARGES

Although a fund with high charges will not necessarily give you a worse return than a fund with low charges, the high-charging fund will have to work a lot harder to deliver you the same return. So it is only worth choosing a high-charging fund if you believe the higher charges are justified by some superior investment strategy.

There are different ways to compare charges, depending in part on the types of fund you choose.

Total expense ratio

The total expense ratio (TER) is basically all the fixed costs over a year of running an investment fund as a percentage of the average value of the fund over the year. Essentially it is the minimum growth rate you would need for your investment just to stand still.

The TER includes the annual management charge, the cost of holding the underlying investments safely, legal costs, publishing reports, and so on. It does not include the dealing charges

Obtaining TERs

Any IFA that you use should be able to provide you with TERs.
- To compare TERs for unit trusts and OEICs, see the Investment Managers Association website at www.investmentuk.org.
- For investment trust TERs, go to the Association of Investment Companies website at www.theaic.co.uk.
- To get the TER for a particular fund, ask the management company or check the fund's literature.

incurred when the underlying investments are bought and sold.

More, importantly, the TER does not include the initial charge or any exit charge. This can have a big impact on your overall return, as the table, below, shows.

TERs for most funds are generally between 1 and 2 per cent. Of this sum, the annual management charge is nearly always the biggest component of the TER.

Examples of the impact of charges

The table shows the value of £1,000 invested if the growth rate before charges is 6 per cent a year. The upper part of the table shows the return after charges where there is no initial charge and the total expense ratio (TER) shown. Compare these results with the lower part of the table where the same TERs are used but there is also an initial charge of 5 per cent.

		Number of years you invest for					
		1	2	3	5	10	15
No initial charge							
TER 1% pa	Value of £1,000 invested	£1,050	£1,103	£1,158	£1,276	£1,629	£2,079
	% pa growth	5.0%	5.0%	5.0%	5.0%	5.0%	5.0%
TER 2% pa	Value of £1,000 invested	£1,040	£1,082	£1,125	£1,217	£1,480	£1,801
	% pa growth	4.0%	4.0%	4.0%	4.0%	4.0%	4.0%
TER 3% pa	Value of £1,000 invested	£1,030	£1,061	£1,093	£1,159	£1,344	£1,558
	% pa growth	3.0%	3.0%	3.0%	3.0%	3.0%	3.0%
Initial charge of 5%							
TER 1% pa	Value of £1,000 invested	£998	£1,047	£1,100	£1,212	£1,547	£1,975
	% pa growth	-0.2%	2.3%	3.2%	3.9%	4.5%	4.6%
TER 2% pa	Value of £1,000 invested	£988	£1,028	£1,069	£1,156	£1,406	£1,711
	% pa growth	-1.2%	1.4%	2.2%	2.9%	3.5%	3.6%
TER 3% pa	Value of £1,000 invested	£979	£1,008	£1,038	£1,101	£1,277	£1,480
	% pa growth	-2.2%	0.4%	1.3%	1.9%	2.5%	2.6%

Reduction in yield

When you invest in unit trusts, OEICs, investment trusts (if you invest through the management company's own savings scheme), pension schemes and investment-type life insurance, you should be given a Key Facts document.

Providing you with a Key Facts document is a requirement of the FSA regulations. The document contains information about the investment in a standard format so that you can easily compare similar investments from different providers.

One of the figures in the Key Facts document is a measure of charges called the reduction in yield (RIY). The RIY shows the return you lose because of the impact of all the charges, including the initial charge. However, in most cases, the Key Facts document includes only the RIY for an investment over a period of ten years. The shorter the period you invest for, the bigger the impact of any initial charge on your investment (see lower section of the table opposite). So the ten-year RIY can seriously underestimate the level of charges you pay if you hold the investment fund for a shorter period.

Case Study   Alan

Alan has narrowed his choice down to two investment funds. Fund A has no initial charge and a TER of 2 per cent a year. Fund B has a 5 per cent initial charge and a TER of 1 per cent. Assuming both achieve 6 per cent a year growth, if Alan invests for five years, the return after all charges from Fund A will be 4 per cent a year (a reduction in yield of 2 per cent a year) and from Fund B it will be 3.9 per cent a year (a reduction in yield of 2.1 per cent). If he invests for ten years, the return from Fund A is still 4 per cent a year, but the return from Fund B improves to 4.5 per cent a year (a reduction in yield of 1.5 per cent) because the impact of the initial charge is reduced.

> **"** The Key Facts document contains information about an investment in a standard format so you can easily compare similar investments. **"**

 To check the RIY for an investment fund, ask the provider or any adviser you are using to provide you with the Key Facts document.

Timing your investment

Ideally, you would buy when investments are low and sell when they are high. But there is no sure way to get the timing right. Regular saving can reduce timing risk but it also reduces your chance of large returns.

Case Study | Pam

Pam invests in a unit trust whose price has followed the pattern that is shown in the table below. She has £400 to invest.

Month	1	2	3	4
Unit price (pence)	90	110	120	85

If Pam had the benefit of hindsight, she would invest in month 4 when the price is at its lowest. She would get £400/0.85 = 471 units at 85p. She would be unlucky to invest in month 3 when the price is at its highest. She would get only £400/1.20 = 333 units at 120p.

If she invested £100 each month, she would get this many units:

£100/0.90 + £100/1.10 + £100/1.20 + £100/0.85 = 403 units.

The alchemy of pound-cost averaging says that this is a bargain because the average unit price over the period is (90 + 110 + 120 + 85)/4 = 101.25p, whereas the average price she has paid is only £400/403 = 99p.

But this comparison of averages does not mean regular saving is the better strategy. It has produced a better outcome for Pam than if she had invested all her money at the highest price. But regular saving also means she has missed the better outcome of investing the full £400 when the price was at its lowest. In either case, she could not know in advance what would be the lowest or the highest price, so pound-cost averaging has removed the risk of making both the best and the worst timing decisions.

Having solved the problem of which fund to choose, you are left with the tricky question of when to invest. The ideal is to invest when the fund prices are low and sell when they are high. But there is no way of knowing at the time when prices have reached their trough or peak. Only hindsight can tell you that.

You can remove some of this timing risk by investing regularly rather than in a single lump sum. This produces an effect called pound-cost averaging. Some pundits describe pound-cost averaging as a sort of alchemy that magically increases the value of your investment. This is not true. By removing timing risk on your way into the market, pound-cost averaging does increase your returns over what they would have been had you invested at the peak of the market, but it reduces your returns relative to what they would have been had you luckily invested at the bottom of the market. In common with other risk-reduction strategies, reducing risk also reduces the potential return.

❝ You can remove some of the timing risk by investing regularly. ❞

Property

Britons have long had a love affair with residential property. More recently, double-digit returns have wooed them into commercial property too. But property is not just about attractive growth. It can be a valuable source of income and a good way to diversify your investments.

Buy to let

For most people, buying their own home has been a very sound investment. So buying other people's homes by becoming a landlord looks equally attractive. But don't overlook the risks.

Soaring house prices over the last decade or so have made residential property seem like a sure-fire way to make money. Not surprisingly then, many people have been drawn into investing in other people's homes as well, by buying properties to rent out. But, as with any investment, you should weigh up the pros and cons carefully before you take the plunge.

" Well-chosen buy-to-let properties can be a good source of income. "

BUY-TO-LET ADVANTAGES

Well-chosen buy-to-let properties can be a good source of income and offer the opportunity of capital gain as well.

The return

The return from a buy to let comes from:

- Income from rents.
- A capital gain or loss when you sell.

This table shows the possibility of a gain is a big factor in the decision to invest.

Why people invest in buy-to-let properties

The table shows the results of a survey by the Association of Residential Letting Agents in 2007 that asked: 'Why did you first decide to invest in residential property?'

Reason	% of respondents
Short-term capital gain (less than five years)	5.5%
Rental income	8.3%
Combined yield from rental income and capital appreciation	45.2%
Create nest egg for long-term future	41.0%

Source: Association of Residential Letting Agents, *The ARLA History of Buy to Let Investment 2001 to 2007.*

Property as an investment

House prices have soared over the last ten years and, according to Mintel, up to 2 million people in the UK now own a second home either in the UK or abroad. Separate research by Baring Asset Management found that over 3 million people plan on using their home to fund their retirement. Before falling sharply in 2008, commercial property had also been riding high, attracting 80 per cent of the total new money going into unit trusts and OEICs in 2006.

> **❝ There is more to property than the chance of a quick capital gain. ❞**

The risks

- The risk with all price bubbles, though, is that they eventually burst. Even so, property may still have a place in your portfolio, because there is more to property than the chance of a quick capital gain.

- Property is primarily a long-term investment that can provide a steady income. In addition, property returns historically move differently from the return from equities – the other mainstay of long-term investment. So property can be a good way to diversify your investments in order to spread your risks.

- Neither capital gains nor income from property are guaranteed and, because individual properties cannot necessarily be sold quickly, sometimes it can be hard to get your money back.

Different ways to invest

The single name 'property' encompasses several quite distinct types of investment:

- Direct investment in bricks and mortar. For private investors this generally means residential property, such as buy to let (see opposite). Commercial properties are just too expensive for the average small investor.

- Property funds that invest direct (see pages 151–4). This is the main way for private investors to take a stake in the commercial property market. Some property unit trusts (PUTs), insurance-based investment funds and, more recently, real estate investment trusts (REITs) are possible choices.

- Property funds that invest in the shares of property companies (see pages 151–4). For example, some PUTs invest in the shares of quoted development companies and/or REITs.

For more about building a diversified portfolio, see Chapter 10.

Gearing

Gearing means the magnification of gains and losses when you borrow to invest (see the case study, below). You might be able to buy a property outright with cash, but most investors take out a mortgage. This is relatively easy because the buy-to-let mortgage market in the UK is well developed, so there are a lot of lenders in this market and a very wide choice of different buy-to-let mortgages. However, at the time of writing, following severe problems in credit markets worldwide, lenders are looking more closely at the risks involved in the loans they make and it is no longer so easy to get a buy-to-let mortgage unless the business plan for your property letting business looks sound.

BUY-TO-LET DISADVANTAGES

Many of the drawbacks of buy to let arise because, unless you are a very large investor, you are likely to have a lot of your eggs in one basket. Therefore, any problems you have with the one, or maybe two, properties you are likely to own can have a big impact on your overall financial position.

Capital risk

Flats and houses are expensive. According to the Association for Residential Letting Agents (ARLA), a third of buy-to-let investors have just one buy-to-let property and only one in six has more than ten properties.

Putting a large amount of money into a single investment is always high risk. Bear in mind that risk is largely symmetrical. So, if the value of the investment rises steeply, your high-risk strategy can pay off handsomely. But, if something goes wrong, you stand to make a big loss.

The risk with a buy-to-let property is not simply a fall in general house prices. You are also vulnerable to risks specific to that property, such as subsidence, the impact of nearby planning applications or a deterioration in the neighbourhood.

> **Case Study** **Vithal**
>
> In 2000, Vithal bought a terraced house in York for £57,000, which he rented out to students. In 2007, he sold the house for £149,000. If Vithal had bought the house outright completely with his own money, he would have a profit of 161 per cent on his initial outlay of £57,000 (ignoring buying and selling costs). In fact, he bought with a mortgage of £42,000, putting in £15,000 of his own money. After repaying the mortgage, he gets £107,000 from the sale, which is a 613 per cent profit on his outlay of £15,000.

 For more information on finding potential areas of growth, see the *Which? Essential Guide Property Investor's Handbook*.

Liquidity

Closely related to capital risk is the problem of getting your money back. It may be impossible to sell a buy-to-let property quickly. You may need to sell at a cut price or wait many months or even years.

Income risk

A residential property will not necessarily produce a steady stream of income. You need to allow for vacant periods between lettings when no rent payments are coming in. You might also have tenants who are late payers. It is crucial that you pick geographical areas and properties that have good letting potential and check out potential tenants carefully.

Costs and time

Your income is not the gross rents the tenants pay. You have to deduct your costs, for example, mortgage payments, buildings insurance and maintenance costs. Unless you live close by and are happy to spend your time showing prospective tenants around, vetting their references, drawing up contracts and sorting out repairs and problems, you will also have to pay fees to a letting agency. An agency typically charges around 10–15 per cent of the gross rent. Most of the costs have to be paid even during vacant periods when you have no tenants.

There are also substantial costs when you buy and sell property, in particular, mortgage arrangement fees, valuation and survey fees, legal costs and estate agents' fees. On purchases, stamp duty land tax can be considerable.

❝ Most costs have to be paid even during vacant periods. ❞

Stamp duty land tax when you buy in 2008-9	
Property price	**Stamp duty land tax rate [1]**
£0–£125,000	0%
£125,001–£250,000	1%
£250,001–£500,000	3%
Over £500,000	4%
[1] Rate applies to whole property price not just the excess over each threshold	

 To check how much stamp duty land tax you will have to pay on a property purchase, use the HMRC calculator at http://sdcalculator.inlandrevenue.gov.uk.

Tax

Your rental income after deducting various costs is taxable. It counts as non-savings income (see Chapter 2), so is taxed at 20 per cent in 2008–9 if you are a basic-rate taxpayer and 40 per cent if you are a higher-rate taxpayer.

Any gain you make when you sell is taxed at 18 per cent. See Chapter 2 for details of how to work out your capital gain for tax purposes. Unlike, say, a unit trust, where you can sell your holding bit by bit to keep each year's gains within your annual allowance, you normally have to sell a property all in one go. This makes it more likely that you will have some tax to pay.

❝Any gain you make when you sell is taxed at 18 per cent. ❞

Case Study Jo

Jo bought a buy-to-let property in 1997 for £80,000 and sold it for £310,000 in 2008. After deducting selling costs and other allowable expenses, Jo has made a gain of £224,000. This is considerably more than his yearly capital gains tax allowance of £9,600 and tax comes to 18% x (£224,000 – £9,600) = £38,592.

 You cannot put direct holdings of property into tax-efficient wrappers, such as ISAs and SIPPs.

Tax if a rental property has been your own home

If at any time a property you rent out has been your own home, you may save some CGT when you come to sell. The gain is apportioned and the part relating to the time you lived there and also the last three years of ownership qualifies for private residence relief and is completely tax free. The part that relates to the time the property was let out may be taxable, but you can claim letting relief. The part covered by letting relief is also tax free. The maximum letting relief you can claim is the lower of the gain that would otherwise be taxed, £40,000 or a sum equal to the private residence relief. See the case study, opposite, for how this might work in practice.

 For more information about the taxation of property see the *Which? Essential Guide Tax Handbook 2008-9*. For more information about letting relief, get free Helpsheet IR283 'Private residence relief' from www.hmrc.gov.uk.

Case Study | Jacek and Emma

Jacek and Emma bought a home in Dorset for £80,000 in 1997. They lived there until 2001 when, because of Jacek's job, they had to move to Birmingham. They kept the Dorset house and rented it out. In 2008, they sold the house for £310,000. Tax on the gain is worked out as follows:

- The basic gain is £310,000 - £80,000 = £230,000
- They deduct allowable expenses (mainly buying and selling costs) of £6,000, reducing the gain to £224,000
- The property was their own home for four years (1997-2001). This and the last three years of ownership qualify for private residence relief, in other words seven of the 11 years. So they get private residence relief of 7/11 x £224,000 = £142,545
- The remaining 4/11th of the gain relates to the letting. This comes to 4/11 x £224,000 = £81,455
- Letting relief is the lower of the gain (£81,455), £40,000 or the amount of private residence relief (£142,545). They deduct £40,000, leaving a taxable gain of £41,455
- They own the property jointly and the gain is split equally between them, in other words £20,727 each
- They each have a CGT allowance of £9,600. They each pay tax of:
$$18\% \times (£20,727 - £9,600) = £2,002.86$$
- Jointly they pay just over £4,000 tax on the gain.

BORROWING FOR BUY TO LET

Most investors cannot afford to buy their rental property outright and consequently rely on a mortgage.

How much?

Buy-to-let mortgages used to be expensive but these days are only fractionally dearer than a normal mortgage. However, the amount you can borrow is normally much less as a proportion of the property's value (called the loan-to-value ratio or LTV). With an ordinary mortgage, you can often borrow as much as 95 or even 100 per cent of the property's value. With buy to let, however, the maximum is usually 85 per cent. This means you need to find a larger deposit than you would for buying your own home.

The amount you can borrow also depends on the lender's assessment of the rental income that the property is likely to generate. Typically, a lender will want to see expected rental income of

125–150 per cent of your monthly mortgage payments. Some lenders, but not all, take into account your income from sources other than your lettings.

Lenders may be unwilling to lend against properties they think cannot easily be resold if you don't keep up your payments. This could be a problem if you are thinking of buying, for example, a former council property or sheltered housing.

You can take out a mortgage secured against your own home and use the money raised to buy a rental property. But failing to disclose the true purpose of the loan is fraud. If the lender finds out, you may be charged a penalty fee and extra interest on the loan. Buildings insurance on the property may be invalid.

If you try to pass off a buy-to-let property as your own home in order to save tax when you sell, this is tax fraud. You risk fines, interest on unpaid tax and possible imprisonment.

Case Study Ann

Ann wants to buy a rental property priced at £200,000. It has been valued at £190,000. If she can get a mortgage for 85 per cent of the valuation (85% x £190,000 = £161,500) she will need to provide a deposit of £38,500.

She's looking at a mortgage from a lender who insists that rental income is 125 per cent of the mortgage payment. The rental income is expected to be £500 a month. This puts a ceiling on her mortgage payment of £500/125% = £400 a month. On this basis, the maximum the lender will give her is £80,000, leaving her to find the remaining £120,000 of the purchase price.

Type of mortgage

Buy-to-let mortgages come in all the same variations as ordinary mortgages. The most basic choice is whether to go for a repayment or interest-only mortgage:

- **Repayment mortgage.** Your monthly payments cover both interest and repayment of the amount borrowed. Provided you keep up the payments, the loan is completely paid off by the

For a detailed guide to buy to let, get the *Which? Essential Guide* to *Renting and Letting*.

end of the mortgage term. You would then receive the full proceeds of the property when it is sold.

- **Interest-only mortgage.** Your monthly payments cover just the interest on the loan. The outstanding balance remains the same throughout the whole mortgage term. Some lenders insist you also make savings each month to build up a lump sum to repay the mortgage at the end of the term. But many lenders don't and you may plan to repay the loan out of the proceeds of selling the property. However, be aware that if the property proceeds were less than the loan, you would have to find money from elsewhere to repay the balance.

 If you choose a **fixed-rate mortgage,** think how you will pay the increased monthly payments if mortgage rates have gone up when your fixed-rate comes to an end.

Jargon buster

Fixed-rate mortgage A mortgage where your monthly payments do not change for an initial period – say, the first two years

" You may plan to repay the mortgage out of the proceeds of selling the property. But if they are less, you have to find the shortfall elsewhere. **"**

Buy to let abroad

With the UK housing market looking overpriced, you may be looking further afield for buy-to-let opportunities, for example, the new East European members of the European Union or the sunny resorts of Spain.

ADDITIONAL PITFALLS

Buy to let abroad has all the advantages and drawbacks of a UK buy to let (see pages 140–4) plus some added dangers. Renting out a foreign property is not an easy route to riches.

Knowing the market

It can be even more difficult to choose geographical areas and specific properties that have good renting potential if you are buying in a country of which you have little personal knowledge and maybe do not know enough of the language to easily find out more.

Having chosen a property, the procedures for buying (and subsequently selling) may be very different from those in the UK. There may be hidden pitfalls, such as being responsible for debts left by the previous owner. It is crucial that you get help from an independent solicitor who has local knowledge and with whom you can talk in detail in a common language. Be wary of using solicitors recommended by developers or estate agents, since they may have a conflict of interest.

Currency risk

There are three main situations in which exchange rate movements could be a concern. These are:

- **At the time of purchase.** There is usually a delay between agreeing the contract to buy and making the payment (or series of payments if, for example, you are **buying off-plan**). If the exchange rate moves between those two dates, you could end up paying more than you had anticipated. You can protect against this by buying a forward currency contract (see the case study, opposite).
- **If you have a foreign currency mortgage.** It is unlikely that a UK lender will agree to give you a mortgage secured against a property abroad. You have two options: take out a mortgage with a lender in the country in which you are buying or take out a sterling mortgage against your UK home and then buy abroad with cash. If you opt for a foreign currency mortgage and you are making the repayments out of

When buying abroad there can be hidden pitfalls – so use a solicitor with local knowledge.

UK income, the sterling amount that you pay will vary with the exchange rate. The problem does not arise if the rental income from the property is sufficient to pay the foreign mortgage payments.

- **When you sell.** Usually you will be paid in local currency. The amount you end up with in sterling will depend on the exchange rate. If, over the period you have owned the property, the exchange rate has moved against you, this will eat into any profit you make on the sale.

Inheritance laws

If you directly own a property abroad, that property will usually be subject to the IHT laws of that country if you die. Many countries have fixed inheritance

Jargon buster

Buying off-plan Buying a property before it is built and on the basis of the plans. Usually you pay a small reservation fee immediately, followed by a deposit of, say, 10–15 per cent on exchange of contracts. There may be staged payments during the building process but the bulk of the balance is due on completion, which might be, say, 18 months to two years later

Case Study Tim

Tim is buying a flat in Spain costing €2120,000. He has paid 10 per cent deposit of €12,000, which cost him £8,571 at an exchange rate of €1.4 to the pound. The balance is due in three months' time. If the exchange rate stays the same, the balance will be £77,143; but if the pound weakens against the euro, the price in pounds will rise. Tim opts to buy a forward foreign currency contract that guarantees he will get the €108,000 he needs in three months' time at an exchange rate of €1.39 to the pound. This fixes the amount he has to pay at £77,698 regardless of what happens to exchange rates in the meantime. He has to pay the foreign exchange broker 10 per cent of the currency cost now and the balance in three months' time.

laws that, for example, dictate that children inherit some portion of the property. This may not be the way you would wish the property to be passed on. Inheritance laws typically apply to people, not to companies. So you may be able to get around the inheritance laws if, instead of owning the property direct, you set up a company in which

 For all aspects of buying a property abroad, including foreign exchange transactions, consider using members of the Association of International Property Professionals (AIPP) www.aipp.org.uk. AIPP operates a code of conduct for members and an independent dispute resolution procedure if things go wrong.

you hold all the shares and get the company to buy and own the property. The company could be based either in the country where the property is situated or offshore. Get advice from a solicitor and/or tax adviser.

Tax abroad

Your solicitor or a tax adviser can advise you on taxes that you must pay at the time of purchase and also any opportunities to save tax. (For example, in France, buying a property and then leasing it back to a rental management company may enable you to reclaim VAT on the purchase price.)

Be aware that many countries levy an annual wealth tax on property – again you may be able to avoid this if you hold your property through a company. Tax might be charged on the value net of any mortgage secured against the property, a factor to bear in mind when deciding whether to take out a foreign currency mortgage or a loan in the UK.

Any rental income is likely to be subject to local tax and also any gain you make when you sell.

UK taxes

If you are a UK resident and consider the UK to be your permanent home (your domicile), you are liable for UK tax on all your worldwide income, including rents from a property overseas and interest on any bank accounts you have opened abroad. This applies whether or not you bring the money into the UK. Similarly, there will be UK capital gains tax on any profit you make when you sell the property. You can usually offset any foreign taxes you have already paid against the UK tax due.

You must report your foreign income and gains each tax year on a tax return. If you do not normally get a return, contact your tax office no later than 5 October after the tax year in which you received the income or gains.

HMRC has been clamping down on UK residents who fail to declare overseas interest and other income. If you are caught, you face fines, interest on unpaid taxes and possible imprisonment.

❝You must report your foreign income and gains each tax year on a tax return.❞

For a detailed guide to buying property abroad, see the *Which? Essential Guide* to *Buying Property Abroad.*

Property funds

Property funds let you invest small sums in a wide range of different properties. With such a fund, you take a stake in a portfolio of many different properties run by professional fund managers.

Property funds come in the same types as described in Chapter 6, for example, unit trusts, investment trusts and insurance funds, and they work as described in Chapter 6. Your return is in the form of dividends (income) paid from the fund and any capital gain or loss when you sell your units or shares. Many property funds can be held through ISAs, SIPPs and other tax-efficient wrappers.

ADVANTAGES OF INVESTING THROUGH A PROPERTY FUND

Property funds help you to spread risk and reduce your workload. They have traditionally been viewed as a sound long-term investment for income investors.

Steady income

At present, nearly all property funds invest in commercial property, such as offices, warehouses and factories, hotels and shops. Commercial leases are often for long periods – say, ten years or more – and typically have upward rent revisions built in. The tenant rather than the landlord is usually responsible for maintaining the property. So commercial property funds tend to have a steady and growing income stream.

A few residential property funds are beginning to spring up. Residential leases tend to be much shorter than commercial ones and the landlord is responsible for maintenance. Therefore, residential funds may have more volatile income and higher costs than commercial funds.

Affordable way to spread risk

The minimum investment is often around £1,000 as a lump sum or £50 per month. This opens up property investment to small investments and regular saving, neither of which is possible with direct investment.

Liquidity

Property funds that invest in shares rather than direct in bricks and mortar can easily pay you when you want your money back, simply by selling shares on the stock market.

Similarly, if you invest in a property fund listed on the stock market, such as a real-estate investment trust, you can sell your shares at any time. The stock exchange ensures that there is a market for your shares, but of course you will not necessarily get the price you want.

With other types of property investment fund, you may not be able to get your money back straightaway (see Lack of liquidity, below).

Easy way to invest overseas

Some property funds are global or specialise in particular geographical areas. The fund managers should have the time, expertise and access to professionals that you might lack when buying rental property overseas.

DISADVANTAGES OF INVESTING THROUGH A PROPERTY FUND

Charges and a lack of liquidity are the main drawbacks to consider and some types of fund may not be as good as you hoped at helping you to diversify risk.

Charges

As with any investment fund, there are charges (see Chapter 6). Buying, selling and managing property is expensive, so the fees and other charges incurred by a property fund that is investing direct in property will be higher than the fees incurred by property funds that invest simply in the shares of property companies.

Lack of liquidity

Some property funds are not listed on stock markets. This includes, for example unit trusts and OEICs (see Chapter 6).

" To avoid unexpected shocks, check the repayment terms before you invest. "

When you want to sell your units, you sell them back direct to the fund management company.

In general, you can sell your units at any time. Most unlisted property funds that invest direct in property keep a proportion of the fund invested in cash and equities (usually shares of property companies). These can be readily sold to raise money to repay investors. Exceptionally, if a lot of investors want their money back all at once, the fund may have to sell some of the underlying properties. This takes time, especially if the fund is to avoid selling too cheaply. So some unlisted property funds are allowed to delay returning your money for up to six months or even longer. To avoid unexpected shocks, check the repayment terms before you invest.

Tax

In general, property unit trusts (PUTs), OEICs that invest in property and also investment trusts have to pay tax on their rental income but not on capital gains they make. You then receive a distribution or dividend with a tax credit of 10 per cent, which cannot be reclaimed. If you are a higher-rate taxpayer, you have extra tax to pay. (See Chapter 2 for more about how dividend income is taxed.)

Insurance-based property funds pay tax on both the rental income and any gains. You cannot reclaim any of the tax the insurer has already paid and might have extra tax to pay if you are a higher-rate taxpayer (see page 38).

This makes most property funds generally unattractive from a tax point of view compared with investing direct in property. However, since the start of 2007, you can invest tax-efficiently in a property fund, provided it is a REIT (see right). During 2008, PUTs and OEICs that meet certain conditions (for example, the fund must invest mainly in real property or shares in REITs and have a reasonably high level of liquidity) will become eligible to be treated in the same way for tax as REITs. These tax-favoured PUTs and OEICs will be known as property authorised investment funds (PAIFs).

A link to equities?

A great advantage claimed for property is that its returns are independent of what is happening to equities, making property a good way to diversify your overall portfolio. This is true for direct investment in property and those funds that are unlisted.

However, experts suggest that where property funds, such as REITs, are listed on the stock market, their share price will tend to move up and down with share prices generally.

REAL ESTATE INVESTMENT TRUSTS (REITs)

A REIT is a UK company listed on the stock market that runs a property rental business. The properties can be commercial and/or residential, based in the UK or overseas. REITs avoid the tax drawbacks of most other UK-based property funds.

Provided the REIT meets various conditions and pays out at least 90 per cent of the profits from its rental business to investors, then the REIT itself pays no tax on the profits and gains from the properties in the fund. You, the investor, are taxed on the income and gains you get from your REIT investment by reference to your personal tax situation in the same way as if you were investing direct in the underlying properties yourself. The table overleaf shows the effect this has on the income you receive.

Income paid out by the REIT is called a property income distribution (PID) and it counts as non-savings income (see Chapter 2). The REIT normally deducts tax at the basic rate. You can reclaim this tax if you are a non-taxpayer. Higher-rate taxpayers have extra to pay. Gains when you sell your shares are taxed in the normal way (see Chapter 2, page 32).

For more information about property funds, contact the Association of Real Estate Funds (AREF) at www.aput.co.uk, or the Investment Management Association at www.investmentuk.org.

Example of how property fund income is taxed (2008–9 tax year)

	Ordinary property unit trust or investment trust	Real estate investment trust (REIT)
Rental income earned by the fund	£1,000	£1,000
Tax paid by the fund	£300	£0
Net income to be distributed to investors	£700	£1,000
Tax deducted before income paid out	£0	£200
Amount received by investor	£700	£800
Amount a non-taxpayer gets after any tax reclaim	£700	£1,000
Amount a basic-rate taxpayer gets	£700	£800
Amount a higher-rate taxpayer gets	£525	£600

If you hold a REIT through an ISA, SIPP or other pension scheme, or a CTF, PIDs are paid without any tax deducted and the return is tax free.

 During 2008, property OEICs that meet broadly the same rules as REITs (for example, holding mainly real property or shares in REITs and having a reasonable level of liquidity so that investors can normally get their money back without long delays) will be able to apply for similar status and also pay PIDs.

❝ The REIT deducts tax at the basic rate. You can reclaim this if you are a non-taxpayer. ❞

 For more information about REITs and other property funds listed on the stock market, contact Reita at www.reita.org.

Income investments

This chapter looks at your options if you have a lump sum to invest, or capital from your home, and want to use it to provide a regular income over the long term. Occasionally, income investing is shorter term – in that case, the savings products described in Chapter 3 are likely to be all you need.

Income and risk

Investing to provide an income poses the twin challenges of securing a high and stable income while protecting both the capital that generates it and the income itself from erosion by inflation.

MANAGING THE RISKS

There are three types of risk to be aware of when investing for a regular income.

Inflation risk

The main risk you face as a long-term income investor is inflation reducing the buying power of your money (see the case study, below). The main ways to overcome inflation risk are:

- **Equities.** Choose shares or share-based investment funds that can provide both income (from dividends) and growth (from increasing share values).
- **Asset mix.** Mix different investments or funds to give you a spread of different assets. Typically, you might use mainly cash, bonds and property in order to provide income and equities for growth.

Case Study Maria

Maria invests a lump sum of £50,000 to provide income throughout her retirement. She is a cautious investor and chooses a building society account. It provides her with a fairly constant £2,500 a year income. Assuming inflation averages 2.5 per cent a year, the chart, below, shows how the buying power of her money changes over time. For example, after 20 years, the £2,500 would buy only the same as £1,526 today.

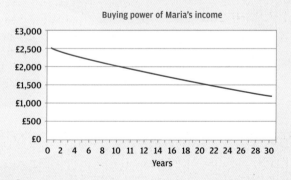

Buying power of Maria's income

- **Special products.** Choose products that automatically give you a spread of different assets.
- **Index-linked products.** Choose products whose return is guaranteed to rise (and fall) in line with inflation.

Longevity risk

Where you want an income to last for the rest of your life, you also face longevity risk – in other words, the risk of living longer than your savings will last. There are two options for dealing with longevity risk: use similar techniques to those described left and above so that you simultaneously invest for growth as well as income; opt for specialist products (annuities) that remove the longevity risk.

Capital risk

Some investments offer an income with no, or virtually no, risk of losing your original capital. These are marked 'low risk' in the table overleaf. Those with no risk are the deposit-type products offered by NS&I, so effectively underwritten by the Government. Similar products offered by banks, building societies and life insurers carry a small risk that the provider might fail. Even then, you would normally be eligible for at least some compensation (see Chapter 10).

If you want a higher income than is offered by these low-risk investments, you will be taking on extra risk, usually extra capital risk. Sometimes these riskier products are marketed to traditionally cautious investors, hungry for extra income, as an alternative to building society savings. Be very clear: a higher-than-normal income always involves extra risk. High-income products will never be as safe as the building society.

Alternatively, you could invest for capital growth (as described, in particular, in Chapters 5 to 7) and cash-in some of your investments at regular intervals to mimic an income stream. This could be tax efficient if you have unused capital gains tax allowance so that capital growth is tax free. But you might have to cash-in investments when their price is low rather than being able to wait until they recover.

❝ Higher-than-normal income always involves extra risk. High-income products will never be as safe as the building society. ❞

For more information about NS&I products, go to www.nsandi.com.

Income-producing investments

Risk level	Type of investment	Income
LOW	Index-linked gilts	Fixed; increases with inflation
	Annuity	Choice, for example, level, increasing, index-linked. Level is vulnerable to inflation
	NS&I fixed-rate bonds	Fixed; vulnerable to inflation
	NS&I income bonds	Variable; vulnerable to inflation
	NS&I pensioners income bonds	Fixed; vulnerable to inflation
	Bank or building society monthly income account	Usually variable; vulnerable to inflation
	Guaranteed income bond	Fixed; vulnerable to inflation
MEDIUM	Gilts	Fixed; vulnerable to inflation
	Some corporate bonds	Fixed; vulnerable to inflation. Risk that company does not pay promised amounts
	Most preference shares	Fixed but no guarantee that full amount or any income will be paid; vulnerable to inflation
	Permanent interest-bearing shares	Fixed; vulnerable to inflation
	Bond-based investment fund	Variable; vulnerable to inflation
	Commercial property fund	Variable; income tends to rise because of upward-only rent reviews (see page 151)
	Distribution funds and bonds	Variable; potential to grow
	With-profits bond	Variable; potential to grow
HIGH	Equity income fund	Variable; potential to grow
	Covered call fund	Variable; potential to grow
	Some ordinary shares	Variable and no guarantee that any income will be paid; potential to grow
	High income bond	Fixed at a high level
	Buy to let	Fixed for short periods; potential to grow; risk of vacant periods with no income
	Equity release scheme	Fixed or variable; can be vulnerable to inflation

Capital	More information
You get back a known sum that increases with inflation if held to redemption; capital risk if you sell on stock market	Chapter 5
You cannot normally get your capital back as a lump sum	page 160
No capital risk; vulnerable to inflation	Chapter 3
No capital risk; vulnerable to inflation	Chapter 3
No capital risk; vulnerable to inflation	Chapter 3
Virtually no capital risk; vulnerable to inflation	Chapter 3
Virtually no capital risk; vulnerable to inflation	page 167
You get back a known sum if held to redemption; capital risk if you sell on stock market	Chapter 5
You should get back a known sum if held to redemption; capital risk if you sell on the stock market. Risk that company does not pay promised amount	Chapter 5
If redeemable, you should get back a known sum if held to redemption; otherwise, capital risk if you sell on the stock market	Chapter 5
Capital risk since you must sell on stock market	Chapter 5
Capital risk since price of units can fall as well as rise	Chapter 6
Capital risk since price of units can fall as well as rise. May be delay in getting money back	Chapter 7
Potential to grow; capital risk since price of units can fall as well as rise	page 168
Potential to grow; capital risk due to possible extra charges if you withdraw when stock market has fallen	page 169
Potential to grow; capital risk since price of units can fall as well as rise	Chapter 6
Some potential to grow; capital risk since price of units can fall	Chapter 9
Potential to grow; capital risk since you must sell on stock market and price of shares can fall as well as rise	Chapter 5
Capital risk since you may lose some or all of your capital if stock markets perform badly. Some protection against smaller market falls	page 170
Potential to grow; capital risk since house prices can fall as well as rise	Chapter 7
You give up a large part or even all of your capital	page 172

Annuities

With an annuity, you buy an income in exchange for a lump sum.
It's a no-turning-back decision because once you have bought the
annuity, either for life or a fixed period of time, you cannot get your
lump sum back.

There are different types of annuity to consider, for example:

- **Temporary annuity.** You buy an income that pays out for a set period of time. It's most commonly used as part of a more complex investment strategy. For example, if an investment requires you to pay in a set sum once a year for the next ten years but you would rather pay a single lump sum upfront, you could use a temporary annuity to fund the regular payments.

- **Lifetime (or permanent) annuity.** This pays out an income for the rest of your life, however long you live. In effect, it combines an income-producing investment with insurance against living longer than your savings would otherwise last.

- **Compulsory purchase (or pension) annuity.** This is the type of annuity you must buy with a pension fund and is usually a lifetime annuity. The full amount of income it produces counts as taxable income.

Case Study Jafari

Jafari has built up a pension fund of £40,000 and wants to start drawing his pension. He needs to maximise his income and is considering two options:

- He could use the whole £40,000 to buy a compulsory purchase annuity. Based on annuity rates in early 2008–9, he could get an income of £3,024 before tax. After basic-rate tax, he would be left with £2,419.
- He could take £10,000 as a tax-free lump sum. The remaining £30,000 would buy a compulsory annuity providing £1,814 income after basic-rate tax. With the £10,000, he could buy a purchased life annuity. This would give him £679 a year before tax, reducing to £647 after tax. Together the two annuities would give him an income of £2,461 a year.

The second strategy would give Jafari an extra £42 a year of after-tax income.

Paying and reclaiming tax on annuities

When you buy a compulsory purchase annuity, your pension is paid through the pay as you earn (PAYE) system. This means the correct amount of tax should have been automatically deducted. PAYE on your pension will be used to collect tax due on any other taxable income you have, such as a state pension. A purchased life annuity is normally paid with tax at the basic rate (20 per cent in 2008-9) already deducted. This counts as savings income and, if your top rate of tax is just 10 per cent, you can reclaim some of the tax already deducted using form R40. If you are a non-taxpayer, you can arrange to receive the payments without any tax deducted by completing form PLA1 (see below).

- **Purchased life (or voluntary) annuity.** A temporary or lifetime annuity that you choose to buy with non-pension scheme money. Each income payment is treated as having two segments. The first counts as a return of part of your original capital and is tax free. The remainder is taxed as income. You can use this tax treatment to your advantage as the case study, left, shows.

HOW MUCH INCOME?

An annuity pays you an income whose level or pattern is usually fixed from the time you first invest. The amount of income you can get is shown by the **annuity rate**. This tells you how much income you will get for each £10,000 you invest. For example, an annuity rate of £670 means you will get £670 a year before tax for each £10,000 you invest.

With most investments, you earn income while aiming to leave your capital intact. An annuity is different because, in effect, you are running down your capital as well as getting a return from investing it. So the income you get from an annuity depends on these broad factors:

- **What return can the annuity provider get from investing your capital?** The money is invested in gilts or similar investments, so the return on gilts is an important factor influencing the annuity rate you are offered. In general, if the return on gilts rises, annuity rates tend to increase.
- **How long will the provider have to pay you an income?** In the case of a temporary annuity, the answer is

 If you need to reclaim tax or ask for gross payments from a purchased life annuity, get form R40 or form PLA1, respectively, from any tax office or the HMRC website: www.hmrc.gov.uk.

161

simply the term of the annuity. The answer is more complicated with a lifetime annuity. Providers cannot know precisely how long you will live, but they can work on the basis of the average life expectancy for a person like you. If the life expectancy of the population as a whole is rising (as is the case now), then annuity rates tend to fall.

- **Your age, gender and health.** In particular, if your health is poor, you smoke or you have worked in, say, a heavy manual job that tends to shorten life expectancy, some providers will offer you a higher income than is standard for a person of your age and gender. This is called an **enhanced annuity** or impaired life annuity.

One life or two?

A single-life annuity pays an income during just your lifetime. A joint-life-last-survivor annuity pays out until the second person of a couple dies. Since a joint-life-last-survivor annuity may have to pay out

for longer, the annuity rate is typically lower than it would be for a single-life annuity. How much lower varies with the age and gender of the second person.

Will the income increase?

The most basic type of annuity provides a level income (hence the name, level annuity) that stays the same year in and year out. Instead you can choose annuities where the income either does or could increase:

- **Escalating annuity.** The income increases by a set percentage each year, say 5 per cent.
- **RPI-linked annuity.** The income changes each year in line with inflation as measured by the Retail Prices Index (RPI). Usually prices are rising, so the income goes up, but very occasionally prices fall and in that case the income would fall.
- **Limited price indexation (LPI) annuity.** The income increases each year in line with inflation but only up to a maximum amount, such as 3 per cent. For example, if inflation was 2 per cent a year, your income would rise by 2 per cent. If inflation was 4 per cent, your income would go up by 3 per cent.
- **Investment-linked annuity.** The income rises and falls according to the performance of an underlying investment fund.

A level annuity is exposed to inflation risk. As prices rise, the buying power of the income falls. But where an annuity provides an increasing income, to make sure there is enough left to pay the higher income later on, the income at the start will be lower.

For example, a 65-year-old man could get a level annuity paying £708 a year or an RPI-linked annuity of £468 a year. If inflation averaged 2.5 per cent a year, it would take 17 years before the RPI-linked annuity income exceeded the level annuity or 11 years if inflation averaged 4 per cent a year.

An investment-linked annuity gives you the option to start with a higher income than you could get from, say, an RPI-linked annuity but with a higher risk that your income could fall.

Research by the FSA shows that a level annuity is the most popular choice. You could save some of the income you get in the earlier years to help you cope with rising prices later on.

Any guarantees?

In general, you cannot get your lump sum back once you have invested in an annuity and the income payments normally stop if you die. That's not a problem if the income is paid out for many years and you feel you have had your money's worth. But if you die shortly after taking out an annuity, the total income paid out will be a lot less than the lump sum you paid. That, of course, is in the nature of insurance – everyone pays, but not everyone claims (see box, below). But there are some options with annuities that help ensure you get a good deal:

- **Annuity with guarantee.** The income continues to be paid out for a set period (usually five or ten years), even if you have died in the meantime. You nominate who you want to receive the income.
- **Capital protection annuity.** The total income payments are guaranteed to at least equal the amount you invested. If you die before that much has been paid out, the balance is paid to your heir(s). For example, if you invest

For an independent comparison of compulsory purchase annuity rates available from different providers, see the FSA comparative tables at www.fsa.gov.uk/tables.

Income investments

£10,000 and all the income payments come to £7,370, your heir(s) get a lump sum of £2,630.

There is a price for these guarantees in the form of a lower income than you would get from the equivalent annuity without any guarantee.

SHOPPING FOR AN ANNUITY

You do not have to buy an annuity from the same provider with whom you have built up your pension savings. There is a big difference in the annuity rates offered by different providers for the same type of annuity and you will often get a higher income if you do shop around. For example, in late 2007, the rates for a level annuity without guarantee for a 65-year-old, non-smoking man ranged from £648 to £720 for each £10,000 invested. It is especially important to shop around if your health or lifestyle is poor. In the example above, the annuity rate for a smoker could be as high as £840.

❝ You will often get a higher annuity if you shop around. Quotes for a non-smoking man ranged from £648 to £720. ❞

Virtually everyone with a pension fund has to buy a compulsory purchase annuity. But only a small number of people choose to buy purchased life annuities. Insurance company experience is that these tend to be people who have a higher life expectancy than average (possibly because people who have money to invest in this way tend to be from higher-income groups that generally have healthier lifestyles and less physically taxing jobs). Therefore, the rates you are quoted for purchased life annuities tend to be lower than the rates for the equivalent compulsory purchase annuity.

AN ALTERNATIVE WAY TO PROVIDE PENSION INCOME

Buying an annuity is not the only way to draw a pension from your pension scheme. You could instead leave your pension fund invested and draw a pension direct from the fund – this is called income drawdown or income withdrawal. It has the attraction that, if you die before age 75, your remaining pension fund can be passed on to your heir(s) either as a continuing pension or a lump sum after tax at a special rate of 35 per cent has been deducted.

Beyond age 75, very high tax charges make passing on your remaining pension fund as a lump sum uneconomic, but

For purchased life annuity rates and for help choosing and buying any annuity, consult an IFA. To find an adviser in your area, see www.unbiased.co.uk.

income drawdown after the age of 75 might still be attractive if, say, you object to annuities on religious grounds. (Some religions, such as the Plymouth Brethren, view annuities as unacceptable gambling on life.)

The drawbacks of income drawdown are that:

- **You don't have the insurance element that an annuity provides.** To guard against your fund running out during your lifetime, there are strict rules on the amount of income you can draw off and your income may have to be reduced.
- **You will be charged by the income drawdown provider** for regular checks that need to be made to ensure that your income is within the limits.
- **Your pension fund remains invested,** so you continue to incur the usual investment charges. For example, if your money is invested in investment funds, you'll incur the charges described in Chapter 6.
- **To beat the income you would have got from an annuity,** you need to invest in investments that are likely to give you a higher return than the gilts and bonds that typically underpin annuity rates. This means investing in equities and, because their value can fall as well as rise, this adds to the risk that your income will go up and down from year to year.

Income drawdown is generally a sensible choice only if you have a six-figure pension fund or you have substantial other sources of retirement income as well. Income drawdown is a complex investment area, so get advice from an IFA.

LONG-TERM CARE ANNUITIES

If disability means that you or a family member needs ongoing help with personal care, you might consider buying an annuity as a way to fund or contribute towards the cost. For example, you might buy an annuity that will pay £1,000 a month every month for as long as care is needed. These annuities are expensive and are most often used by older people who are able to sell their home or take out an equity release scheme (see page 172) to raise the lump sum needed to buy the annuity. If the person's life expectancy is low, they are likely to qualify for an enhanced annuity. Typically, care will be provided in a residential care or nursing home. Provided the annuity income is paid direct to the care provider, the income is tax free. Get advice from an IFA.

“ You might consider buying an annuity as a way to fund or contribute towards the cost of ongoing help with personal care. ”

Insurance bonds

Many insurance products are designed to provide you with an income. Tax rules are at the heart of decisions about whether they are the most suitable choice for you.

THE DRAWBACKS OF INSURANCE BONDS

We have already seen that life insurance policies can be used as investments (see Chapters 2 and 6). Single-premium policies, where you invest one lump sum at the outset, are typically called bonds and the special tax treatment makes them particularly suited to providing an income. However, the tax rules also mean they are not the most tax-efficient investment for many people. The tax treatment is described in Chapter 2, but it is worth recapping the main features here:

- The insurance company has paid tax on both income and gains from the underlying investments that you cannot reclaim. The pay outs you get always count as income and there is no further tax for you to pay unless you are a higher-rate taxpayer.
- A higher-rate taxpayer may have to pay extra tax of 20 per cent on a pay out. But you can take up to 5 per cent of the premium you paid out of the policy as income each year without any higher-rate tax bill at that time. Instead any tax is due when the policy finally ends and is based on your tax position at that time. If you do not draw the full 5 per cent in any year, you can carry the remainder forward to boost the income you draw in later years without any immediate tax bill.

By contrast, a unit trust or investment trust, although it pays tax on income from the underlying investments, does not pay tax on any gains. The gains are

Insurance bonds are not suitable for non-taxpayers and starting-rate taxpayers. People with unused capital gains tax allowance might do better to look at other types of investment funds, such as unit trusts.

To check out many of the insurance bonds available, see the FSA's comparative tables www.fsa.gov.uk/tables (follow the link to 'investment bonds'). You can buy bonds direct from the insurers who issue them or through an IFA.

taxable in your hands but, since you have a generous capital allowance (£9,600 in 2008–9), the gains are likely to be tax free. Even if you do pay tax on the gains, it is at a rate of 18 per cent from 2008–9 onwards, whereas an insurance company will have paid tax at up to 28 per cent on gains that have been made by the investments held through an insurance bond.

The upshot is that, if the investment involves significant capital growth, most investors are likely to get a higher after-tax return from an investment fund held as a unit trust, open-ended investment company (OEIC) or investment trust rather than through an insurance bond.

WHEN TO USE AN INSURANCE BOND

Insurance bonds could be worth considering if:

- The underlying investment fund produces mainly income and you are a basic- or higher-rate taxpayer.
- You are investing for income and your income is within the range where you are losing age allowance (see Chapter 2, page 29). This is because the 5 per cent income withdrawals from an insurance bond do not count at the time they are drawn as income for the purpose of working out age allowance. But the bond proceeds plus the earlier

5 per cent withdrawals will count as income for the year the bond ends and so could cause you to lose age allowance then.

The rest of this section looks at the main types of insurance bond that you are likely to come across as income-producing investments. Be aware that financial advisers generally receive substantially more commission if they recommend that you invest in an insurance bond rather than a unit trust or OEIC. Unfortunately, this could influence their advice (see Chapter 10 for more details).

GUARANTEED INCOME BONDS

These are insurance bonds that pay a fixed income for a set term – usually between one and five years – and then return your capital in full, making them

> **Case Study** Jane
>
> Jane, who is a higher-rate taxpayer, invests £20,000 in an insurance bond. Each year, she can draw an income of up to £1,000 (5 per cent of the premium she paid) with no higher-rate tax to pay at the time. If she draws only £400 in one year, she can carry forward the unused £600 and draw, say, £1,600 in another year without breaching the 5 per cent rule.

 For details of guaranteed income bonds available, see personal finance magazines, such as *Money Management* and *Which? Money*. To find out about NS&I products, see the website www.nsandi.com.

a low-risk investment suitable for cautious investors, provided you are happy to tie your money up for the full term. Often you can choose between monthly or yearly income. You must normally invest your money for the full term with no option to get your money back early. They are an alternative to some NS&I products (see Chapter 2) or gilts (see Chapter 4).

In the past, some guaranteed income bonds have been based on annuities, which alters the tax treatment (see page 161), but annuity-based income bonds are not usual these days.

DISTRIBUTION BONDS AND FUNDS

These are investments designed to produce income but with some potential for your capital to grow.

Distribution bonds

These are insurance bonds that have no set term, but should be viewed as medium- to long-term investments suitable for balanced investors (see Chapter 1) who are comfortable with the fact that their capital is not 100 per cent secure.

Your money is invested in a fund that holds a spread of different assets. Traditionally, it was invested 60 per cent in the bond asset class (for income) and 40 per cent in equities (for growth), and so sometimes these bonds are called 60–40 bonds. Income from the investments is separately identified and you choose whether to draw off all this income, just part of it with the rest being reinvested, or a larger sum. If the income from the underlying investments is not enough to cover fully the level of income you have chosen, you will eat into your capital.

- **The usual tax rules apply** (see page 166), so the insurance company has already paid tax on the income that cannot be reclaimed. If the level of income you choose is more than 5 per cent a year of the sum you invested, there may be extra tax to pay if you are a higher-rate taxpayer.
- **You can usually choose how often to draw the income,** for example, monthly, quarterly or half-yearly, and you may also be able to take out small additional lump sums without penalty.
- **You can cash in your bond at any time,** but there may be penalty charges if you do this within the first few years of purchase.

Whether or not you get back your capital in full depends on the performance of the underlying investments, the life insurer's charges (see page 125) and the amount of income you have drawn.

Distribution fund unit trusts and OEICs

In recent years, some unit trusts and OEICs have been developed specifically to rival insurance distribution bonds. These unit trusts, which typically have the word 'distribution' in their name, also spread your money roughly 60–40 between bonds and equities with income being separately identified and available to draw off.

- **If you hold distribution units** (see page 120), you receive the income earned by the underlying investments.
- **If you hold accumulation units** (see page 120), the income is reinvested.

Unit trust and OEIC distribution funds are the same risk level as distribution bonds – in other words, suitable for balanced investors – but have tax advantages: as described on page 166, the taxation of capital gains is more favourable; and unit trusts and OEICs can be held through ISAs (see Chapter 2).

When you look at listings in newspapers or on websites of unit trusts and OEICs, they are grouped in sectors similar to those outlined on pages 127–32. Distribution funds do not have their own sector and may appear, for example, in the 'cautious managed', 'equity and bond income' or 'equity income' sectors (see Chapter 6).

WITH-PROFITS BONDS

These bonds can provide an income with some potential for capital growth. Your money is invested in an underlying fund on a with-profits basis (see page 131). You choose the level of income you want – because of the tax rules for insurance bonds, 5 per cent is a popular choice.

> ## Jargon buster
>
> **Cautious managed** Type of managed fund that aims for a level of risk acceptable to so-called cautious investors. (However, the industry definition of a cautious investor is closer to the definition of balanced investor that we use in this book.) The manager switches the balance between asset classes according to the aims of the fund and stock market conditions
>
> **Equity and bond income** Type of investment fund that invests in a mix of bonds and shares designed to produce a high level of income
>
> **Equity income** Type of investment fund that invests mainly in the shares of listed companies and aims to provide some growth and a fairly high level of income

If the underlying investments do not grow enough to fund your income in full, you will be eating into your capital. You can usually get your money back at any time but watch out for charges. There is no guarantee that you will get all your capital back.

With-profits bonds have gained a bad reputation in recent years, largely because they have in some cases been sold as

To check out the details of different unit trusts and OEICs, visit the Investment Management Association website at www.investmentuk.org, or a fund comparison site, such as www.trustnet.com.

low-risk investments when, in fact, they are medium-risk. The risks materialised when the stock market crashed between 2000 and 2003, leaving many investors either locked into poor returns or suffering big capital losses if they tried to get their money back. But, provided you understand the nature of this investment, it might be worth considering.

HIGH INCOME BONDS

These aim to provide a higher-than-average income with full return of your capital after a set term of, say, three or five years. But – as investors whose bonds matured during the period 2000–2003 found out – there is no guarantee that you will get your money back in full. You could make a substantial loss or even lose your money altogether.

❝ Don't view high income bonds as an alternative to the building society - they might be useful if you see them as an alternative to direct investment in the stock market. ❞

High income bonds should not be viewed as an alternative to the building society – they are in a different risk category altogether. However, they might be useful if you understand them to be an alternative to direct investment in the stock market.

Many of these high income bonds are set up as insurance bonds, in which case the usual tax rules apply as described on page 166.

High income bonds (also sometimes called structured products) use complicated techniques to deliver both a high income and the possibility of returning your capital in full. For example, the bulk of your money might be invested in reasonably low-risk investments (such as corporate bonds) that will grow over the fixed term by enough to return your capital. The remainder is used to buy derivatives (see Chapter 9) to pay for the income you get. The return from the derivatives depends on the performance of a stock market (or with more complicated products, several stock markets or a selection of shares). If the return is insufficient, the income you have had is effectively clawed back by reducing the capital you get back at the end of the term. The case study, opposite, shows an example of how this could work in practice. But high income bonds work in a variety of different ways, so you always need to check the terms of any particular bond carefully.

Case Study Alan

Alan has £50,000 to invest and a choice of three income investments:

- Building society account offering 5 per cent and full return of his capital.
- Direct investment in shares offering around 7 per cent income and the possibility of capital growth or loss.
- Investment in a high income bond offering 10 per cent income and full return of his capital provided the stock market does not fall by more than 30 per cent over the next five years. If the stock market does fall by more than 30 per cent, Alan will lose 2 per cent of his capital for each 1 per cent stock market fall – for example, if the stock market fell by 40 per cent, Alan would lose 2 x 40% = 80% of his capital and would get back only 20p for every £1 invested.

Ignoring tax, the table shows some possible outcomes for each investment over the next five years. The last column looks at what would happen if the stock market fell by 50 per cent (as the UK market did between 2000 and 2003). The high income bond is a disaster because he would lose all his original capital compared with leaving his money in the building society (though he has had a high income in the meantime). But if Alan had been choosing between shares and the high income bond, the middle column shows that the bond offers some protection against a falling stock market compared with direct investment in the stock market.

What might happen to Alan's investment

	Stock market rises by 50 per cent	Stock market falls by 30 per cent	Stock market falls by 50 per cent
Building society account	£2,500 a year income £50,000 capital returned	£2,500 a year income £50,000 capital returned	£2,500 a year income £50,000 capital returned
Shares	£3,500 a year income £75,000 capital returned	£3,500 a year income £35,000 capital returned	£3,500 a year income £25,000 capital returned
High income bond	£5,000 a year income £50,000 capital returned	£5,000 a year income £50,000 capital returned	£5,000 a year income All capital lost

Equity release schemes

In retirement, you might find yourself asset-rich-income-poor with less income than you would like but a lot of capital tied up in your home. One way to convert your home into income would be to move to a cheaper place and invest the capital released.

However, if you don't want to move or can't find a cheaper home, an equity release scheme might be the answer. Equity release schemes let you raise a lump sum or income from the value of your home without moving. There are two basic types of scheme: lifetime mortgage or a home reversion scheme. Both can be used to raise a lump sum, income or a combination of both.

RISKS

Equity release schemes are complex products. Get advice and make sure you understand any scheme before going ahead. Whatever scheme you choose, be aware that:

- You will always get far less capital out of your home than the total capital that you give up. The equity release provider generally has to wait many years to get the money back and, in effect, charges you for the loss of use of the money over that time and the

risk that it might not get all of the money back if house prices fall.

- **Close family, as well as you, understand the terms of the equity release agreement** because any inheritance from you will inevitably be much smaller than they may have been expecting.

- **Income and lump sums from an equity release scheme can affect your entitlement to state benefits,** such as pension credit and council tax benefit, and the amount of tax you pay (for example, if you lose age allowance – see Chapter 2). Get advice from an IFA or a benefits

Check what happens if your circumstances change - for example, you want to move, marry or have a carer move in with you.

An IFA can help you decide whether an equity release scheme is suitable for you and, if so, to compare and choose the best scheme for your circumstances. Always use a specialist adviser.

adviser, such as your local Citizens Advice Bureau.

- **With a home reversion scheme, ownership of part or all of your home transfers to the equity release provider.** You become a tenant and should check very carefully your rights and obligations under the tenancy agreement, in particular your responsibility for keeping the property in good repair. Get a solicitor to check the agreement.
- **With a home reversion scheme, the** amount of capital you release and the amount you give up depend crucially on the value put on your property. Therefore it is essential that you arrange for your own independent valuation.

LIFETIME MORTGAGE

You take out a mortgage against your home but it differs from a normal mortgage in two ways:

- **Capital repayment.** The loan is repaid only when you die or move permanently into a care home. If you have a partner, the mortgage can be set up to run until the second of you no longer needs the home.
- **Interest.** Schemes work in a variety of ways but, most commonly, you do not pay any interest on the mortgage during your lifetime. Instead, the

interest (which is usually charged at a rate fixed for the life of the loan) is added to the amount you owe and only paid when you die or move permanently into care. This is often called a roll-up mortgage.

Rolling up the interest on a loan means the amount you owe grows significantly (see the table, overleaf). This may leave little or nothing to pass on to your heir(s). In effect, you are using up your capital to provide cash or income now.

There are two ways to use a lifetime mortgage to provide income:

- **Take the whole loan in one go as a lump sum,** which you then invest, for example, in any of the income-producing investments listed in the table on pages 158–9.
- **Draw down the loan bit by bit to mimic a stream of income.**

You will pay less interest using the second method because in the early years you owe less than if you were to draw down the loan in one go.

❝Equity release schemes are complex products. Get advice.❞

 To find a solicitor, see Useful addresses on page 216. To find an IFA, contact www.unbiased.co.uk.

How a roll-up mortgage could grow

The table shows how much you would owe if you take out a mortgage for £50,000 at an interest rate of 7 per cent.

Number of years since taking out the mortgage	Amount you owe
Start	£50,000
1	£53,500
2	£57,245
3	£61,252
4	£65,540
5	£70,128
10	£98,358
15	£137,952
20	£193,484
25	£271,372

HOME REVERSION SCHEME

With a home reversion scheme, you sell part, or all, of your home to the home reversion company in return for a lump sum. You retain the right to carry on living there until you die or move permanently into a care home either rent free or for a trivial rent. If you have a partner, the scheme can be arranged to run until the second of you no longer needs the home. You can invest the lump sum in any of the investments listed in the table on pages 158–9 to provide yourself with income.

From the reversion company's point of view, it is making an investment of the lump sum it gives you. The investment will earn no income, so the reversion company expects to get all the return from its investment when the scheme comes to an end. It does this by giving you a lump sum now that is a percentage of the value of your home and when the scheme ends, taking a higher percentage of the proceeds from selling your home. Once again, you are effectively giving up your capital in return for cash or income now, which means that you will have less or even nothing to pass on to your heir(s).

TAKE ADVICE

Any mortgage or sale of your home is a major decision with big financial and legal implications. It is essential that you get advice from both a solicitor and an IFA.

An IFA should assess your particular circumstances to see if equity release is suitable for you, advise on the choice between a lifetime mortgage and home reversion scheme and recommend the best provider.

As part of this process, the IFA must advise you about the effect on any state benefits and tax or refer you to another specialist.

 For more information about equity release schemes, get Age Concern's free factsheet FS12, 'Raising Income or Capital From your Home', available from www.ageconcern.org.uk .

Unusual investments

Antiques, traded options, spread betting, hedge funds or business angels – these are some of the less usual investments you might consider. They could help you to diversify risk and some are tax efficient – but bear in mind that does not guarantee you will make any money.

Collectables

Collectables are tangible objects, such as antiques, art, rare books, coins, wine and classic cars. Some people claim they can be an alternative asset class because the return on collectables, such as art, has virtually no correlation with the return on equities, property, bonds or cash.

Some experts suggest that putting some of your money into collectables helps you to spread your risks. Others argue that since most collectables produce no income and their prices are set largely by changing tastes and fashion, they cannot be analysed and valued in the same way as mainstream assets, which makes collectables a poor investment.

If you are investing purely as an investment, collectables are a high-risk choice. Don't risk money that you cannot afford to lose and be prepared to invest for the long term. Do your homework or get advice on what to buy and be aware of dealing and ownership costs. The good news is that, if you do make a profit, gains on collectables are treated favourably for tax purposes.

HOW TO INVEST

In general, be prepared to pay high upfront costs for collectables. Depending on the type of item you are buying, there are four main ways to buy:

- **At auction.** You'll pay a buyer's premium, which ranges from around 15 to 25 per cent on top of the hammer price. When you sell at auction, there is a seller's commission and you may have to pay for your entry in the auction catalogue.
- **From dealers or galleries.** Mark-ups can be high, for example, around 50 per cent for art. Choose dealers who belong to a recognised trade association, such as the British Antique Dealers Association, the Association of Art & Antiques Dealers (LAPADA) or

> **❝ Most collectables produce no income and their prices are set largely by changing tastes and fashion. ❞**

For a wealth of information about buying at auction, visit www.bonhams.com, www.christies.co.uk and www.sothebys.co.uk. For seriously classic car auctions, see www.coys.co.uk.

Art

In recent years, the fashion has shifted away from old masters and towards contemporary artists. You don't have to invest millions – investments from £1,000 upwards are possible. Indigenous art from countries, such as Russia and China, is also popular as newly wealthy buyers emerge from those areas. To find out more about investing in art, try the following websites: www.affordableartfair.co.uk, www.artasanasset.com and www.artprice.com.

Society of London Art Dealers (which, despite its name, covers the whole of the UK) (see below). With, for example, wine investing, expect to pay broker's commission when you sell.

- **Direct from the artist** in the case of contemporary art. You will save the dealer's commission.
- **From private sellers.** This is more risky. Check that you are happy that the items they are selling are genuine and appropriately priced.

However you buy, you are normally responsible for the costs of transport and insurance to your home or other destination. Bear in mind the ongoing costs of ownership, for example,

insurance, security and storing the item in the correct conditions.

Do not buy and sell through people who contact you out of the blue. You will be laying yourself wide open to scams and frauds. Collectables do not count as investments for the purposes of financial regulation, so there are no complaints or compensation schemes to help you if things go wrong. All you can do is report any fraud or theft to the police.

TAX AND COLLECTABLES

If you buy and sell antiques, wine, art or other collectables on a regular basis, HMRC might argue that you are trading in them. In that case, you will be charged income tax on the profits you make as if you are running a business.

Provided you do not count as a trader, any profits you make from collectables are subject to CGT, not income tax. Moreover, gains on collectables are tax free if they are from:

- **A private car.** This exemption would cover most classic, vintage and veteran cars.
- **A wasting asset.** This is an item whose original predictable life is 50 years or less – even if its actual life turns out to be longer. This exemption covers wine, whisky and other consumable items.
- **An asset worth £6,000 or less when you dispose of it.** To prevent

 The websites for dealer trade associations are: www.bada.org (British Antique Dealers' Association), www.lapada.org (Association of Art & Antiques Dealers) and www.slad.org.uk (Society of London Art Dealers).

you artificially exploiting this exemption, items that form a set are treated as a single asset, even if you split the set and sell the parts separately.

If you dispose of an item worth more than £6,000, special rules apply that may reduce your tax bill. Your taxable gain is the lower of either the profit you actually make or five-thirds of the excess over £6,000 (see the case study, below).

You can get tax relief for losses (by setting them against gains you make on other assets – see page 32), but losses on chattels worth over £6,000 are restricted by replacing your actual sale proceeds with the £6,000 figure.

Wine

Unlike most collectables, wine is normally held purely as an investment. Although you could drink it, even opening the original case can damage the value. Wine has to be stored well, so many investors never even take it home, but leave it stored with the wine broker from whom they made the purchase (for a fee, say, of £8 a year per case). There have been numerous wine scams with investors paying over the odds for near worthless wines, usually in response to cold calls. Do your homework carefully – for example, using www.wine-searcher.com for wine-price information and to locate dealers.

Case Study Amy

In 2008-9, Amy, an avid collector, sells the following assets:

- A 1964 Alfa Romeo Spyder for £30,000, making a gain of £10,000. Because the Alfa is a private car the gain is tax free.
- Twenty cases of 1989 Pomeroy Cuvée Louise Rose at £65 a bottle, making a profit of £7,000. This gain is tax free because the wine is a wasting asset.
- A painting for £5,800. The £2,000 gain is tax free because the sale price was below the £6,000 threshold.
- A set of Georgian silver candlesticks for £7,000 that Amy had bought five years ago for £5,000. Her actual gain is £2,000 but under the special rules she is taxed on £7,000 - £6,000 x 5/3 = £1,666. This is well within her annual allowance for the year (£9,600 in 2008-9).

Amy also sold a Victorian chest of drawers, for which she had originally paid £7,000, at just £5,000. Her actual loss was £2,000. But under the CGT special rules, the loss is restricted to £6,000 - £7,000 = -£1,000.

Derivatives

Derivatives are complex investments that derive their value from some other underlying asset(s), typically commodities, shares or a stock market index. Examples are traded options, futures, warrants and covered warrants.

Derivatives give you the opportunity to profit from movements in the price of the underlying asset during a specified period of time. Derivatives typically have a term of a few months up to a year, but a few are available for terms of up to, say, five years. The more volatile the underlying asset, the greater your opportunities for profit.

THE BASICS OF DERIVATIVES

Derivatives originated in the farming world as a way of reducing risk. Imagine yourself as a farmer planting a crop that will be ready for sale in six months' time. Before you plant, you would like to be sure that you will be able to sell the crop and the price you'll get. Therefore you enter into a contract with a buyer whereby you promise to deliver a set amount of crop on a fixed date in future at a price set now. The buyer similarly commits to taking delivery on the future date at the agreed price.

Jargon buster

Covered warrant Similar to a traded option (see below). Issued by an investment bank, it gives the holder the right to buy an underlying asset on or by a set date at a set price. Covered warrants have been specifically designed to give private investors easy access to derivatives. Critics claim they are more expensive than traded options

Forward A contract that obliges one party to deliver an underlying asset on or by a specified date at a set price and the other party to accept delivery on those terms (for example, the currency contract on page 149)

Future A forward contract that can be bought and sold on the stock market

Traded option Similar to a future, but the buyer of the contract has the right – not the obligation – to buy or sell the underlying asset either on or by a set date at a set price

Warrant Issued by a company, it gives the holder the right to buy that company's shares on or by a set date (or on a series of dates), at a set price

 For information about traded options and futures, go to www.euronext.com.

The pros and cons of derivatives

Pros	Cons
• You can make money from a fall in the price of the underlying asset as well as a rise. • You can benefit fully from a rise or fall in the price of the underlying asset, yet invest only a fraction of the amount you would if buying or selling the asset (an effect called gearing – see page 124).	• Derivatives offer a short window during which to make any profit and you can lose all of the capital you invest. With some derivative strategies, you can lose even more, but these strategies are generally not suitable for private investors. • The underlying asset might produce income (for example, dividends from shares), but you do not get any income from derivatives. • They require your full attention - they are not buy, hold and hope investments. You need to actively play the market. If that level of attention is not for you, you could instead consider funds that use derivatives (see page 184).

If, in the meantime, the market price for the crop rises, the buyer has a valuable contract because he or she will be able to buy the farmer's crop at one price and immediately sell it on the market for a higher price. But, rather than hanging on until the date set in the contract, the buyer could sell his contract for an immediate profit to someone else. What is changing hands here is the contract – the derivative – not the underlying asset.

Most investors never take delivery of any underlying assets and either sell the contract on the stock market or get out of the investment by buying another contract that exactly cancels the first one. Where a contract derives its value from a stock market index or some other index, there is no delivery of underlying assets (since it would be impractical to provide small tranches of the 100 or more shares or other assets that make up the index). Instead, when the contract ends, settlement is made in cash with a set number of pounds being paid for each point of the underling index. All covered warrants are settled for cash, regardless of whether the underlying asset is an index, shares, commodities or currency.

Risk

Derivatives are a way of shifting risk from one person or institution to another. Bear in mind that risk is largely symmetrical with a risk of loss being balanced by the opportunity for profit, so risk can be attractive to investors. In the farming example, the farmer is reducing risk. The derivative contract means that he gets a known, fixed sum for his crop. He is insured against the risk of a price fall, but also cannot benefit from a price rise. The buyer of the derivative contract has taken over the risk. If crop prices rise, the buyer stands to make a profit from the contract, but if crop prices fall he could lose all his money.

Types of contract

There are many different types of derivative contract, but the two most basic are:

- **Call contract.** This gives you the right to buy the underlying asset on or before a set date at a set price. You might buy this type of contract if you expect the price of the underlying asset or index to rise.
- **Put contract.** This gives you the right to sell the underlying asset on or before a set date at a set price. You might use it if you expect the price of the underlying asset or index to fall.

Different derivative contracts can be combined to build more complex investment strategies.

Tax

Unless you trade so often that HMRC think you are running a business, profits you make from derivatives count as capital gains. You may have to pay CGT if your total gains exceed your annual allowance (£9,600 in 2008–9).

Case Study Claire

Claire expects the stock market to rise and decides to invest in covered warrants. The FTSE 100 Index is standing at 6400. She buys call warrants that give her the right to 'buy the market' at 6500 at any time during the next month. The stock market price of the warrants is 3p each and she invests £3,000. Settlement will be at one-tenth of a penny for each index point. Whether or not Claire makes a profit depends on what happens to the stock market over the next month.

If the index reaches this level during the month	Value of each warrant	Profit or loss per warrant	Claire's overall profit or loss	Percentage return
6500 or less	0p	3p loss	£3,000 loss	100% loss
6530	30 x £0.001 = 3p	0p	Money back. No gain or loss	0%
6550	50 x £0.001 = 5p	2p profit	£2,000 profit	67% profit
6600	100 x £0.001 = 10p	7p profit	£7,000 profit	133% profit

Covered warrants (but not other types of derivative) may be held through a SIPP, in which case, gains will be tax free.

There is no stamp duty when you buy derivatives (as there would be if you were buying underlying shares).

HOW TO INVEST

You buy and sell derivatives through a stockbroker. Choose either an execution-only service or one that includes advice (see page 100). The broker must check whether you seem to have training or experience to understand these investments. If you don't, the broker will give you a warning letter to that effect, but ultimately whether or not to invest is your choice. If you go ahead despite the warning, you cannot later claim you were sold unsuitable investments.

The broker charges commission when you buy and sell. There is also a spread between the (higher) price at which you

" You buy and sell derivatives through a stockbroker who must check whether you have the training or experience to understand these investments. "

can buy a derivative contract and the (lower) price at which you can sell.

SPREAD BETTING

Spread betting is a type of gambling that is a form of derivative trading. It is offered by some online bookmakers and stockbrokers and is a gamble on numbers. The numbers might be, for example, the future level of a stock market index, share price, commodity price, currency rate, or the number of goals scored in a football match.

Risk

Spread betting is very similar to buying traded options and covered warrants, but more risky because you can lose more than you invest.

How spread betting works

The bookmaker either starts with the current value or takes a view on the most likely outcome, with a margin of error either side, called the spread. The upper end of the spread is the offer price at which you 'buy' the index. The lower end of the spread is the bid price at which you 'sell' the index. You buy if you bet the outcome will be higher than the spread and sell if you bet it will be lower. You receive or pay so much per point once the outcome is known (see the case study, opposite). You can bet on movements within a day or over a longer

 For information about warrants and covered warrants, go to www.londonstockexchange.com. For information about traded options and futures, go to www.euronext.com. See Chapter 5 for more about finding and using a stockbroker.

period. You have to put up some money upfront (called a margin) to cover potential losses and may have to deposit further money if the bet starts going against you.

The key differences between spread betting and traded options or covered warrants are:

- **Your losses are unlimited** unless you use a **stop-loss**.
- **Profits count as the proceeds of gambling** and are tax free.
- **You don't pay commission** to any broker (all the charges come out of the spread).
- You can usually bet smaller amounts.

Jargon buster

Stop-loss Way to protect yourself from unlimited losses. You instruct the bookmaker to close your bet once the underlying index reaches a level you set. You may have to pay extra (in the form of a wider spread)

Unusual investments

❝Spread betting profits are tax free. ❞

Case Study **Irene**

The FTSE 100 Index opens at 6400 and a bookmaker is quoting a spread of 6397 to 6403 for the day. Irene thinks the stock market will fall during the day so she 'sells' at 6397. She decides she would like to gamble £10 per index point. Irene can take a profit or cut her losses at any time during the day or she can let the bet run to the end and settle up then. The table shows some possible outcomes.

Index closes or Irene takes a profit/cuts losses at	Profit or loss
6450	Irene loses (6450 – 6397) x £10 = £530
6400	Irene loses (6400 – 6397) x £10 = £30
6350	Irene makes a profit of (6397 – 6350) x £10 = £470
6300	Irene makes a profit of (6397 – 6300) x £10 = £970

Hedge funds

Most of the investment funds in Chapter 6 aim to make you money mainly by buying investments, holding them and selling at a profit. This approach is called 'long' investing and it can work well in rising markets. Hedge funds add an array of other strategies to profit from falling markets as well.

As you have already seen in this chapter, there are different ways to make money from investments, including techniques that work in falling markets. Hedge funds, also called alternative investment funds, use derivatives and other complex strategies to try to boost gains and/or deliver returns even when markets fall. If you are attracted to these strategies but don't want to be an active derivatives trader, hedge funds could be the answer.

WHAT IS A HEDGE FUND?

There is no precise definition of a hedge fund. It is generally taken to mean a fund that has the following parameters.

- **Uses derivatives** and takes short positions.
- **Uses gearing** to magnify returns (but also losses).
- **Has the freedom to use a very wide range of assets and strategies** that may include, for example, bonds, equities and commodities, exploiting small differences in price between similar investments (called arbitrage), swapping investments for others that produce different capital or income streams (called swaps), speculating on price movements during takeovers and mergers, and so on.
- **Tends to have higher-than-normal charges,** often including performance fees for managers.

You have seen earlier in this chapter how derivatives produce a return over a set period of time. Many of the strategies used by hedge funds mean taking a position that will come to fruition over a set period of months or even a couple of years. For this reason, it is common for hedge funds (and therefore funds of alternative investment funds (FAIFs) – see box,

---

Jargon buster

Long position Buying and holding assets in the hope of selling them later at a profit. This can be achieved either by buying the assets direct or using derivatives (see pages 179-83)

Short position Selling assets in the hope of buying them back later at a lower price and so realising a profit. The fund may borrow the shares to sell from other investments funds (for a fee) or use derivatives (see pages 179-83) to create a short position

---

below) to put restrictions on getting your money back:

- Commonly, you will be locked into the investment for an initial period of, say, one or two years.
- You will usually have to give anything from 90 days to 12 months notice to get your money back.
- You might be restricted to getting back only a proportion of your money at a time, say 20 or 25 per cent.

Hedge fund fees are higher than for conventional investment funds. For example, a performance fee of, say, 20 per cent of the profits made and a 2 per cent annual management charge are typical.

The examples overleaf illustrate a few of the types of hedge fund available, but this is a very diverse group. And increasingly conventional funds, like those outlined in Chapter 6, are adopting some of the hedge funds' strategies, so the distinction between different types of fund is tending to blur.

RISK

Some hedge funds use derivatives as insurance to offset the risks that are inherent in the underlying assets they hold. Others are exploiting risk to find superior returns. As always, risk and reward go hand-in-hand. So if a fund promises higher-than-average returns, the flip side is that you will lose money if the strategies fail.

Most investment funds can make money in a rising stock market, so the real test of hedge funds is whether they can really deliver something extra in hard times.

It is also claimed that hedge funds have a low correlation with equity and bond performance, so act as a separate asset class that can help you to spread the risks of your overall portfolio. But when problems have emerged with some large companies' shares or in the bond markets, it seems that hedge funds have

Fund of alternative investment funds (FAIFs)

Most professional and private investors who invest in hedge funds do not do so direct. Instead they invest in a FAIF. The fund manager researches and puts together a portfolio of different hedge funds. The advantage for investors is that they are delegating complicated research to professionals. The disadvantage is that you must pay for two levels of management. For example, the FAIF manager might take an annual management fee between 1 and 1.5 per cent of the value of the fund and possibly a performance fee of, say, 10 per cent of the return on top of the fees charged by the individual hedge funds.

Most hedge funds and FAIFs are based offshore for tax reasons, but this means the funds are not subject to UK regulation and consumer protection rules (see page 204). However, the FSA plans to give the go-ahead for UK-regulated FAIFs, set up as unit trusts and OEICs, probably from 2008, and the government is removing tax disincentives.

been hit too. So it is not clear that the claimed lack of correlation really is as good as expected.

SOME HEDGE FUNDS

There are various types of hedge fund. Here are descriptions of three of them.

Absolute return funds

These funds (also called target return or total return) aim to produce a consistently higher return than you can get from putting your money in cash, such as the investments described in Chapter 3. The funds use various strategies, for example:

- **Bond-based funds.** These invest mainly in corporate bonds to produce income and use derivatives to protect the fund from market downturns.
- **Diversified funds** invest in a broad spread of asset classes and mix long and short positions to keep the fund value stable.

If you are a cautious investor who would normally choose savings accounts, bear in mind that absolute return funds mean taking on extra risk and might not be suitable.

Covered call funds

These use derivatives to create a higher, more stable income than you would get from a conventional equity-income fund. In return, you give up some potential for capital growth.

The fund buys equities (a traditional long position). It also sells call options (see page 181). A call option gives the buyer the right to buy the underlying shares at a pre-set price. The seller of the option is obliged to deliver the shares at that price if the option is exercised. The price the buyer pays for the option provides extra income for the fund. When the stock market is stable or falling, the option is unlikely to be exercised, so the fund keeps the extra income and the shares. If the stock market is rising, options are more likely to be exercised, so the fund then has to sell the shares at the pre-set price limiting its own ability to benefit from the rising market.

130/30 funds

These aim to combine traditional long investing with short selling to boost the overall return. Typically, the fund manager:

- **Invests 100 per cent of the fund** in shares and investments expected to rise in value.
- **Sells shares it does not own** (for example, borrowing them from another fund for a fee) that are expected to fall. The value of the shares sold comes to 30 per cent of the fund's value.
- **Uses the money raised from selling shares** to invest in more shares whose value is expected to rise.

Overall then, the fund has bought (taken a long position in) shares worth 130 per cent of the fund's original value and sold shares worth 30 per cent of its value. Provided the manager's share selections turn out to be good, the fund makes extra money from the short sales and magnifies the gains from its long position. If not, losses result.

Business angels

The Government encourages people to invest in new and growing businesses by offering a range of tax incentives. These are high-risk investments because government statistics show that 30 per cent of new businesses do not survive beyond their third year.

Even if a business does not fail, it may be many years before investors see a return on their money and it can be hard to find a buyer if you want to sell your stake. So do not get carried away by the tax reliefs – they may be far outweighed by the losses you make. On the other hand, every IBM, Sainsbury's and Google started small, so the potential profits from being an earlier backer are huge.

MAIN TAX INCENTIVES

These schemes all focus on investment in unquoted trading companies, which for tax purposes includes shares listed on the London Stock Exchange's Alternative Investment Market (AIM) and the PLUS-quoted market (see Chapter 5) as well as companies with no listing on any market.

The definition of a trading company excludes, for example, companies involved in banking, share-dealing, insurance, accountancy, legal services, farming, market gardening, running hotels and other property-related businesses.

Income tax loss relief

Normally, if you sell shares at a loss, you would get relief from CGT by offsetting the loss against gains made on other assets (see Chapter 2). But if you make a loss as a result of investing in the shares of an unquoted trading company, you can instead claim income tax relief on the loss by setting it against:

- Income for the tax year in which you make the loss and
- Income for the previous tax year.

From 6 April 2008, CGT is charged at a single rate of 18 per cent, whereas basic and higher-rate taxpayers pay income tax at 20 and 40 per cent, respectively. This makes income tax loss relief more attractive than CGT relief for these taxpayers.

You have 22 months from the end of the tax year in which you make the loss to claim this relief. For example, if you make the loss in 2008–9, you must

For further details about tax reliefs available when investing in new businesses, see www.hmrc.gov.uk. For information about venture capital trusts, contact the British Private Equity and Venture Capital Association at www.bvca.co.uk.

187

claim relief by 31 January 2011. Make your claim either through your tax return or in writing to your tax office.

Enterprise investment scheme

Under the enterprise investment scheme (EIS), you get immediate tax relief on £500 or more that you invest direct in the shares of an unquoted trading company, provided you hold the shares for at least three years. You can also invest in EIS companies through an investment fund, in which case investments less than £500 also qualify for relief.

The maximum investment from 2008–9 (subject to European Commission approval) is £500,000 a year. Up to £50,000 of this can be carried back and set against your income for the previous year for investments made in the first six months of a tax year.

Income tax relief is given at a rate of 20 per cent, but the maximum relief cannot exceed the total income tax you pay for the relevant tax year. You have just under six years from the end of the tax year in which you make the investment to make your claim. For example, if you invest in 2008–9, you must claim EIS relief by 31 January 2015.

In addition, provided you have held the shares for at least three years, any capital gain you make on their sale is tax free.

If you make gains on the disposal of other assets, you can put off the tax bill if you reinvest the proceeds of the sale in an EIS investment.

Venture capital trust

A venture capital trust (VCT) is an investment trust quoted on the stock exchange. It invests in the shares of unquoted trading companies and so gives you a stake in a portfolio of small and growing companies.

Provided you hold the VCT shares for at least five years, you get income tax relief at a rate of 30 per cent on up to £200,000 a year invested in VCTs and there is no CGT on any gain you make when you sell the shares. Dividends you get do not count as income and so also get tax relief.

Income tax relief on the amount you invest is given in the same way as for EIS investments (see above left).

Case Study   Leslie

In 2008-9, the tax bill on Leslie's income is £78,000. In November 2008, Leslie buys £100,000 of shares in an unquoted company issuing shares through the EIS scheme. The shares qualify for tax relief of 20% x £100,000 = £20,000. This is subtracted from his tax bill, leaving him to pay income tax of £58,000 for the year. If he does not hold the EIS shares for three years, he will have to repay the £20,000 tax relief he has had.

 To find out about opportunities to invest through the enterprise investment scheme, contact British Business Angels Association at www.bbaa.org.uk.

Building your portfolio

Given the huge array of different investments, picking the ones that will help you meet your personal financial goals can seem daunting. This chapter outlines some approaches you could adopt. If this is too hands-on for you, consider delegating the detailed decisions to fund managers or a financial adviser.

10

First principles

A portfolio is a collection of investments chosen to give you the best possible chance of meeting a financial goal given an acceptable level of risk. Rules of thumb can help, but the ideal portfolio is personal to you and your goals.

YOU AND YOUR GOALS

Chapter 1 looked at financial planning as a structured process that starts with identifying your financial goals and moves through stages to acquiring appropriate financial products for meeting those goals. Some goals can be met with insurance products, mortgages or other loans. But many involve saving or investing either a lump sum or on a regular basis. The appropriate strategy for achieving each savings or investment goal depends on a variety of factors:

- **The timescale involved** – is this a short-, medium- or long-term goal?
- **The importance and flexibility of the goal.** Are there severe consequences if you miss a specific target?
- Your instinctive attitude towards risk (as revealed, for example, by the quiz in Chapter 1).
- **What other resources you have to fall back on,** such as earnings, money tied up in your home, a possible inheritance.
- **The extent to which taking on extra risks** improves the chances of meeting your goal (often referred to as the risk premium).

You put your strategy into practice by choosing specific investments, in other words, a portfolio. So the factors left are also the key determinants behind your choice of portfolio.

ASSETS OR INVESTMENTS?

Some 20 years ago, a seminal piece of academic research showed that over 90 per cent of the variation in pension fund performance from year to year was due to the asset allocation of the funds rather than the particular stocks and shares the fund managers picked.

There has been much debate since and critics have pointed out that, even

Jargon buster

Asset allocation The proportions in which a portfolio is spread across different asset classes, such as cash, bonds and shares

Risk premium The extra return you get from an investment, such as shares, compared with the return from a risk-free investment (for example, very short-term loans to the UK Government)

if the pattern of performance is largely determined by asset allocation, different funds still turn in a markedly different performance by the end of any given term. Therefore, other factors are also important, for example, charges, stock selection and investment timing. But research suggests that active fund management (picking stocks and deciding when to buy and sell) far from enhancing performance, on average, reduces it below the level it would have been had a fund been invested purely on the basis of asset allocation.

The practical messages from the academic research are:

- Stock picking cannot consistently and predictably improve performance.
- There is no way consistently to predict which investment markets are about to rise and which are about to fall.

This leaves asset allocation as the most important factor determining investment performance that you can control.

ASSET ALLOCATION AND GOALS

The idea behind asset allocation is very simple. You spread your money across several asset classes that tend to behave differently from each other (see the table, below). When economic and financial conditions cause one asset class to fall, other classes tend to be unaffected or to rise. This should reduce the volatility (in other words, risk) of your portfolio but means sacrificing some potential return (see case study, overleaf).

There is a constant interest in other types of investment that behave independently of the main asset classes. This gives a range of possible asset classes that include those given overleaf.

Correlation between the main asset classes

The table shows the extent to which different asset classes move in line with each other. If they move perfectly in line, they have a score of 1.0. The closer the figure is to 0, the lower the correlation. A minus score shows that, when one of the assets rises, the other falls.

Asset class	Correlation between asset class on the left and this asset class:			
	Property [1]	UK equities	Gilts	Cash
Property [1]	1.0	0.19	0.04	-0.27
UK equities	0.19	1.0	0.65	0.08
Gilts	0.04	0.65	1.0	0.17
Cash	-0.27	0.08	0.17	1.0

[1] Direct investment in commercial property

Source: Investment Property Database Limited. Based on data for 1970 to 2006. © Investment Property Databank Limited and its licensors, 2008. All rights reserved.

- Cash (see Chapter 2)
- Bonds (see Chapters 4 and 6)
- Equities (see Chapters 5 and 6)
- Property (see Chapter 7)
- Hedge funds (see Chapter 9)
- Collectables (see Chapter 9)
- Commodities (see Chapters 6 and 9).

You need to consider the asset allocation appropriate to each of your goals. Asset allocation should be based on the factors already identified on page 190, namely timescale, the importance and flexibility of the goal, your attitude towards risk, what other resources you have, and the risk premium for different asset classes.

With a medium- or long-term goal, it will usually be appropriate to spread your investment across more than one asset class creating a diverse portfolio. With short-term goals – in other words, savings or investments for a period of five years or less or money that you may need back at short notice – it is normally not appropriate to take capital risk, so you should usually be fully invested in the cash asset class.

ALTERING THE ASSET ALLOCATION

The asset allocation that you start out with may cease to be suitable as time goes on. This can happen for a variety of reasons. For example:

- **Changing attitude towards risk.** When you are young and earning, you can afford to feel fairly relaxed about risk because you have the scope and time to replace any losses. Therefore you may be comfortable with a high proportion of your investments in equities and other relatively high-risk products that give you the chance of high returns. As you get older, you may become more cautious and be more inclined to focus on preserving your wealth rather than growth. As a result, you may want to switch progressively more of your money into cash and bonds.
- **Changing financial goals.** Many goals involve an initial phase where you are investing for growth followed by a second phase where you are drawing an income or cashing in the investment. As the end of the first phase approaches, your initial long-term goal gradually changes into a medium- and then a short-term goal. Where you continue to invest

Case Study Evan

Evan has £10,000 to invest for ten years or more. If the average expected return from cash is 3 per cent a year and, from equities, 6 per cent, the table shows the overall return he might get given different allocations between the two asset classes.

Asset allocation		Yearly return on portfolio	Value of £10,000 after 10 years
Cash	Equities		
90%	10%	3.3%	£13,886
70%	30%	4.0%	£14,780
50%	50%	4.6%	£15,674
30%	70%	5.2%	£16,568
10%	90%	5.7%	£17,462

during the second phase, the asset allocation suitable for growth may need to be replaced by one suitable for producing income.

- **Change in other resources.** You may have been happy with a high level of risk and return while working but if, say, your earnings stop because of long-term illness or redundancy, you made need to shift your portfolio towards lower-risk assets.

You should review the asset allocation from time to time and adjust as necessary for changes like these. In theory it would also be sensible to change your allocation if the risk premium on one or more asset classes shifts. But, in practice, you have no way of knowing if there has been a change. The risk premium refers to the average additional return measured over long time periods. It does not mean a temporary rise that is likely to reverse later on. Piling more money into an asset class because it is temporarily booming undermines the whole risk-spreading philosophy of asset allocation.

Rebalancing

Your investments will not all grow at the same rate. This means that over time the asset allocation of your portfolio will drift from the allocation you started with. Some experts recommend that you regularly rebalance your portfolio so that the original allocation is restored, but this is a controversial view.

Rebalancing could involve taking any of the following steps.

- **Selling some of the assets** that have performed best and using the proceeds to buy more of the assets that have performed less well.

- **Investing an additional lump sum** in the assets that have performed least well, so that the extra you invest offsets the fall in value and restores the proportion of your portfolio invested in these assets to the original level.

- **If you are saving regularly,** shift the split of your new savings going into each asset class.

Supporters of rebalancing say it forces you to buy-low/sell-high, which is the ideal way to make money from a long position. Critics say this is akin to pulling up the flowers and watering the weeds. But, since, over the long term, you would expect equities to outperform other asset classes, if you do not rebalance at all, there will be a built-in tendency for the overall level of risk in your portfolio to drift upwards.

Unless you are saving regularly, rebalancing is likely to involve extra costs as you buy some investments and sell others, possibly in quite small quantities. Some experts recommended that you rebalance every six or twelve months so that you do not drift too far from your original allocation (and risk level). Others suggest you rebalance whenever an asset class has deviated from the starting point by more than an amount you specify (say five percentage points above the target level). Given such frequent adjustments, the extra costs could be significant.

Rose

Rose is investing for growth but is a cautious investor. At the outset she invested 60 per cent of her portfolio in equities and 40 per cent in cash and bonds. When she reviews her portfolio, she finds that the equities have performed better than the cash and bonds. As a result she now has 70 per cent of her portfolio invested in equities and only 30 per cent in cash and bonds. This is a higher-risk position than she feels comfortable with, so Rose sells some equities, realising a good profit on them, and reinvests the proceeds in cash and bonds.

SOME BASIC PORTFOLIOS

There are no hard and fast rules for building the perfect portfolio. What is right for one person and their goals will be wrong for another. There are some broad ideas you can take as a starting point. But you need to think whether they suit you and adapt them as necessary. If you are using an adviser, he or she will probably have some similar outline portfolios that you can discuss and adapt.

Rule of thumb

A very crude idea is that the percentage of your portfolio invested in low-risk cash and bonds should match your age. For example, if you are aged 20, put 20 per cent in cash and bonds with 80 per cent in equities. If you are 70, put 70 per cent in cash and bonds and 30 per cent in equities. This works on the notion that appetite for risk reduces as you age and the investment timescale reduces, but it does nothing to match your portfolio to the other factors outlined on page 190.

The FTSE APCIMS portfolios

The Association of Private Client Investment Managers and Stockbrokers (APCIMS) is a trade body. It has joined with FTSE, the company responsible for producing stock market indices, to create some model portfolios and performance indices based on these portfolios as a guide to what private investors might expect from their investments. There are three different portfolios:

- **An income portfolio** for investors seeking income.
- **A growth portfolio** for growth investors.
- **A balanced portfolio** for investors seeking combined income and growth.

APCIMS carries out a quarterly survey of its members to find out what asset allocations they are recommending for different types of client. The FTSE APCIMS portfolios are based on the survey results. The table opposite shows the three portfolios as they stood in June 2007.

You can check the latest FTSE APCIMS portfolios at the websites of either the Association of Private Client Investment Managers and Stockbrokers (www.apcims.co.uk) or FTSE (www.ftse.com).

A balanced portfolio is different from the way the term 'balanced' has been used in this book to mean a position on the risk scale between cautious and adventurous investing.

The FTSE APCIMS portfolios

Asset class	Income portfolio	Growth portfolio	Balanced portfolio
UK shares	45%	50%	45%
International shares	10%	30%	22.5%
Bonds	35%	5%	17.5%
Cash	5%	5%	5%
Commercial property	5%	5%	5%
Hedge funds	0%	5%	5%
Total	100%	100%	100%

Bear in mind that these benchmark portfolios are just a guide and may not suit you given your own attitude towards risk, resources and other factors.

Asset allocation tools

Many advisers use asset allocation tools – computer-based calculators that produce a recommended allocation according to the answers you give to a variety of questions. Simplified versions are available free on some websites – usually US ones (see below).

FROM ASSETS TO INVESTMENTS

Having decided on your ideal asset allocation, you need to choose specific investments in each asset class. Guidance is to diversify as much as possible so that performance in your portfolio mimics as closely as possible performance of the whole asset class rather than being dominated by one or two companies or sectors that skew your return.

As we have seen (Chapter 6), an efficient way for small investors to gain a spread of investments is to invest in funds. If the academics are right that active fund management on average reduces fund performance (see page 191), tracker funds might be the best choice for your core assets. But investment funds cover a very wide choice of sectors and investments, giving you plenty of scope for more adventurous investing too.

❝ Diversify as much as possible so that your portfolio mimics performance of the asset class. ❞

For an example of an asset allocation tool, see the Iowa Public Employees Retirement System calculator at www.ipers.org/calcs/AssetAllocator.html, which focuses on saving for retirement.

Building your portfolio

Manage your own portfolio

A do-it-yourself approach is feasible provided you have time and a genuine interest in investing. Joining an investment club can make the process more enjoyable and enable you to pool ideas and expertise.

You might opt to manage your own portfolio of investments if some or all of the following apply:

- **Your savings or investment goals are very straightforward,** such as short-term saving using cash assets.
- **You enjoy learning** about and managing investments.
- **You have the patience to read the small print** that comes with products so that you really understand what is involved.
- **You are happy asking questions** if you don't understand something.
- **You have time to monitor your portfolio** regularly and to make any necessary adjustments.

There is a huge wealth of resources available to help you. These include:

- **Books** about the detail of analysing and picking shares, investment strategies, dealing in options, reading the financial pages, and so on. You will find many useful guides by browsing in a good bookshop or on websites such as Global Investor (http://books.global-investor.com) or Amazon (www.amazon.co.uk).
- **Websites.** Exchanges, stockbrokers, specialist information sites, government websites, trade bodies and so on all often include a lot of free guidance and information.

66 You might opt to manage your own investments if you have time to monitor your portfolio regularly. 99

 Some useful websites for investors include www.hemscott.com, www.iii.co.uk, www.londonstockexchange.com and www.trustnet.com.

INVESTMENT CLUBS

An investment club is a group of people who decide to pool their money to buy and sell shares and other investments together. They meet regularly to discuss and make investment decisions and there is usually a strong social side to the club.

If you think it is hard developing a portfolio just for yourself, imagine how much more difficult it could be to get agreement across a whole group. Nevertheless, joining forces with friends, family, work colleagues or neighbours to invest collectively in the stock market can have advantages:

- **Affordability.** By pooling your money you can create a diverse portfolio with a smaller stake per person than if you were investing on your own.
- **Information and experience.** This can be pooled, particularly where members have different work backgrounds and interests. Their joint knowledge of different sectors of the economy may be extensive.
- **Considered decisions.** You will have to discuss your ideas and win over the rest of the group, so your decisions might be more sound than if made on your own.
- **Education.** If you are new to stock market investing, this can be a good way to learn how it's done and may help you gain confidence to go it alone later on.

If you simply wanted an affordable way to buy into a diverse portfolio,

investment funds would be a more obvious route (see Chapter 6).

The overall financial goal of the group is invariably growth. For the club to work harmoniously, it is important that you all have a similar attitude towards investing, particularly regarding risk. Typically, members will have their main financial planning (see Chapter 1) sorted out and be fairly relaxed about taking risks with their investment club money.

&& For the club to work harmoniously, it is important that you all have a similar attitude towards investing. 99

Starting and running a club

There are no set laws or rules to which you must conform. But, because money is involved, it makes sense to put the club onto a formal footing right from the start. You should have a constitution, officers (chairperson, treasurer and secretary), a separate bank account for the club funds, good accounting procedures and clear rules about the ownership and rights of each member, including what happens if they leave the club. You don't have to reinvent the wheel. An organisation, Proshare Investment Clubs (PIC), has for many years been providing resources and support for investment clubs, including a definitive handbook on how to set up and run one.

PIC recommends that clubs should have between three and twenty members and that you buy your first investment once the club has a total paid-in sum of, say, £1,000. The rules should specify how much and how often members invest. Typically, members might pay in a lump sum to get the club started and a regular sum, say £25 a month, after that.

Who owns what?

PIC recommends that clubs use a unit valuation system, which means that:

- Members are allocated units in line with the amount they invest.
- Once the club starts to invest, the value of each unit is recalculated once a month by taking the club's total assets and dividing by the number of units issued.
- New units are bought at the most recently calculated unit value.

Tax

No special tax rules apply to investment clubs. Each member is responsible for tax on their own share of the return from the investments. Unlike, say, a unit trust, you cannot invest in an investment club through an ISA.

Case Study | The Optimists Club

Five friends decide to set up an investment club, The Optimists. They invest as follows:

- An initial investment of £100 from each member. The club has £500. This is divided into 500 £1 units.
- A monthly investment of £25, which buys each member 25 £1 units each month.
- By the fourth month, the club has £1,000 and makes its first investment. Each member has 200 units.

- In the fifth month, the investment has grown to £1,100. The new unit price is £1,100 / 1,000 = £1.10. Each member makes their usual monthly investment of £25, which now buys £25 / £1.10 = 22.73 new units.

 For more information about setting up an investment club, contact Proshare Investment Clubs at www.proshareclubs.co.uk.

Getting help

If you do not feel confident choosing or running your own portfolio, you can get help. There are three main options: invest in an appropriate type of fund, make your own decisions, but with help from an adviser, or use a discretionary investment manager.

USING FUNDS

Investment funds, such as those outlined in Chapters 6, 7 and 9, are not just possible ingredients in your portfolio. Some funds are a ready-made portfolio in themselves, giving you a spread of assets from different classes. Different funds offer different portfolios for different purposes, for example:

- **Asset allocation/managed funds** invest in a range of assets, including cash, bonds, property and equities (see the table, overleaf, for details).
- **With-profits funds.** Insurance-based funds that give you a return largely based on the performance of a wide range of investments, including bonds, property and equities (see page 131).
- **Lifestyle funds,** typically used for pension savings, CTFs and other goals where you are saving towards a long-term target date. These adjust the asset mix automatically as the end of the chosen investment term approaches (see page 132).
- **Multimanager/fund of funds** hold a selection of other investment funds. These can be expensive because of the double layer of charges (see page 132).

It is important that you check the aims and strategies of any particular fund before you invest to make sure that they offer the type of portfolio you are looking for. Make sure that the investment goals and aspects such as risk and tax treatment are suitable given your personal preferences and circumstances.

> **❝ Some funds are ready-made portfolios, giving you a spread of assets. ❞**

See Chapters 2 and 6 for guidance on the tax treatment of different investment funds.

Investment funds that give you a ready-made portfolio

Risk	Name of fund	Type of fund	Investment aim	Investment rules applying to fund	
				Allocation to equities [1]	Other allocation rules
HIGHER	UK equity and bond	Unit trust or open-ended investment company (OEIC)	Immediate income	20% to 80%	20% to 80% in UK fixed interest [2]. At least 80% UK assets
	Defensive	Insurance or pension	Income or growth [3]	Maximum 35%	At least 85% sterling-based assets
	Cautious managed	Unit trust or OEIC	Growth	Maximum 60%	At least 30% in fixed interest and cash. At least 50% in sterling- and euro-based investments
		Insurance or pension	Income or growth [3]	20% to 60%	At least 60% in sterling-based assets
	Distribution	Insurance or pension	Immediate income	20% to 60%	At least 50% in sterling-based assets
	Balanced managed	Unit trust or OEIC	Growth	Maximum 85%; at least 10% non-UK equities	At least 50% in sterling- and euro-based investments
		Insurance or pension	Income or growth [3]	40% to 85%	At least 50% in sterling-based assets
	Flexible managed	Insurance or pension	Income or growth [3]	Maximum 100%	At least 20% in sterling-based assets
LOWER	Active managed	Unit trust or OEIC	Growth	Maximum 100%; at least 10% non-UK equities	Discretion to hold high proportion of non-equity investments (such as fixed interest and cash)

[1] Equities include, for example, preference shares and convertibles (corporate bonds that can be exchanged for shares on set future dates on pre-set terms)

[2] Fixed interest is the collective name for gilts and corporate bonds

[3] When held through an insurance policy, you have the option to draw an income (see pages 40 and 166–71)

GETTING INVESTMENT ADVICE

If you are a confident investor, you might be happy to buy or arrange your own investments without getting any advice. This is variously called dealing on an execution-only or direct offer basis. The investment decisions are yours alone and you have no comeback if it turns out that an investment is unsuitable for you.

If you are less confident, it makes sense to seek advice. This could be from a product provider, the provider's tied agent or an independent adviser, such as an IFA or stockbroker.

It is illegal for firms to market or sell investments or give advice about them to UK investors unless they are authorised by the FSA. Provided a firm is authorised, you are protected in a variety of ways (see page 204). Some of the investor protection rules specifically relate to advice, in particular:

- **Suitable advice.** The adviser must only recommend products that are suitable for you, given your circumstances and attitude towards risk.
- **Know the customer.** In order to give suitable advice, the adviser must gather enough information about you. Usually, he or she will do this by carrying out a fact find.
- **Complaints procedure.** If the advice turns out to be unsuitable, there are formal channels through which you can complain.
- **Compensation.** You have the right to compensation if you lose money because of unsuitable advice. If the firm has gone out of business owing you money, a compensation scheme may step in to pay you redress.

Product provider

You might decide to take out an investment direct with a provider – for example, an insurance company or a unit trust or investment trust management company. Unless you are investing on a direct offer basis, the salesperson you deal with will carry out a fact find and, on the basis of this, recommend the most suitable products from the provider's range. If the provider has no suitable products, the salesperson should tell you this. He or she might be able to offer you an 'out-of-range' product from another provider.

The salesperson is likely to be paid a salary and possibly commission based on the number or value of products he or she sells. Either way, you indirectly pay for the advice because the cost is built into the product's charges.

Tied agent

Tied agents sell the products of one or more particular providers. Agents range from small firms to large high street

See page 204 for more about investor protection rules. To make sure that a firm is authorised by the FSA, check the FSA register at www.fsa.gov.uk/register.

banks and building societies. At the start of your dealings with the firm, it should make its tied status clear and tell you which products it can offer.

The adviser should then carry out a fact find and offer you a suitable product from its range or tell you if it has nothing suitable. Tied agents get commission from the provider each time they sell a product. You indirectly pay the commission through the charges for the product.

Independent financial adviser (IFA)

IFAs can give you advice on the whole of your financial planning or just a particular aspect or goal. They range from single practitioners working from home through to large firms and subsidiaries of the high street banks. To qualify to use the name 'independent', an IFA must:

- **Be able to recommend any product on the market,** so should be able to find you the best deal available.
- **Let you pay for the advice by fee if you want to.**

Traditionally, most IFAs were paid by commission, in other words, a payment from the provider whose product they sell you. Indirectly, you pay the commission through the charges for the product. Many IFAs do still get commission, though you might be able to negotiate a rebate, so that part of the commission is refunded to you either as

---

Commission versus fees

The advantage of paying for advice by fee is that the adviser gets paid regardless of whether or not he or she sells you a product. This means there is no incentive for the adviser to sell you products you don't need or to base recommendations on which providers pay the highest commission. So you can therefore be more confident that the advice really is independent. On the other hand, the fee can seem large – between £50 and £200 an hour is typical.

Although commission might be equally large, paying it gradually through the product charges is painless and makes the advice on the face of it seem free. Of course, the advice is not really free. You generally pay upfront or through other charges for the product or through an exit charge or surrender charge if you cancel the investment within the first few years.

For a list of IFAs, contact IFA Promotion at www.unbiased.co.uk. To find a stockbroker, use the find-a-broker service on the London Stock Exchange (www.londonstockexchange.com) or contact APCIMS at www.apcims.co.uk.

a cash sum or through enhanced product terms. But increasingly, IFAs either charge you a fee based on the time they spend on your case or give you the option to pay that way if you want. Any commission from product providers is then deducted from the fee.

Stockbrokers

Stockbrokers specialise in direct investment in stock market investments, such as shares, gilts, corporate bonds, traded options and covered warrants. If you want advice about these, a stockbroker is usually a better choice than an IFA. Many stockbrokers also offer advice about investment funds, especially investment trusts and exchange-traded funds (ETFs) that you buy and sell on the stock market. There are different services that you can pay for:

- **Execution-only service.** If you are confident making your investment decisions, you might opt for this service in which case you do not get any advice.
- **Execution-and-advice service,** which generally costs a bit more. The cost of the advice is normally bundled into the commission that you pay each time you buy and sell through the broker.

The form of advice varies – for example, the broker might just comment on your proposed trades. Alternatively, the firm might phone or email you with suggestions. You might be sent information on a regular basis – for example, analysts' reports and recommendations, news about current issues and so on.

USING A DISCRETIONARY INVESTMENT MANAGER

A discretionary investment manager, also called a portfolio manager, does not just give you advice. The firm takes over managing your investments, making your investment decisions for you and handling most of the administration and paperwork.

Discretionary management is usually an option only if you have a fairly substantial sum to invest, say, £100,000. But some firms will accept portfolios as low as £20,000 though you should then expect your money to be put into investment funds rather than direct holdings of shares and other stock market investments. Discretionary management firms that act for private investors tend to be stockbrokers, banks, some IFAs or specialist firms.

Normally you pay for the service through an annual fee that is typically a percentage of the value of your portfolio. You will also pay dealing charges and other transaction fees when investments in your portfolio are bought and sold.

 Contact APCIMS at www.apcims.co.uk for details of members offering discretionary investment management.

Protection for the investor

In general, it is illegal for any firm to carry on a financial business in the UK unless it is authorised by the FSA. Provided you deal only with authorised firms, you benefit from various levels of protection.

To become authorised, a firm must be solvent, prudently operated and run by honest and competent people. In many cases, there are also rules that set out how a firm should do business including what information you must be given.

Authorised firms must also have formal complaints procedures and belong to the Financial Ombudsman Service (FOS) (www.financial-ombudsman.org.uk), which is an independent body that resolves disputes between firms and their customers. As a last resort, if an authorised firm goes bust owing money to its customers, there is a compensation scheme that may step in to pay redress.

Provided you deal with an authorised firm, you benefit from all the above investor protection. If you deal with a firm that is not authorised, you might have no protection at all if something goes wrong.

> **Authorised firms must also have formal complaints procedures.**

MAKING A COMPLAINT

If you have problem with a financial product or service or advice from an authorised firm, first complain to the firm involved. If its initial response is not satisfactory, ask for details of its formal complaints procedure.

If you are not happy with the formal response or there has been no response within eight weeks, you can take your case to the FOS. This is a free dispute-resolution service that has been designed for consumers to use without the need for any legal representation. The ombudsman can order a firm to put matters right, including ordering awards of up to £100,000.

If you are unhappy with the ombudsman's verdict (or as an alternative to going to the ombudsman), you can bring a court case against the firm. But, in general, going to court will be a lengthier and more costly process than using the FOS.

 Before you do business with any financial firm, make sure it is authorised by checking the FSA Register at www.fsa.gov.uk/register.

Exemption from authorisation

In some cases, financial firms may legally deal with the UK public even though they are not directly authorised by the FSA:

- Appointed representatives. If a firm is acting as the tied agent of an FSA-authorised firm, the agent (called the firm's appointed representative) does not have to be authorised. Instead the firm that is authorised is responsible for regulating its appointed representatives.
- EEA authorised firms. These are firms operating from another country in the European Economic Area (which is made up of the European Union plus Iceland, Liechtenstein and Norway). These firms are regulated by their home country, which offers similar standards of investor protection to the UK. If anything goes wrong, you deal with the complaints and compensation systems in the home country not the UK's.

If, instead of 'authorised', you see 'appointed representative' or 'EEA authorised' against a firm's entry in the FSA Register, it is safe to do business with that firm.

COMPENSATION

If you have lost money because of an authorised firm's dishonesty or negligence, normally you would seek compensation from the firm (with the help of the FOS or courts as described above). But your chances of getting money from the firm evaporate if the firm goes out of business. In that situation, you can make a claim to the Financial Services Compensation Scheme, which might refund you some or all of the money you have lost. See the table, overleaf, for details of the maximum you can claim.

❝ The Financial Ombudsman Service is free and has been designed for consumers to use without legal representation. ❞

For more information about the FOS, go to www.financial-ombudsman.org.uk. For further details about the Financial Services Compensation Scheme, see www.fscs.org.uk.

Compensation from the Financial Services Compensation Scheme

Type of investment involved	Level of cover	Maximum payment
Deposits (such as bank and building society accounts)	100% of the first £35,000 [1]	£35,000
Pensions, annuities and investment-type life insurance	100% of the first £2,000; at least 90% of the remainder	Unlimited
Other investments (such as unit trusts, shares)	100% of the first £30,000; 90% of the next £20,000	£48,000

[1] At the time of writing (December 2007), the Government was reviewing this limit and method of protecting deposits

Investment risk

In general, the law and FSA rules do not protect you from investment risk. It is in the nature of many investments that you might lose money and that is a risk you accept in return for the chance of making a higher return. However, if you have relied on investment advice and the adviser failed to make sure that you understood the risks you were taking, you might have a valid complaint if you lose money as a result.

❝ It is in the nature of many investments that you might lose money and that is a risk you accept for a higher return. ❞

Glossary

Accrued income: The part of a gilt or bond price that represents built-up interest which will be paid to the purchaser at the next payment date.

Annual equivalent rate (AER): The true interest rate you get over a year (assuming the rate does not change, if it is variable). Use the AER to compare the returns on different accounts.

Annuity: An investment where you exchange a lump sum for income, usually for life.

Asset allocation: The proportions in which a portfolio is spread across different asset classes, such as cash, bonds, property and equities.

Bid price: The (lower) price you get when you sell shares, units or derivatives contracts. The difference between this and the (higher) offer price at which you buy is, in effect, a charge you pay.

Bond: Investment where you lend to a company, government or other organisation and can sell the loan on the stock market.

Buying off-plan: Buying a property before it is built. Usually you pay a small reservation fee immediately, followed by a deposit, possibly staged payments during the building process and the balance on completion.

Buy to let: Property that you buy in order to let out to tenants.

Call contract: A derivatives contract that gives you the right to buy an underlying asset on or before a set date at a set price. You might buy this contract if you expect the price of the underlying asset or index to rise.

Capital risk: The risk of losing some or all of the money you originally invested or some or all of the profits you have made so far.

Cash: Commonly used in the investment world to refer collectively to savings-type products that earn interest.

Cash settlement: Exchanging cash when a derivative matures or is exercised instead of delivering the underlying asset.

Closing price: Broadly the last price at which a stock was bought or sold on the most recent trading day.

Corporate bond: Investment where you lend to a company and can sell the loan on the stock market.

Coupon: With a gilt or other bond, the amount of interest you get each year expressed as a percentage of the nominal value.

Covered warrant: Similar to a traded option. Issued by an investment bank, it gives the holder the right to buy an underlying asset on or by a set date at a set price. Covered warrants have been specifically designed to give private investors easy access to derivatives.

Derivative: A contract that gives you the obligation or right to buy or sell some underlying asset at a set price on or by a set future date (called the exercise date). The value of the contract varies with the price of the underlying asset and the time left until the exercise date. Many derivatives contracts can be bought and sold before the exercise date and so provide an investment regardless of whether the underlying asset is ever bought or sold.

Earnings per share (eps): The company's profits after various deductions, such as tax, divided by the number of ordinary shares.

Enhanced annuity (impaired life annuity): An annuity that pays a higher-than-average income because your life expectancy is lower than average, which can be due to poor health or lifestyle.

Equities: Another name for shares or share-based investments.

Exercise: With derivatives, taking up your right to buy or sell the underlying asset. With share options, going ahead and buying the shares.

Final-salary scheme: Type of occupational pension scheme where your employer promises you a pension worked out as a proportion of your pay at or near retirement.

Forward: A contract that obliges one party to deliver an underlying asset on or by a specified date at a set price and the other party to accept delivery on those terms.

Friendly society: Basically an insurer owned by its customers.

Friendly society tax-efficient plan: Investment-type life insurance policy from a friendly society that produces a largely tax-free return. But the maximum you can invest is very low at just £270 a year.

FTSE 100: An index that is calculated as a weighted average of the share prices of the 100 largest companies quoted on the London Stock Exchange. It is often used as a measure of the performance of the stock market generally.

Fund of funds: An investment fund that holds a selection of other investment funds. Can be expensive because of the double layer of charges.

Fund supermarket: Usually a website, but sometimes a phone-based service, that lets you invest in a wide range of investment funds from different providers. You can either hold the funds direct or invest through a wrapper (a stocks and shares ISA or SIPP) operated by the supermarket provider.

Future: A forward contract that can be bought and sold on the stock market.

Gilts: The common name for bonds issued by the British Government.

Gross: An amount of income before any tax has been taken off. Alternatively, the amount of an expense or outgoing before tax relief has been taken off.

Group personal pension: A personal pension that you can join through work. Your employer chooses the provider and may have negotiated some special features, for example, lower charges.

Hedge fund: An investment fund that can use a much wider range of investment techniques than other funds, enabling it, for example, to make money when the stock markets are falling.

HM Revenue & Customs (HMRC): The government department responsible for managing the UK tax system.

Indexation allowance: An allowance that ensured you did not pay capital gains tax on gains due purely to inflation over the period 1982 to 1998. Abolished from 6 April 2008.

Level annuity: An annuity where the income you get stays the same year after year. The drawback is that the buying power of the income falls as the general level of prices rises.

Life expectancy: The length of time you are expected to live based on the average experience for people of your current age and often other factors (such as your gender and health).

Lifestyle funds: These are typically used for pension savings, child trust funds and other goals where you are saving towards a long-term target date. They adjust the asset mix automatically to reduce risk and lock in previous gains as the end of the chosen investment term approaches.

Lifetime annuity: Investment where you give up a lump sum and in return get an income for life. Once purchased, you cannot change your mind and get your lump sum back.

Listed: Describes a company whose shares are traded on a formal stock exchange.

Long position: Buying and holding assets in the hope of selling them later at a profit. This can be achieved either by buying the assets or derivatives.

Long term: Usually defined as ten years or more.

Managed funds: Investment funds that invest in a range of assets, including cash, bonds, property and equities.

Market capitalisation: A way of valuing a company by multiplying the number of ordinary shares it has issued by the current share price.

Market price: The price at which you buy and sell gilts, shares or other investments traded on a stock market.

Medium term: Approximately five to ten years, but not very precisely defined.

Means-tested state benefits: State benefits that you can get only if your income and savings are low, for example, pension credit, council tax benefit and housing benefit.

Mid price: The point halfway between the bid and offer price.

Multimanager funds: An investment fund that holds a selection of other investment funds. Can be expensive because of the double layer of charges.

National insurance: A tax you (and employers) pay while you are working that also entitles you to claim various state benefits. In some situations where you cannot work – for example, you are caring for young children or you are ill – you get credits.

Net: The amount of income left after tax has been taken off. Alternatively, an amount you pay after tax relief has been taken off.

Nominal value: A unit used as a reference for quoting information about gilts and some other investments. For gilts, the standard unit is £100.

Occupational pension: A pension from a scheme run by your employer, who pays some (or occasionally all) of the cost of providing the pension.

Offer price (also called the ask price): The (higher) price you pay when buying shares, units or derivatives contracts. The difference between this and the (lower) bid price at which you sell is, in effect, a charge you pay.

PAYE: System for automatically collecting tax through deductions direct from your pay or pension.

PAYE tax review form (P810): A form you may have to fill in every few years if you pay tax through PAYE to check that the correct amount of tax is being deducted from your pay or pension.

Personal pension: A pension scheme that you usually arrange for yourself and that stays with you even if you change jobs.

Put contract: A derivatives contract that gives you the right to sell an underlying asset on or before a set date at a set price. You might use it if you expect the price of the underlying asset or index to fall.

Quoted: Describes shares that are traded on a formal stock exchange or any other stock market, so that trading establishes a price for the shares.

Real: Describes the value left after any increase due to inflation has been stripped out (or any decrease due to falling prices).

Real estate investment trust (REIT): A type of investment fund that invests in commercial and/or residential property. Tax on the rental income from the properties in the fund is payable by reference to your personal tax situation rather than that of the fund.

Recognised stock exchange: A UK or overseas market for trading in shares, which is on a list kept by HMRC. To be on the list, a UK exchange must be regulated by the FSA and, for an overseas exchange, by an equivalent regulator in its home country.

Redemption yield: The return from a gilt or bond. It is the coupon and any gain or loss at redemption expressed as a percentage of the market price.

Risk premium: The extra return you get from an investment, such as shares, compared with the return from a risk-free investment (for example, very short-term loans to the UK Government).

RPI-linked annuity: An annuity where the income you get increases each year in line with inflation. The drawback is that the starting income is lower than you would get from an annuity that is not RPI-linked.

Running yield (or income yield): With a gilt or other bond, the coupon as a percentage of the market price.

Salary sacrifice: Arrangement, which has tax advantages for both you and your employer, where you give up some pay and, in return, your employer provides you with non-cash benefits, for example, paying more into your pension scheme.

Self-invested personal pension (SIPP): Type of personal pension where you choose how to invest your savings.

Settlement system: Administrative arrangements to ensure that, when a share, bond or derivatives transaction takes place, money is delivered to the seller and the investments are registered to the buyer.

Share: A part-ownership of a company that can be sold to another investor.

Short position: Selling assets in the hope of buying them back later at a lower price and so realising a profit. Investment funds typically borrow the shares to sell from other investments funds (for a fee) or use derivatives to create a short position.

Short term: Usually defined as five years or less.

Spread: The difference between the bid and offer prices for a share, unit or derivatives contract. Also, in spread betting, the range of values against which you bet.

Spread betting (or index betting): A type of gambling that is a form of derivatives trading, offered by some online bookmakers and stockbrokers.

Stakeholder scheme: A personal pension that meets set conditions, for example, a cap on charges and low minimum contribution.

State pension age: The age at which you can start to receive your state pension. Currently, 65 for men and 60 for women, but increasing gradually to 68 for all.

Stop-loss: Way to protect yourself from unlimited losses when buying and selling shares or derivatives. You instruct the broker or bookmaker to close your position once the relevant share price or index reaches a level you set.

Taper relief: Allowance that reduced the amount of capital gains tax you paid according to how long you had held an asset, with higher relief for business assets. Abolished from 6 April 2008.

Tax relief at source: Treating a payment that qualifies for tax relief as being a net-of-tax amount. Tax relief is then added. For example, if you pay £80 into a personal pension, the pension provider claims £20 tax relief from HMRC and adds it to your scheme.

Tax return: Form you may have to fill in each year with information about your income and other details so that you pay the correct amount of tax.

Tax year: Runs from 6 April to the following 5 April.

Traded option: Derivatives contract, similar to a future, but the buyer of the contract has the right – not the obligation – to buy or sell the underlying asset either on or by a set date at a set price. The traded option contract can be bought and sold on the stock market.

Trust fund: A legal arrangement where someone holds investments or other property not for their own use but for the benefit of someone else.

Warrant: Issued by a company, it gives the holder the right to buy that company's shares on or by a set date (or on a series of dates), at a set price.

With-profits funds: Insurance-based funds that give you a return largely based on the performance of a wide range of investments, including bonds, property and equities.

Useful addresses

Accountants

For a list of members in your area contact:

Association of Chartered Certified Accountants
2 Central Quay
89 Hydepark Street
Glasgow G3 8BW
Tel: 0141 582 2000
www.acca.co.uk

Institute of Chartered Accountants in England and Wales
PO Box 433
Chartered Accountants' Hall
Moorgate Place
London EC2P 2BJ
Tel: 020 7920 8100
www.icaew.co.uk

Institute of Chartered Accountants in Ireland
CA House
83 Pembroke Road
Dublin 4
Tel: (00 353) 1 637 7200
www.icai.ie

Institute of Chartered Accountants of Scotland
CA House
21 Haymarket Yards
Edinburgh EH12 5BH
Tel: 0131 347 0100
www.icas.org.uk

Association of International Property Professionals (AIPP)
94 New Bond Street
London W1S 1SJ
Tel: 020 7409 7061
www.aipp.org.uk

Association of Investment Companies (AIC)
9th Floor
24 Chiswell Street
London EC1Y 4YY
Tel: 020 7282 5555
www.theaic.co.uk

Association of Private Client Investment Managers and Stockbrokers (APCIMS)
114 Middlesex Street
London E1 7JH
Tel: 020 7247 7080
www.apcims.co.uk

The Association of Real Estate Funds (AREF)
Tel: 07720 343 792
www.aput.co.uk

Bank of England base rate
www.bankofengland.co.uk/monetarypolicy

British Business Angels Association
New City Court
20 St Thomas Street
London SE1 9RS
Tel: 0207 089 2305
www.bbaa.org.uk

British Insurance Brokers Association (BIBA)
14 Bevis Marks
London EC3A 7NT
Consumer helpline: 0901 814 0015 (calls charged at 25p per minute)
www.biba.org.uk

The British Private Equity and Venture
Capital Association
3 Clements Inn
London WC2A 2AZ
Tel: 020 7025 2950
www.bvca.co.uk

The Chartered Institute of
Taxation
12 Upper Belgrave Street
London SW1X 8BB
Tel: 020 7235 9381
www.tax.org.uk

Child Trust Fund Office
Waterview Park
Mandarin Way
Washington NE38 8QG
Tel: 0845 302 1470
www.childtrustfund.gov.uk

Citizens Advice Bureaux
Look in *The Phone Book* under 'Citizens
Advice Bureau'
www.citizensadvice.org.uk
www.adviceguide.org.uk

Computershare Investor Services
The Pavilions
Bridgwater Road
Bristol BS99 6ZW
Gilts enquiries: 0870 703 0143
Gilts publications: see Debt Management
Office below
www.comptershare.com

Consumer Direct
Tel: 08454 04 05 06
www.consumerdirect.gov.uk/

Debt advice
Citizens Advice Bureau
See separate entry above

Consumer Credit Counselling Service
Wade House
Merrion Centre
Leeds LS2 8NG
Tel: 0800 138 1111 (freephone)
www.cccs.co.uk

National Debtline
Tel: 0808 808 4000 (freephone)
www.nationaldebtline.co.uk

Debt Management Office (DMO)
Eastcheap Court
11 Philpot Lane
London EC3M 8UD
Tel: 0845 357 6500
www.dmo.gov.uk

Ethical Investors Group
Montpellier House
47 Rodney Road
Cheltenham GL50 1HX
Tel: 01242 539848
www.ethicalinvestors.co.uk

Ethical Investment Research Services
(EIRIS)
80–84 Bondway
London SW8 1SF
Tel: 020 7840 5700
www.eiris.org

Euronext
Cannon Bridge House
1 Cousin Lane
London EC4R 3XX
Tel: 020 7623 0444
www.euronext.com

Financial Ombudsman Service (FOS)
South Quay Plaza
183 Marsh Wall
London E14 9SR
Tel: 0845 080 1800
www.financial-ombudsman.org.uk

213

Financial Services Authority (FSA)
25 The North Colonnade
London E14 5HS
FSA consumer helpline: 0845 6061234
www.fsa.gov.uk
Consumer website:
www.moneymadeclear.fsa.gov.uk
Comparative tables: www.fsa.gov.uk/tables
FSA Register: www.fsa.gov.uk/register

Financial Services Compensation Scheme
7th Floor
Lloyds Chambers
Portsoken Street
London E1 8BN
Tel: 020 7892 7300
www.fscs.org.uk

FTSE
12th Floor
10 Upper Bank Street
Canary Wharf
London E14 5NP
Tel: 020 7866 1800
www.ftse.com (portfolios)
FTSE4Good:
www.ftse.com/Indices/FTSE4Good_Index_
Series/index.jsp

HM Revenue & Customs (HMRC)
For local tax enquiry centres look in *The
Phone Book* under 'HM Revenue &
Customs'
For your local tax office, check your tax
return, other tax correspondence or check
with your employer or scheme paying you a
pension
www.hmrc.gov.uk
Form R40 (claim back tax):
www.hmrc.gov.uk/individuals/fgcat-
claimingarepayment.shtm
Share schemes:
www.hmrc.gov.uk/shareschemes/employee
_schemes.htm

Stamp duty calculator:
http://sdcalculator.inlandrevenue.gov.uk
Probate and inheritance tax helpline:
0845 302 0900
www.hmrc.gov.uk/cto

**Independent financial adviser (IFA) - to
find one**
IFA Promotion
Tel: 0800 085 3250 (freephone)
www.unbiased.co.uk

The Institute of Financial Planning
Whitefriars Centre
Lewins Mead
Bristol BS1 2NT
Tel: 0117 9345 2470
www.financialplanning.org.uk

**Independent financial advisers
specialising in annuities**
The Annuity Bureau
Tel: 0845 602 6263
www.annuity-bureau.co.uk/

Annuity Direct
32 Scrutton Street
London EC2A 4RQ
Tel: 0500 50 65 75 (freephone)
www.annuitydirect.co.uk

Hargreaves Lansdown Annuity Supermarket
Tel: 0845 345 9880
www.h-l.co.uk/
pensions_and_retirement/annuities.hl

WBA Ltd
Tel: 020 831 4711
www.williamburrows.com

Insurance broker - to find one
Look in *The Phone Book* under 'Insurance –
Intermediaries'
See entries for British Insurance Brokers
Association (above) and Mylocaladviser.com
(right)
To check an intermediary is authorised,
contact the FSA Register (see above)

Investment Management Association (IMA)
65 Kingsway
London WC2B 6TD
Information line: 020 7269 4639
www.investmentuk.org

Islamic Bank of Britain
PO Box 12461
Birmingham B16 8NH
Tel: 0845 6060 786
www.islamic-bank.com

London Stock Exchange
10 Paternoster Square
London EC4M 7LS
Tel: 020 7797 1000
www.londonstockexchange.com
Find a stockbroker:
www.londonstockexchange.com/en-gb/
pricesnews/education/resources/broker/

Money Management magazine
From larger newsagents
Subscriptions and back copies: 020 8606 7545

Moneyfacts
Moneyfacts House
66–70 Thorpe Road
Norwich NR1 1BJ
Subscriptions: 0845 1689 600
www.moneyfacts.co.uk

Mortgage broker
See The Phone Book under 'Mortgages'
Use www.mylocaladviser.com,
www.searchmortgagebroker.co.uk or
www.unbiased.co.uk
To check an intermediary is authorised,
contact the FSA Register (see left)

Mylocaladviser.com
www.mylocaladviser.com

National Savings & Investments
Tel: 0845 964 5000 (calls charged at local rate)
www.nsandi.com
NS&I index-linked savings certificates calculator:
www.nsandi.com/products/ilsc/calculator.jsp
NS&I unclaimed premium bond prizes:
www.nsandi.com/products/pb/
haveYouWon.jsp
Pensioners guaranteed income bond calculator:
www.nsandi.com/products/pgib/calculator.jsp

Pension calculators
Association of British Insurers and Financial Services Authority
www.pensioncalculator.org.uk

MoneyTrail
Age Concern England
Astral House
1268 London Road
London SW16 4ER
www.ageconcern.org.uk/moneytrail

Pension Protection Fund
Knollys House
17 Addiscombe Road
Croydon
Surrey CRO 6SR
Tel: 0845 600 2541
www.pensionprotectionfund.org.uk

The Pension Service
For your local office, look in The Phone Book under 'The Pension Service'
Tel: 0845 60 60 265
www.thepensionservice.gov.uk
State pension forecast:
www.thepensionservice.gov.uk/atoz/
atozdetailed/rpforecast.asp (But for people reaching state pension age on or after 6 April 2010, the forecasting service has been suspended until autumn 2008)

The Pensions Advisory Service
11 Belgrave Road
London SW1V 1RB
Tel: 0845 601 2923
www.thepensionsadvisoryservice.org.uk

Pensions Ombudsman
11 Belgrave Road
London SW1V 1RB
Tel: 0207 834 9144
www.pensions-ombudsman.org.uk

Personal Inflation Calculator
www.statistics.gov.uk/pic

PLUS Markets
Standon House
21 Mansell Street
London E1 8AA
Tel: 020 7553 2000
www.plusmarketsgroup.com

Proshare Investment Clubs
4th Floor
Bankside House
107 Leadenhall Street
London, EC3A 4AF
Tel: 0906 802 2222 (calls are charged at 60p per minute)
www.proshareclubs.co.uk

Reita
c/o British Property Federation
1 Warwick Row
London SW1E 5ER
Tel: 020 7802 0109
www.reita.org

Safe Home Income Plans (SHIP)
83 Victoria Street
London SW1H 0HW
Tel: 0870 241 6060
www.ship-ltd.org

Solicitor – to find one
Look in *Yellow Pages* under 'Solicitors' or contact the following professional bodies for a list of their members in your area:

Law Society
113 Chancery Lane
London WC2A 1PL
Tel: 0870 606 2555
www.lawsociety.org.uk

Law Society of Northern Ireland
40 Linenhall Street
Belfast BT2 8BA
Tel: 028 9023 1614
www.lawsoc-ni.org

Law Society of Scotland
26 Drumsheugh Gardens
Edinburgh EH3 7YR
Tel: 0845 113 0018
www.lawscot.org.uk

Stockbroker – to find one
See separate entries above for Association of Private Client Investment Managers and Stockbrokers and London Stock Exchange

Tax advisers – to find one
See 'Tax advisers' in *Yellow Pages* and separate entry for Chartered Institute of Taxation above

Zopa
3rd Floor, Radiant House
36–38 Mortimer Street
London W1W 7RG
www.zopa.com

Index

absolute return funds 186
additional voluntary contribution (AVC)
    scheme 81–2
adventurous investors 14
Alternative Investment Market (AIM) 98
annual equivalent rate (AER) 52–3
annuities 160–5
    with guarantee 163
    income amount 161–4
    as insurance 163
    lifetime 77
    long-term care 165
    paying and reclaiming tax on 161
    as a pension income 164–5
    risk level 158–9
    RPI-linked 19, 162
    types of 160–1
annuity rate 161, 162
asset allocation 190, 191–3, 195
    funds 199
asset classes 22, 191
assets 190–1, 195
Association of Investment Companies 123
Association of Private Client Investment
    Managers and Stockbrokers
    (APCIMS) 194–5, 203
Association of Real Estate Funds (AREF) 153
Association of Trust Companies 135

bank accounts 55, 58–9
    monthly interest 65, 158–9
    versus NS&I products 60
    bed and breakfasting 108
bonds 7, 114, 127–8
    asset classes 22

capital 61
children's bonus 63
corporate 16, 17, 158–9
distribution funds and 158–9
escalator 59
fixed-rate 61, 65, 158–9
guaranteed equity 62, 158–9
income 65, 158–9
insurance *see* insurance bonds
pensioners' guaranteed income 65
premium 66–7
with-profits 158–9
budget calculator 10
building society accounts 55, 58–9
    monthly interest 65, 158–9
    versus NS&I products 60
business angels 187–8
buy-to-let property 140–50
    borrowing for 145–7
    overseas 148–50
    risk level 158–9
    and tax 144

capital bonds 61
capital gains (or losses) 94
    exchange-traded funds (ETFs) 121
    gilts 111
    investment trusts 123
    unit trusts 120
capital gains tax (CGT) 28, 31–3
    investment funds 133
    shares 94
    tangible moveable property 41
    tax tips 47
capital protection annuity 163–4

capital risk 6, 15–16, 22
    buy-to-let property 142
    gilts 110
    income and 157
    pensions 74–5
    savings 51–2
    shares 94
cash 11, 127
    asset classes 22
    definition 19
    real investment returns 20
    risk of keeping 16
children's bonus bonds 63
children's savings accounts 55
child trust funds (CTFs) 43, 45, 63
collectables 176–8
    gains on 41–2
compensation 205–6
complaints 204
convertibles, bonds 114
Co-operative Bank 57
corporate bonds 16, 17, 158–9
covered call funds 158–9, 186
credit union accounts 56
CREST 101
cumulative preference shares 97

Debt Management Office (DMO) 112–13
debt problems 11
deep-discount bonds 114
defined benefit occupational pension
    schemes 78–9
demutualisation 106
dependants, considering 23, 34, 47
deposit-based investments *see* saving(s)
derivatives 179–83
    spread betting 182–3
    tax 181–2
discount broker 120
discretionary investment manager 203
distribution funds and bonds 158–9,
    168–9
diversification 22, 195

dividend income 21, 28, 38, 92–4
    exchange-traded funds (ETFs) 121
    foreign 38
    gilts 110
    investment trusts 123
    unit trusts 119

easy access accounts 55–7, 58, 64
Ecology Building Society 57
emergency funds 55
employer's contributions, pensions 72, 79
enhanced annuity 162
enhanced money market fund 127
enterprise investment scheme (EIS) 188
equities *see* shares
equity income fund 158–9
equity release schemes 158–9, 172–4
escalating annuity 162
escalator bonds 59
ethical investments 57, 99, 129–30
exchange-traded funds (ETFs) 121–2, 126

Financial Ombudsman Service (FOS) 204
financial pages, reading 107
financial planning 10–14, 50–4
Financial Services Authority (FSA) 15, 51,
    201
Financial Services Compensation Scheme
    (FSCS) 51–2, 75
fixed interest savings certificates 59–60
fixed-rate bonds 61, 65, 158–9
fixed-rate interest 53–4
fixed-rate mortgages 147
fixed/variable risk 15–16
Fraud Compensation Fund 75
friendly society tax-efficient plan 125
FTSE APCIMS portfolios 194–5
FTSE4Good 99
FTSE 100 Index 97, 98
fund management company 86
fund of alternative investment funds (FAIF)
    185
fund supermarket 86

gearing 124, 142
gilts 7, 112–13, 127–8
    inflation risk 19
    real investment returns 20
    risk 17, 110, 158–9
goals 7, 190
    and asset allocation 191–2
    defining 10
    timescales 20–1
group personal pension 78
growth, investing for 24–5, 58–63
growth company 97, 98
guaranteed equity bonds 62, 158–9
guaranteed income bonds 167–8

health considerations 11, 24
hedge funds 98, 184–6
help, getting 199–203
high income bond 158–9, 170
home reversion scheme 174

impaired life annuity 162
income
    investing for 24, 26, 156–74
    and risk 156–9
    savings for 64–5
    see also dividend income
income bonds 65, 158–9
income tax 28–31
independent financial advisers (IFAs) 202–3
indexation allowance 31
index-linked investments 16
    gilts 113, 128, 158–9
    real investment returns 20
    risk 17, 19
    savings certificates 60–1
individual savings accounts (ISAs) 43–4, 56
    easy access 58
    for income 64
    versus pensions 73
    tax and 44, 47, 134
inflation 16–18
inflation risk 15–16, 19

gilts 110
    income and 156–7
    pensions 75–6
    savings 54
inheritance laws on overseas property
    149–50
inheritance tax 28, 34
insurance-based funds 124–5, 126, 134
insurance bonds 166–71
    distribution bonds and funds 158–9,
      168–9
    guaranteed income bonds 167–8
    high income bonds 158–9, 170
    with-profits bonds 158–9, 169–70,
      199
interest 37, 52–4
    see also saving(s), income
interest-only mortgages 147
interest-rate risk
    gilts 110
    savings 53–4
interest yield, gilts 111
investing
    amount available for 24
    for growth 24–5
    improving decisions on 8
    for income 24, 26
    preparing for 11–14
    process of 7–8
    reason for 7
investment clubs 197–8
investment funds 16, 116–38
    risk 17, 158–9
    types of 119–26
    using for your portfolio 199–200
investment-linked annuity 162
Investment Management Association 135
investment trusts 122–4, 126
investors
    protection for 204–6
    types of 14
Islamic Bank of Britain 57
Islamic bonds (sukuk) 113

219

junk bonds 114

life insurance 11, 38–40, 124–5
lifestyle funds 199
lifetime annuity 77
lifetime mortgage 173–4
limited price indexation (LPI) annuity 162
listed shares 97–8
loan-to-value ratio 145
London Stock Exchange 97–8, 100, 121
longevity risk 15–16, 157, 76–7

market capitalisation 98
market value reduction (MVR) 131
Money Management 135
money market funds 127
money purchase occupational pension
        schemes 79–80
Money Trail 77
monthly interest accounts 65, 158–9
mortgages
    for buy to let 145–7
    lifetime 173–4
Mudaraba savings account 57
mutual funds 7

national pension scheme 83–5
National Savings & Investments (NS&I)
    versus banks and building societies 60
    capital bonds 61
    children's bonus bonds 63
    easy access account 56
    fixed interest savings certificates 59–60
    fixed-rate bonds 61, 65, 158–9
    income bonds 65, 158–9
    index-linked savings certificates 60–1
    inflation risk 19
    investment account 56
    pensioners' income bonds 65, 158–9
    premium bonds 66–7
    risk 17, 51
net asset value (NAV) 122
newspaper financial pages 107

nominee accounts 101
non-savings income 28
notice accounts 58

occupational pensions 70, 71, 78–80, 81–2
130/30 funds 186
open-ended investment companies (OEICs)
        120–1
    distribution fund 168–9
    investment funds comparison 126
    see also property unit trusts (PUTs)
ordinary shares 96
over-50s account 59
overseas investment 129
    investment funds 117
    property 148–50, 152

P810 form 42
Pay As You Earn (PAYE) 42, 71
pension compensation schemes 75
pensioners' guaranteed income bonds 65,
        158–9
pension protection fund 75
pensions 43, 70–3
    new national scheme 83–5
    provider failure 74–5
    and risk 74–7
    tax and 47, 70–2, 134
    work-based 78–82
    see also self-invested personal pensions
        (SIPPs); specific type
performance statistics for comparing funds
        135
personal equity plans (PEPs) 43, 44
personal pension 71, 86–90, 124–5
    group 78, 87
    stakeholder 78, 87, 88
    see also self-invested personal pensions
        (SIPPs)
PLUS Markets plc 97–8
PLUS-quoted market 98
portfolios, building 190–206
postal share dealing 103

preference shares 96–7
premium bonds 66–7
privatisation 106
product providers 201
property 128, 140–54
    asset classes 22
    buy to let *see* buy-to-let property
    pension schemes and 89
    property funds *see* property funds
    risks 17, 141
property funds 151–4,158–9
property unit trusts (PUTs) 152–3

R40 form 36–7
real estate investment trust (REIT) 44,
    128, 153–4
real investment returns 20
real terms 6
redeemable preference shares 97
redemption yield, gilts 111–12
reduction in yield 137
Reita 154
repayment mortgages 146–7
Retail Prices Index (RPI) 17–18
    see also RPI-linked annuities
retirement annuity contract 71
risk quiz 12–14
risk(s) 6–8, 15–18
    bonds 110
    derivatives 180–1
    equity release schemes 172–3
    gilts 110
    hedge fund 185–6
    income and 156–9
    investment funds 133
    managing 19–22
    and pensions 74–7
    property 141, 142
    protection from 206
    savings 51–4
    shares 94–5
    tax-free savings and investments 36
    see also specific risk e.g. capital risk

roll-up mortgage 173–4
RPI-linked annuities 19, 162

salary sacrifice, pension top-up 82
Save As You Earn (SAYE), shares 105–6
saving(s) 7–8
    access to your money 54
    accounts *see* savings accounts
    amount available for 24
    amount you can invest 54
    financial planning 50–4, 58–63
    how deposits work 51
    improving decisions on 8
    income 28, 36–8, 64–5
    interest-rate risk 53–4
    saving to meet a target 18
    sharia-compliant and ethical 57
    tax 54
savings accounts 50–1, 55, 55–7,58
    risk 17, 51–4
    shopping around for 50
    *see also specific institution; specific type
        of account*
scams 15
self-invested personal pensions (SIPPs) 43,
    45–6, 87, 88–90, 134
settlement system 101
share-based investments 40–1
    see also shares
share identification rules 108–9
share incentive plan (SIP) 105
share reorganisations 99
shares 128–31
    asset classes 22
    buying and selling 100–7
    definition 19
    inflation risk 156
    listed 97–8
    nominee accounts 101
    ordinary 96
    paperwork 95
    preference 96–7
    prices 103

Index

shares (*cont.*)
    real investment returns 20
    rewards 92–4
    risks 17, 94–5, 158–9
    and tax 108–9
    unlisted 98–9
    unquoted 99
    see also stockbrokers
sharia law 24, 57
shortfall risk 15–16, 18, 20
    pensions 74
    savings 54
Smile Bank 57
spread betting 182–3
stakeholder pension scheme 78, 87, 88
stamp duty land tax (SDLT) 143
state pension 70
stockbrokers 100–1, 203
stock exchange, recognised 98
stock market investments 92–114
    see also share-based investments;
        shares; *specific investments*
sukuk 113

tangible moveable property 41, 89–90
taper relief 31
tax 24
    business angels and 187–8
    buy-to-let property and 144
    capital gains *see* capital gains tax (CGT)
    children and 34
    collectables and 41–2, 177–8
    derivatives and 181–2
    dividend income 38
    -efficient shareholdings 94
    -efficient wrappers 43–7
    -free savings and investments 35–6
    gains on share-based investments 40–1
    inheritance *see* inheritance tax
    investment funds and 133, 134
    life insurance and 38–40
    overseas property and 150
    pensions and 70–2

    property and 150
    property funds and 152–3
    savings and 54
    shares and 108–9
    taxable savings income 36–8
    telling the revenue 42
tax-efficient special savings account
    (TESSA) 43, 44
tax relief at source 29
term accounts 58–9
tied agents 201–2
top-slicing relief 39
total expense ratio (TER) 135–6
tracker funds 130
tracker rate interest 53–4
traded option 179
traditional money market fund 127
Triodos Bank 57
trust fund 106
trusts, setting up 34

unit trusts 7, 119–20, 126, 168–9
unlisted shares 98–9
unquoted shares 99

variable rate interest 53–4
venture capital trust (VCT) 188

warrants 179, 181, 182
wine 178
with-profits bonds 158–9, 169–70, 199
work-based pensions 78–82
    see also occupational pensions
wrap accounts 7, 48
wrappers 43–7, 119

yearly investment limits
    child trust funds (CTFs) 45
    individual savings accounts (ISAs) 44
    self-invested personal pensions (SIPPs)
        46

Zopa 67–8

Which? Books

Other books in this series

Property Investor's Handbook
Kate Faulkner
ISBN: 978 1 84490 051 0
Price: £10.99

Property Investor's Handbook is the essential read for both the would-be and the more experienced investor. From buy to let and off-plan to new-build and buying overseas, this book is packed with practical advice and tips on how to plan and research your investment and back-up plans should things go wrong, plus the latest information on renovation, property funds and syndicates.

Tax Handbook 2008/9
Tony Levene
ISBN: 978 1 84490 045 9
Price: £10.99

Make sense of the complicated rules, legislation and red tape with *Tax Handbook 2008/9*. Written by *The Guardian* personal finance journalist and tax expert Tony Levene, this essential guide gives expert advice on all aspects of the UK tax system and does the legwork for you. It includes information on finding the right accountant and how to get the best from them, advice on NI contributions, tax credits for families and the self-assessment form. An indispensable guide for anyone who pays tax. This new edition also contains updates from the 2008 budget and guidance on how green taxes could affect you.

Wills and Probate
Paul Elmhirst
ISBN: 978 1 84490 033 6
Price: £10.99

Wills and Probate provides clear, easy-to-follow guidance on the main provisions to make in a will and the factors you should consider when drafting these. The second part of the book provides step-by-step guidance on probate, making the process as straightforward and trouble-free as possible. By being aware of key changes and revisions and avoiding the common problems and pitfalls, you can limit delays, avoid disputes and save tax.

Which? Books

Which? Books provide impartial, expert advice on everyday matters from finance to law, property to major life events. We also publish the country's most trusted restaurant guide, *The Good Food Guide*. To find out more about Which? Books, log on to www.which.co.uk or call 01903 828557.

" Which? tackles the issues that really matter to consumers and gives you the advice and active support you need to buy the right products. **"**